A Personal Selection
from 20 Years of Columns from
The New York Times

Nelson Bryant

I L L U S T R A T I O N S   B Y   G L E N   W O L F F

A FIRESIDE BOOK
Published by Simon & Schuster Inc.
New York · London · Toronto
Sydney · Tokyo · Singapore

OUTDOORS

SIMON AND SCHUSTER/FIRESIDE

Simon & Schuster Building
Rockefeller Center
1230 Avenue of the Americas
New York, New York 10020

SIMON AND SCHUSTER, FIRESIDE and
colophons are registered trademarks of Simon &
Schuster Inc.

Designed by Black Angus Design Group
Manufactured in the United States of America

10 9 8 7 6 5 4 3 2 1
10 9 8 7 6 5 4 3 2 1 PBK.

Library of Congress Cataloging in Publication Data

Bryant, Nelson.
    Outdoors : a personal selection from 20 years of columns from the
    New York times / Nelson Bryant : illustrations by Glen Wolff.
        p. cm.
    "A Fireside book."
        1. Hunting. 2. Fishing. I. New York times. II. Title
    SK33.B881115 1990
    799—dc20   89-77884
                                                            CIP

ISBN 0-671-70807-4
        0-671-69372-7 PBK.

THESE ARTICLES HAVE BEEN PREVIOUSLY PUBLISHED
IN *The New York Times.*

Contents

CONTENTS

CONTENTS

Introduction

More than seventeen years ago, John Gude, a literary agent, persuaded me and American Heritage Press that a selection of my "Wood, Field and Stream" columns from *The New York Times*—I had then been at it for less than four years—would be a worthwhile publishing endeavor. I was flattered, and even entertained a notion of substantial financial reward. That did not happen, but the reward was enough to purchase an acre of land, to pay for the digging of a cellar hole and for a new chain saw with which I cleared the white oak woods for my homesite.

That home has been sold, the chain saw is faltering, and copies of that first book, *Fresh Air, Bright Water*, are scarcer than volunteers for a night patrol into enemy territory, a scarcity that has not enhanced their value.

More talented newspaper columnists than I have discovered that—with few exceptions—collections of their outpourings do not have wide appeal, and this is particularly true of those who write about fishing and hunting. For readers who seek to follow the chronicler's lead to the letter, timeliness is all-important. A lure or bait that worked one year may be of little value the next, or the fish themselves, particularly if they are a migratory species, may not return to the same spot the following spring or summer. There is also the inescapable truth that some of what one is peddling is yesterday's news. Change is the name of the game, and the journalist is its servant.

Many years ago, I began to try, whenever possible, to fashion essays that—while including a substantial dollop of practical information—also captured the mood, the lasting qualities, of the adventure. Many of the pieces in this book—I chose fewer than 100 columns from a total of about 2,500—are of that genre, and sometimes there is no "how to" advice at all, just a celebration or examination of one man's relationship with the natural world, with loved ones, with time passing. I am grateful to the *Times* for allowing me to indulge in these digressions which have occasionally appeared in verse form, usually at Christmastime or at the advent of a new year.

Although more than 5 percent of the 2,500 columns were devoted to things ecological—including acid rain; the loss or degradation of tidal and inland wetlands; the survival struggles of striped bass and Atlantic salmon; the ubiquitous presence of polychlorinated biphenyls in lakes, rivers, and oceans; and the long but successful fight to require the use of non-toxic steel pellets for waterfowling—none of them is included. Lack of space was a factor in this decision, as was an awareness of the ever-shifting nature of such issues. New assessments and discoveries may make yesterday's story obsolete. This is essentially the province of the daily press, the magazines, and radio and television, although a book devoted entirely to an environmental threat—such as Rachel Carson's *Silent Spring*—can call a generation to action.

As one might expect, some of the people encountered in these pieces are no longer alive. I have not made notice of this. They were alive when I wrote about them, and I chose to remember them that way.

This harvest of "Outdoors" columns—for reasons I cannot recall, "Outdoors" replaced the "Wood, Field and Stream" appellation about a decade ago—may enable me to purchase a new chain saw and perhaps finance a week's Atlantic salmon fishing in Iceland. A less-fanciful combination would be a Seamaster reel for saltwater fly fishing and a week in pursuit of bonefish on the gleaming flats of Christmas Island. At the very least, I'll have something new of my own doing to add to the *Times*'s next request for an update on my biography. For seventeen years, the only change I've occasionally had to offer was the birth of yet another grandchild.

Wood, Field and Stream: Time of Soaring Dreams

Once upon a time, my daughters, there was a boy who beheld the earth with a wonder much like yours.

Each dawn was promise, each season a delight, and the world, for all its anguish, was good to know.

Those were the years when the boy could spend an entire August afternoon, nibbling watercress and watching trout hover above the pebbles in a brook, a time when the years that lay ahead seemed inexhaustible, a time of soaring dreams. It was the time when a gull's cry, muted by fog and distance, could call the boy down miles of empty beach alone, his thoughts as wide as the Atlantic.

And it may startle you to know that your father, who was once the boy, still feels the tug of moonlight through pines or across the shining water and marvels at the first lilies of spring.

The secret I would have you know this Christmas Eve is that even though the years will steal your fresh beauty, it need only be, in truth, a minor theft. What you must guard against is that jaded state wherein there is nothing new to see or learn.

Marvel at the sun, rejoice in the rhythmic

wheeling of the stars and learn their names, cry aloud at the swelling beauty of an orchid in the white oak woods, or December's first snow; slide down the wind with a hawk and cherish the smell of woodsmoke and mayflowers, or the caress of a warm wool blanket; tarry by a stream where willows bend and flee tedium's gray embrace.

Cherish laughter and whimsy, but battle unrelentingly for what you know is right and be aware that the thieves of wonder can enter any heart.

This does not mean that you will forever walk in fields of flowers where sweet birds sing, although there is no father who has not, for a time at least, wished this for his girls.

You will love and be loved, hurt and be hurt, and you will know despair and taste regret, but if your father's wish is answered, you will accept all this and ask for more.

Look back, my girls, but not too often, and more to learn than to regret, for regret grows fat as hope grows lean.

Less wise than loving, striving to make words replace some deeds undone, your father wishes you a happy Christmas.

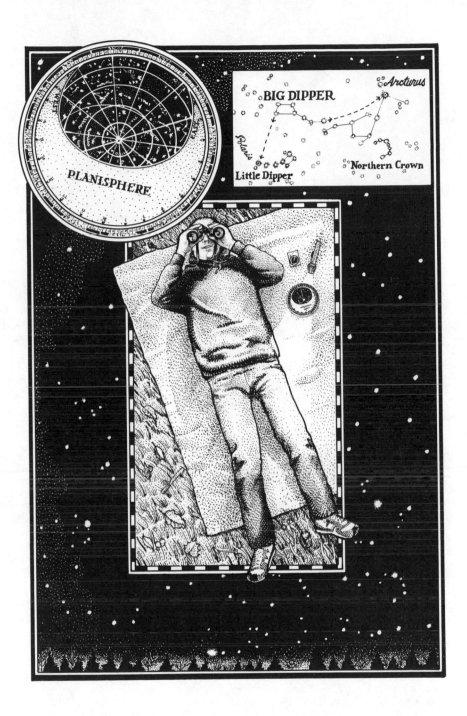

PLANISPHERE

BIG DIPPER

Arcturus

Polaris

Little Dipper

Northern Crown

SPRING

Trout Rituals

One might be tempted, because so little time remains to get one's equipage in order, to say to hell with preparations for the April 1 opening of the New York State trout season.

There is an appealing insouciance and considerable merit in that attitude. Streams will be high and cold—certainly the latter, anyway—many lakes and ponds will be frozen and the real reason for observing the ritual has little to do with catching fish. Why not wait until the day before the event, fling a snarl of gear into the trunk of the car and depart in time to toss down a few toddies with fellow anglers at some murky bar in the boondocks that evening?

Following the above approach, it wouldn't be until one was sloshing through the muck—or snow—the following morning, that one would wonder if one's waders had deteriorated over the winter. A brief sortie into the frigid water will provide the answer, and if leaks do exist one has an acceptable excuse for calling it quits and reclining against a boulder in the wan April sun.

Trying to locate small flaws in hip boots or waders before they are used is an infuriating endeavor at best. A large rip caused by the barbed wire fence under which one crawled to reach a pool in a farmer's pasture is eminently obvious and a pleasure to mend. The leaks that often defy detection are pinholes made by briars, or cracks caused by the material growing old. The late Sparse Grey Hackle advocated testing waders in a bathtub, but deep down I think he knew that most modern tubs don't even hold enough water for proper bathing. Even if one's tub is sufficiently commodious, that approach has a serious weakness because a tiny hole that might not leak when it was just below the surface of the water could do so when exposed to the greater pressure created by deeper water. Another leak-finding technique that is often recommended involves sitting in a dark room running a flashlight around the interior of one's waders, and if one pursues this diligently at least half of the holes will be located before the batteries fail. The most efficient approach is to stride purposefully into the stream on opening day and wait for icy trickles to develop. While one is at it, one should go as deep as possible in order to find all the leaks in one baptism. When that has been accomplished, go ashore, change socks and make the necessary repairs. In addition to patches and cement, the repair kit should include some paper toweling to dry off the areas to be repaired, and a felt-tipped marking pencil with which to circle them.

If one does not plan far ahead for opening day, one is almost certain to leave the proper flies—small nymphs in the main—for that time of year behind, but it's possible that they can be borrowed from a fellow angler who had to leave the stream because his legs were aching intolerably from the cold.

If one discovers that he hasn't the proper tippet material to affix to the end of his leaders, it really doesn't make much difference because in less than an hour after beginning to fish, numbed fingers won't be able to fashion either of the two knots—blood or double surgeon's—needed to accomplish that. In years long gone when I trembled with pleasure at the thought of opening day, I was able to extend my knot-tying period to noon by immersing my fingers and thumbs in a cup of hot coffee. More recently, I have found it necessary to empty my thermos into my stomach in the first half hour.

It is possible that April 1 will also reveal that the finish on one's flyline has cracked or peeled in several places—which will make long casts impossible—or that one has forgotten to bring along a sinking line, or at least one with a sinking tip, both helpful in getting the aforementioned nymphs close to the bottom where semitorpid trout are feeding and resting, mostly the latter. Both of these situations are irritating, but not catastrophic. In all probability, most of the successful fly fishermen will be making casts of no more than twenty feet—lobbing out leaders weighted with a brace of split shot just above the fly. A long toss isn't needed and the split shot will do the job—although removing all grace from the act of casting—just as well as the sinking lines.

On opening day two years ago, one of the dozen or so fly fishermen present at Cairn's Pool, which is in one of the no-kill stretches of the Catskills' Beaverkill, was not even pretending to use a conventional casting technique. His reel was filled with monofilament line and with the help of split shot he was getting his nymph where he wanted it. He had caught and released a dozen nice browns in that manner. The technique was effective, but, to this observer at least, it was a blend of cane pole angling and ice fishing.

Some of the fly fishermen at Cairn's had caught trout the day before. They weren't breaking the law because it allows year-round fishing for the species in all no-kill stretches of various streams and in many lakes and ponds. The Beaverkill has two such stretches and the Willowemoc, which joins it at Junction Pool in Roscoe, has one. These areas offer excellent angling for large, holdover trout. This year the lower no-kill stretch on the Beaverkill, which originally began a mile upstream of the iron bridge in Horton and ended six-tenths of a mile below it, has been extended downstream about five-eighths of a mile, carrying it past Jim and Joyce Petersen's Silver Fox Tavern and Beaverkill Cabins. Mr. Petersen, who is a member of Manhattan's Theodore Gordon Flyfishers, recently completed arrangements with the state for this extension. This new no-kill stretch may do much to ease the discomfort of April angling on the Beaverkill: when fishing waters bordered by the Petersen holdings, one would only be a short haul from the just-renovated Tavern's brass rail bar and restaurant.

Although a handful of fly fishermen may be found on no-kill sections of the Beaverkill every month of the year, the average angler needs a starting date to furnish the anticipation that fathers action. And no matter how disorganized one may be the first day out, that is what April 1 is all about.

Sportsman's Spring-Cleaning

An outdoorsman who suffers from the pack-rat syndrome will eventually be choked by clutter whether his digs are modest or grand. At that point, he must begin to discard certain items, not only to gain breathing room, but also to save time lost in bouts of nostalgia while poking through his hoard.

This isn't as easy as it sounds, even when an object is of little practical value.

Recently, while throwing away some trout flies that were frazzled beyond repair, I came upon an ugly wet fly weighted with several turns of copper wire that I tied nearly forty years ago, when I was still in college. It worked the first time I used it, but never again. When it surfaced the last time, I was again reminded of that one trout, a 16-inch brown caught in a deep pool on New Hampshire's Mascoma River.

In that era, sinking fly lines didn't exist, and even if they had existed, I couldn't have afforded anything more than the floating level line that I was casting with a fiberglass rod I had made from a kit purchased from Herter's for about $12. (It was only last year that I gave that rod—and this hurt a little—to one of my grandsons.)

I had created the fly because I was sure that there were big browns in the depths of that pool that I couldn't reach with an ordinary offering. The fish took on the third or fourth cast. I played it with care in the bat-filled dusk, and was so delighted when I finally had it in hand that I fished no more that evening.

Last week, I threw that fly into the waste basket, an act that emboldened me to remove three grain sacks of books from my library on the outdoors. Most were tedious works dealing with technical and overworked aspects of hunting or fishing, but none involved waterfowling, a subject that has yet to be drowned in words.

The attack on the books—thousands more remain—cleared a substantial space for a poetry shelf. The winnowing slackened, but it will resume, starting with taxidermy texts. The only thing I will stuff into a fish, bird or mammal that I catch or shoot is spiced bread crumbs or oysters.

There are more than two dozen works devoted to survival or building emergency wilderness shelters that need to be culled. I need instruction on surviving in the workaday world, not the forest primeval. If I get caught in a blizzard up north in winter, I'll crawl under an old hemlock and fall asleep.

On the other hand, I'm going to keep my five books on building log cabins. I've helped others erect cabins, but one of my never-ending fantasies has been to have one of my own, to purchase a few hundred acres of mature spruces and build a cabin from some of them, a cabin that would have a year-round spring or brook nearby.

Why else would I have a broadax, a slick, a 3-pound hatchet, a double-bitted ax, a froe, an adze, two big drawknives, a log scriber, a heavy-duty breast drill, a long boat builder's hand auger, a block and tackle and a snatch block stashed away?

My collection of pots and pans for camping or outdoor cooking has gotten out of hand. There are mess kits and cups from the armies of at least four countries, amassed when today's marvelous backpacking cookware wasn't available. They will have to go, but I don't know if I can relinquish the huge sheet-metal frying pan—it is 20 inches in diameter—that hangs in a toolshed.

Some twenty-five years ago, I saw a picture of a Wyoming

guide squatting by a campfire preparing breakfast for his sports in such a pan, and instantly knew that I needed one. That same year, I purchased an old-fashioned Dutch oven—it has a flat cover with a raised lip on which one may pile embers when cooking out of doors—that sits in a corner of the cellar where I put it twenty years ago, slathered with cooking oil to prevent rust. I used the oven a dozen times before I put it away. The pan has never been touched by fire, but one doesn't lightly discard something in which forty-eight pullet eggs can be fried at one time.

I have been giving some of my rifles and shotguns to my sons, but there is one fowling piece I've used only four times to which I still cling. It is an antique muzzle-loading, double-barrelled shotgun that is somewhere between 28 and .410 gauge. It is effective out to no more than twenty yards, having no choke at all in either barrel—something I didn't know when I bought it on Cape Cod about fifteen years ago at the start of a trip that was to include Wilson's snipe shooting in South Carolina.

When I arrived at the half-flooded meadows where the snipe lurked, I decided to use the muzzle-loader. My companions laughed at me, saying that the birds would be out of range of my little gun. They would have laughed harder had they known how it was choked, that pellets fired from it would cover the side of a chicken house two car lengths away.

We marched across the huge meadow, each man at least 150 yards from the next, and after firing three shots at fast-flying snipe that sprang from the grass about thirty yards distant, without touching a feather, I knew I was in trouble. I also knew that while the others could not see whether I was succeeding, they could certainly count my shots.

Fate intervened. A drove of about a dozen of the birds that I did not see until the last second flew directly in front of me about 15 yards distant. I fired one off-balance shot, and birds showered down from the sky—five or six of them, I believe. Those snipe, plus two others that I got with one shot each at a similar range, made me high man for the morning, and my ratio of shots fired to birds bagged was better than anyone else's. I let my friends marvel at my apparent skill for several weeks before spilling the beans.

A gun with such a history isn't easily given away.

Fly Patterns
for Trout

An urge to simplify, to choose a few dozen artificial flies that will enable him to catch trout under all conditions, lurks in the heart of many a fly fisherman.

This is a desire that will never be fully realized, but if one is not held captive by the dry fly—a tradition that was started by the British angler-author, F. M. Halford, in the latter part of the last century—one can take his share of fish while using only a tiny fraction of the thousands of patterns currently being proffered to trout.

One should focus on the time-tested flies, whether wet, dry, nymph, streamer or bucktail.

It was no accident that one of the two successful fly fishermen I encountered recently at opening day of New York State's trout season had taken three good-sized rainbow trout on a Gold-Ribbed Hare's Ear nymph. The Hare's Ear—or something quite like it—has been luring trout to the creel for more than two centuries. The Hare's Ear began as a wet fly, with dry and nymphal versions following.

In 1935 when the Derrydale edition of Preston Jennings's *A Book of Trout Flies* first appeared it was the first American work that, among other things, accurately identified some of the aquatic insects found in many of this country's streams. In the edition Jennings observed that "For upstream fishing, a trimmed Hare's Ear wet fly with only the stubs of the wings left on, is about as good a Nymph as has come to the attention of this writer."

A measure of the popularity of the Gold-Ribbed Hare's Ear may be had from the Orvis Company's recent announcement that "The Hare's Ear sells three times as many as its closest competitor for the most popular nymph."

Alert to a hot item, Orvis is offering a special—boxed selection of seventeen Hare's Ear flies, both nymphs and dries. That same announcement observes that the assortment "will suggest most kinds of aquatic insects."

It was that quality of suggestion rather than precise imitation that, according to Chauncy Lively in a piece on the Hare's Ear in the February issue of the Pennsylvania Angler, drove Halford to abandon the pattern "because he could not find a precise explanation for its success," a case of the tail wagging the dog. (Lively's article includes detailed instructions for tying a classic rough-bodied Hare's Ear nymph using dubbed fur from a hare's ears and mask. Single copies of the magazine may be had for 80 cents postpaid from the Pennsylvania Fish Commission, 3532 Walnut Street, Harrisburg, Pa. 17109.)

Most artificial flies, particularly nymphs and dry flies, are intended to suggest or represent the various forms of aquatic insects upon which trout feed. Another group, the streamers and bucktails, either resemble certain bait fish or are simply so-called "attractors," bearing little similarity to any specific forage fish but intended to stimulate a trout into striking.

The so-called wet flies—which were all that were used for hundreds of years—are difficult to pin down. Certain patterns fished fast or slow, near the surface or deep, might at one time suggest a nymphal or emerging insect and at another an injured minnow.

A list of basic trout flies for the Northeast should certainly include the Hare's Ear nymphs and dries.

A few tiny midges—No. 22, 24 or smaller, and in light and dark shades—should be among one's flies. There are times on both lake and stream when surface-feeding trout focus on hatches of such insects to the exclusion of all else. The size of the fly is the most critical factor when this occurs, and it is sometimes possible to take a slightly larger fly, such as a No. 18 or 20, and make it acceptable to the fish by removing much of its original dressing with scissors or nail clippers.

Important floating imitations of May flies include the Light Cahill, Quill Gordon, Red Quill, Hendrickson, March Brown, Adams and Grey Fox. In the most recent edition of his small but invaluable "Streamside Guide" (Nick Lyons Books/Winchester Press), Art Flick wrote that the Quill Gordon is of great importance to anglers, "Because it is the first May fly of any size to appear in spring." In the Catskills, one can expect to see it emerging by early May.

May fly nymphs—including those of the March Brown and Hendrickson—are important, and one should also have a few stone fly nymphs in hand. Although some of the dry flies, among them the Adams, intended for use during May fly hatches will work when trout are feeding on emerging caddis flies, the latter—because they are an important source of food for trout in many streams—deserve to be specifically represented in your fly box in both dry and nymphal versions. To learn more about this, *The Caddis and the Angler* by Larry Solomon and Eric Leiser (Stackpole) will serve you well.

Every fly fisherman should have the Royal Wulff in various sizes. This fly, which is essentially an attractor, floats well, doesn't come apart readily and is highly visible to the angler, an important consideration when one is fishing on rough water or in failing light.

Although most of today's fly fishermen seem to prefer using dry flies or nymphs, a great many trout are still being taken with various wet flies, streamers and bucktails. In his *Streamside Guide*, Flick wrote that the only bucktail he carried with him was the Black-Nosed Dace.

As one who enjoys working big streams with such flies—I find it fun to throw a long line and fish a sunken fly blind—I would add the Edson Tiger, both light and dark, the King of the Waters, the Black Ghost, the Muddler Minnow, the Mickey Finn and the Alexandra. The last-named is an ancient pattern that one rarely sees in use in this country, and it is an excellent fly for fishing still waters: lakes, ponds and reservoir.

Having long been a devotee of still water fly fishing in remote brook trout ponds in Northern New England, I cannot resist mentioning an attractor fly invented by a friend of mine that has often been extremely effective.

I call it Vic's Special. It is tied on a No. 10 or 12 long-shanked hook. The body is red fluorescent floss with a butt of peacock herl and a tag of golden pheasant tippets. The wings are a swatch of hair—which pulsates when the fly is retrieved in short jerks—from the tail of a gray squirrel. It resembles nothing I have ever seen in still or moving water, but it catches fish, particularly brook trout, which, admittedly, are not known for their sophistication.

On Pleasures of
Fishing for
Connetquot Trout

Settling on the top of a dead tree 30 yards
away, an osprey watched me struggle to cast
my fly against a near gale.

Apparently he had already caught his supper, for he paid no attention to the trout that
were occasionally rising before us in the wind-
ruffled water.

The pond I was fishing is alongside the
upper reaches of the Connetquot River, a
lovely, spring-fed stream that rises in west-
central Long Island and flows south into Great
South Bay. Once the exclusive province of
well-to-do sportsmen of the Southside Club, it
is now within a state park, and for five dollars
one may fish it for four hours and keep three
trout.

I had spent half an hour on the river,
working either nymphs or wet flies over long,
green streamers of starwort that, anchored to
the bottom, provide magnificent cover for
trout, but the wind was so strong I was having
difficulty controlling my casts.

It was then that Willie Kolenek, who began
working for the Southside Club nearly fifty
years ago, happened by and suggested that I
try the pond, a portion of the old stream bed
of the Connetquot which was diverted by the

club because in running through a bog, it picked up too much silt.

At the foot of the pond, where there is a concrete dam, Willie showed me where to wade. "Stay in the middle where the old stream ran, and feel your way along," he said, "or you'll go up to your neck in muck."

When the water was even with my thighs, I learned that there was a substantial leak in the right leg of my waders, but with Willie watching me I could not turn back and kept moving out as the icy water climbed.

For twenty minutes, after which my mentor left, I did nothing, the rising trout I could see being out of range, but then they moved closer and I was fast to a nice brook trout of fourteen inches.

My hands were so numbed with the cold it was difficult to hold his writhing, muscular body while removing the hook, but eventually he was in my creel and two more of similar size soon joined him.

The osprey had been watching me throughout, and I had the feeling that he now regarded my endeavors with more respect. This bird could have been one of a nesting pair in Connetquot River State Park that made use of an artificial tree erected for them by the Long Island Lighting Company. A fire last April destroyed the dead tree the ospreys had been using, and Gil Bergen, the park's manager, asked the utility for help. A tall pole with a circular platform on top of it was erected, and the birds soon made use of it. It was necessary, Bergen said, to nail some branches on top of the platform to give the birds a start with their home-making.

Leaving the pond in the gathering dusk, I encountered John Driscoll, an East Norwich, N.Y., lawyer who, upon learning I was saving my trout to take to friends, gave me the one he had caught.

Driscoll is one of many area anglers who sometimes slip away from their jobs late in the day for a bit of emotional rejuvenation on the Connetquot, as is Dr. Frederick (Bud) Wright, a Huntington, Long Island, veterinarian, who took Bergen and me to lunch at George Remmer's Snapper Inn in Oakdale. (Adding to the meal's pleasure for me was the chance to chat with Dana Lamb, an angling author whose work I have long admired, who was dining at an adjacent table with a friend.)

The Snapper Inn is a first-rate seafood restaurant that should be remembered by those who visit the Connetquot.

Those planning to fish the Connetquot should make reservations ahead of time, for a beat (a specific section of the stream). Only fly fishing is permitted.

The park (telephone number [516] 581-1005) has a section of the stream reserved for the handicapped that is readily accessible by wheelchair. On the main lower pond, the site of a grit mill built in the eighteenth century, one may, if one obtains the beat that embraces it, go forth in a rowboat for trout.

The park raises its own trout, browns, rainbows and brookies, and about 30,000 are taken from its waters each year. Many of the fish are holdovers from previous years, and every once in a while a brown trout of 12 pounds or more is caught.

A program of events for school children and adults goes on throughout the summer, including nature walks—deer, ducks and Canada geese are always to be seen—and evening vigils in April to watch the courtship flights of woodcock.

Those driving to the Connetquot from Manhattan could take the Cross Island Parkway immediately after crossing the Throgs Neck bridge. Follow Cross Island to the Southern State Parkway and take Exit 44 to the Sunrise Highway east. The entrance to the park is about a mile east of that exit on the north, or westbound, lane of Sunrise, so one has to drive a short distance past that entrance in order to make a turn, into the west-bound lane.

The Oakdale station of the South Shore branch of the Long Island Rail Road, where cabs are available, is about a mile from the park. One has to take the Long Island Rail Road to Babylon, then change to the South Shore line.

Still Waters Provide an Alternate Trout Site

For centuries, and until very recently, all the books devoted to fly fishing for trout dealt with stream and river angling and ignored lakes and ponds, which are often more rewarding.

This is not to suggest—at least for many fly fishermen—that still-water angling can fully match the pleasure of studying and working a lovely stream where all is sweet sound and motion. But there are many occasions when streams are fished out, too low, too crowded, or when the trout they contain are too small to keep.

I think, for example, of a little, rock-strewn creek in central Vermont that has always been loaded with wild brook trout. In that stream, a trout on every second or third cast isn't unusual, but few are over 5 inches long, and a 5-inch fish released this year may be no larger a year hence. The stony bed of the stream doesn't provide suitable habitat for aquatic insects upon which the trout and certain species of smaller forage fish feed.

But in the Adirondacks, in northern Maine, north and central New Hampshire and to a lesser degree in Massachusetts (mostly on Cape Cod), Vermont and Connecticut, there are many lakes and ponds where one-pound brook trout are not unusual. Some of these lakes also hold much larger brown and rainbow trout and a few even offer splake (a cross between brook trout and lake trout). In the deeper lakes one will also find lake trout, but they cannot, except in early spring, be taken by a cast fly or a fly trolled on a fly line. As the surface water warms, lake trout go deep and can only be reached with a trolled wire line, a so-called downrigger, or one of the planing devices that takes a lure or fly deep when it is trolled.

There are days when the still-water fly fishermen can catch trout on the surface on a dry fly, but more than two-thirds of the time he will be terribly handicapped if he confines himself to that approach. This is particularly true in summer when most of the trout spend their time in cooler, deeper water. At such times, one may have to get his fly down 10 to 20 feet or more.

There are many types of sinking fly lines available for still-water fishing. The best bet is probably the one that sinks the fastest.

Fly rods for still water can be as light and delicate as one wishes, but the more powerful rods and heavier lines—No. 7, 8 or 9 outfits—enable one to cast farther.

Ideally, one should also bring a smaller rig—No. 5 or 6—for a floating line and dry fly fishing to still waters. There are occasions near sundown and thereafter when trout will rise through super-heated surface water and feed voraciously on hatches of aquatic insects. Having a dry fly rod all rigged saves the precious time required to put a reel of floating line on the big rod.

Learning to successfully fish the various lakes and ponds is not easy. There are no obviously attractive holding spots for trout such as pools, eddies downstream of boulders or pocket water.

In some of the small, relatively shallow spring-fed ponds in summer, the trout may be concentrated about those springs over a few square yards of the bottom.

When most of a trout pond is truly warm, 70 degrees or above, the angler must locate the cold water, so a so-called stream thermometer is an essential part of his equipment. Brook trout, for example, are comfortable and active in water between 50 and 60 degrees.

I am thinking of a little mountaintop lake in New Hampshire

which has provided me with many brook trout of more than a pound, plus one 2-pounder. A friend and I took good fish from it for several years but it wasn't until we located some springs welling up from the bottom that we could do this consistently. The cold water area on the bottom probably doesn't cover more than a 30-yard square, but when it was found we fished it again and again in midsummer with sinking lines and never failed to catch trout.

Many of the trout ponds in the Adirondacks, Maine and New Hampshire are truly remote and often the forest grows to the water's edge. The bottoms of these ponds are often muck, and that, plus the short-side trees, leaves no room for a back cast. In that situation, some sort of flotation is needed and either a light-weight canoe or an inflatable raft must be portaged in. I have tried the inflatable one-man "donut," or inner tube, affairs. They are acceptable if the depth around the shore is such that one can top-toe along on top of the muck with most of one's weight sup-ported by the tube, but if one's feet are off the bottom one is virtually immobilized and subject to every vagrant twist of wind.

A word of caution on inflatable rafts: it has been my experience that those advertised as two-man affairs are just about the right size for one fly fisherman, who needs, among other things, plenty of room for his loose coils of line.

Some lakes and ponds have firm walking in the shallows and at the right time of year they can be successfully fished by a wading angler. Still others can be reached by conventional or four-wheel drive vehicles and then, of course, one can luxuriate in a relatively large and comfortable craft.

Because most summer still-water fly fishing involves sinking lines, those who embark on it should have a good supply of wet flys, nymphs and streamers. In the last-named category, I have found the Muddler Minnow, the Alexandra, the Mickey Finn, the Hornberg and the Careless Coachman good choices with which to begin. The Careless Coachman, created by a friend and me for still-water trout, has red or orange fluorescent floss body, a tail of golden pheasant tippets and is topped off with gray squirrel tail.

The best way to attack an unfamiliar lake is to ask questions of someone who knows it. Lacking such information, if someone is lucky enough to have a canoe and a companion, a good approach is to paddle along the shore with the paddler trolling a fly and the other angler casting toward the shore. (Be sure, however, to check the state's angling regulations for that body of water. Maine, for example, has some trout ponds in which only fly casting, no trolling, is permitted.) If either gets a hit, stop paddling so both can work the area thoroughly with cast flys.

There are times when no amount of casting will produce a fish, but one will pick up trout with considerable regularity while trolling. This usually occurs when the water temperature is right for trout at all depths. And what works on one lake may not work on another.

Eleven years ago I had the pleasure of fishing a loch in northern Scotland with Professor Frederick H. Stewart of the University of Edinburgh. The brown trout in the lake, which averaged well over a pound, were very dour, to use the professor's phrase, and on the first day only one responded to my long casts from shore. Professor Stewart did no better than I on that day, although his approach was different. He fished the surface water from a drifting skiff, making very short casts with a Grouse and Claret wet fly on the end of his leader and any large and bushy fly as a dropper. Professor Stewart, who had first visited that moor loch and others in Caithness County with his wife, the novelist Mary Stewart, and me, tried for those trout a few more times together and he always did better than I, but he observed that "one never really knows when those fish will take. I have never been able to discover a feeding pattern."

Happily, not all trout are so dour.

Slipping out of my pack on the south shore of 48-acre Bourn Pond in the Lye Brook Wilderness Area of the Green Mountain National Forest, I was content.

Nearly three years ago, a friend had told me of the spot. I had resolved to visit it, but, as is so often the case, circumstances intervened.

Several times I drove by the forest on my way to trout fishing on the Battenkill or to woodcock or grouse hunting, but there was never enough time to run down maps of the region and to find out what ponds in the area might offer the best angling.

Finally, an invitation from Bart Jacob of Dorset, Vermont, to attend a meeting of the Ruffed Grouse Society in nearby Grafton provided another chance to be close to the spot. To pass by it once again was unthinkable.

My urge to visit the area was born of a lifelong desire to angle for trout in a truly wild setting whenever I can.

There are many to whom fishing in moving water is all-important, but over a period of thirty years I have come to regard remote trout ponds with great affection. They do not offer the excitement of a stream or a river, and in July, August, and part of September in the Northeast, one is usually confined to working with a sinking line, probing for trout that have sought out the deeper, colder water. The delight of a fish taking a floating fly is rarely experienced during the dog days of summer, but the sights and sounds—save, perhaps, for a passing airplane—of civilization are erased. One sees beavers prowling a shallow bay, or hears a loon's cry or the moaning of wind in the mountains.

Measured by its distance—about 3 miles—from the end of the access road, Bourn Pond is only reasonably remote, but its wilderness qualifications are otherwise untainted, and it receives large annual stockings, dropped by air, of yearling brook trout. In each of the last two seasons, for example, some 6,000 trout were added.

Some of these fish grow to respectable size. Chatting with a ranger, Nort Phillips, at the Manchester, Vermont station of the United States Forest Service on my way to the area, I learned that a 16-inch brookie had been taken out of Bourn this summer.

Accompanied by two friends, Bill Cairns of Manchester and Tony Atwill of Dorset, I visited Bourn the following day. One can reach the edge of the Lye Brook Wilderness from a settlement called East Kansas, which is a few miles east of Arlington. An excellent dirt road, suitable for ordinary cars, leads up the mountain to Access Point 9, where one picks up the trail to the pond. The access point may also be reached from the west end of the same road in Stratton. In winter, the road is plowed only part way up the mountain on either side. Cross-country skiers often visit the Lye Brook area from either side of the ridge.

When we arrived at the access point, three young men were removing a canoe and packs from a pickup truck, and we wondered if they were planning to portage the canoe all the way to Bourn.

The trail itself is a cinch, winding north with very few ups and downs, woods and shallow flowages occupied by beaver. We saw none of those animals, but were rewarded by the paw print of a good-sized bear in a muddy spot.

The rangers have paid a good deal of attention to this trail: log or sawn-timber walkways are built across the swampy areas and log ripraps contain portions of the trail, which may be damaged by spring washouts. Both the trail and the area around Bourn Pond are free of man's debris, and one hopes this is as much a result of the new environmental consciousness as it is the work of Forest Service personnel.

Reaching the pond, we set about blowing up our inflatable rafts, because it is virtually impossible to fish the place successfully from shore.

Our rafts were all the same, each made by the American Safety Company. When these lightweight craft—they weigh only a little over 5 pounds each, complete with aluminum-plastic oars—were introduced a few years ago, back-packing anglers greeted them with delight. They are no longer being manufactured, however, and this is a pity, for nothing presently on the market up to this writer's knowledge, is even half as light or durable.

A stiff northerly breeze whipped across the pond as we launched, driving scattered clouds before it, and I looked in vain for signs of rising trout. I had not really expected to see any, for we had arrived at midday, and in such waters during summer and early fall, trout usually do not feed on the surface except in early-morning or at dusk.

Cairns, one of the East's most accomplished fly-casters and fly-fishermen, was the first to connect. He—as were Atwill and I—was fly-fishing with a sinking line. The fish was barely 6 inches long, clearly one of the yearlings planted in July.

Before venturing on the lake, I had found a good-size rock to serve as an anchor and was diligently searching for the deeper spot, which I had been told by the ranger station was about 20 feet down. The surface water was unpleasantly warm, about 70 degrees, for brook trout, and I was hoping to find a deep, cool area. Using Thoreau's thesis, advanced in *Walden*—that the deepest part of the pond is often where imaginary lines, connecting its longest and widest parts, intersect—I found one spot about 18 feet deep.

But the water was just as warm on the bottom as it was on top.

As I continued my search, the three canoeists paddled by, apparently headed for the Adirondack-type shelter at the north end of the pond. (There is another shelter at the south end, where the trail first reaches the lake.)

It would be gratifying to report that we eventually found where the trout were concentrated, but such was not the case. We took a few small fish in two hours, but that was all, and we had to leave the pond at two-thirty to allow time for me to get to my ruffed grouse conclave.

Hurriedly deflating my raft, I was reminded once again that the most important element and successful angling is being on the spot at the right time. By the end of the first week in October, Bourn should be chilled sufficiently for the trout to be ranging freely at all depths.

Vermont's trout season runs through October 28, providing a splendid opportunity for fishing during one of the most rewarding and delightful times of year, a time when the hills are aflame, the bugs and mosquitoes are gone and the trout are feeding hungrily before the onset of winter. There is, by the way, no restriction of trout fishing with lures or bait—as opposed to fly-fishing—in Vermont.

Fishing the Bourn

Chub Cay, the Bahamas. Standing knee-deep in a tidal stream, I first saw the bonefish when they slipped out of the blue-green water in the channel and came across a lite-colored bar 100 yards away.

Long and gray, they moved slowly upcurrent, more than a hundred of them, and I shouted a warning to my three nearby fishing companions, the Bahamian guides, Stanton Johnson and Alfred Dawkins, and Jack Samson, the managing editor of *Field and Stream* magazine.

Watching a school of bonefish move toward you across the shallows or flats is much like watching a flight of bluebills swinging in toward the decoys. It is hunting and fishing together, and the tension is almost intolerable.

One must wait until the fish are within casting range and drop the fly or lure a few feet in front of them. To cast too far is disaster, for the fish will spook. To cast too short can also be disastrous, for the fish may never see the lure. (If one is using bait, such as shrimp or cut conch, the latter error is not as critical, for there is a good chance the fish will smell it and pick it up.)

When the fish were about 75 feet away, I made my cast and the fly fell within a few feet of three of them. Two moved toward the fly, then turned away and before I could retrieve my line they were going by me on both sides and I remained motionless, not wanting to spoil it for Samson and the others.

His offering received the same treatment, however, and I turned and watched the two guides, 40 yards upstream from me, as they flipped shrimp in front of the fish. A group of perhaps twenty bonefish was crowding Dawkins and he inched backward, step by step, in a semicrouch, endeavoring to keep the bait in front of them.

The four of us took no fish from that school, but a few minutes later Mrs. A. J. McClane, who was fishing farther upstream with her husband, *Field and Stream*'s fishing editor, hooked and landed an 8-pounder on spinning gear. And after all the bonefish had passed by, another member of our party, Mrs. Georgie Moore Lapham of Delray Beach, Florida, hooked and released a good-sized bonnet shark.

A strong westerly wind had kept us off the extensive bonefish flats along Chub Cay, a remote and lovely island in the Berry chain, the first of our two days of fishing there. On the second day we chose the interior waters of the tidal stream once again because we had seen bonefish of better than fifteen pounds there.

Chub Cay, owned by Crown Colony Group of 730 Fifth Avenue, New York, is open to a limited number of guests who may fly in aboard their own aircraft or the club's plane, or by commercial flights from Nassau. Also, there is usually room for visiting yachts in the club's 73-berth marina.

Arriving on our second day there was the schooner *Red Cat* out of Martha's Vineyard, Massachusetts, skippered by a friend, Stanley Hart. As the wind softened to a caress against the failing light from the west, Samson and I sat on the deck of the *Red Cat* with Hart, his wife, Maria, their seagoing eleven-month-old daughter Sloan and a crewman, Ricky Behr, and drank a toast to that day in June when they would sail home to another lovely island 1,400 miles north.

Alewives:
A Forgotten Fish

Considerably smaller than the better-known shad and equally bony, the alewife, also known as herring, buckeye, sawbelly, grayback and gapereau, was once welcomed with open arms by Northeast seacoast residents whose winter food supplies were running short.

Alewives were salted, smoked, pickled and baked and there was even a lively trade in the salted variety of the West Indies.

Today, except for a few men who catch them for their roe—which, to my taste at least, is superior to that of the shad—and for lobster bait, or as chum for more highly-prized species, alewives are paid little attention.

A few countrymen still use alewives to make their gardens grow. Two of these fish, the females emptied of their roe, of course, buried under a hill of squash or corn or a tomato plant provide excellent fertilizer. In the Northeast, most of the alewives have usually completed their spawning runs and departed before a garden can be planted, so one must have his plot plowed and harrowed in early April and must plant the fish before the vegetables, marking the spots where they are buried with sticks.

Virtually any reasonably clean stream or river entering into salt water attracts alewife runs, although some of these waters may have been rendered useless for this purpose by dams a short distance upstream. Alewives, which can grow to more than 15 inches long and weigh over a pound, will enter tiny brooks or rivers as large as the Potomac or the Hudson.

Their spawning appears to take place in the slower stretches of such streams, or, in the case of the bit rivers, smaller tributaries to them. There is, for example, a substantial alewife run in the Hudson's tributary, the croton, and another a few miles upstream in Popolopen Creek, which enters from the Hudson's west shore just above Bear Mountain Bridge.

Those who have gone after alewives in a specific stream can count on the fish following the same schedule year after year. If you contemplate prospecting a stream for the first time and it is a small one, now is the moment—from New Jersey north to Massachusetts—to begin looking for the fish.

If the run is large, you will see the alewives by the dozens or the hundreds in many pools or you may observe them skittering upstream, sometimes nearly flat on their sides, through the shallows. The fish leave evidence of their passage in such shallows: the rocks in the shallow water scrape off a few silvery scales which lie gleaming on the bottom.

The brilliant quality of alewife scales spawned a short-lived industry in Massachusetts during and after World War I, when their iridescence was extracted to make, among other things, costume jewelry.

The casual alewife hunter needs nothing more than a dipnet and a pair of boots, and the fish can even be captured by snagging them with a large, bare, treble hook and spinning or bait-casting gear.

The alewife's close relatives, the shad, will hit an artificial fly or a tiny lead jig known as a shad dart, and the alewife will respond to a small fly, say a No. 12 streamer with a gold or silver body topped off with white bucktail or white hackle.

The alewive's spawning range extends from Florida to the Gulf of St. Lawrence and overlaps that of a very similar species, the blueback herring. Both may spawn in the same streams, and adult contingents of both may remain in the streams until early summer.

Their roe and flesh are equally good, and the latter is best when the fish first come in from the sea.

The blueback is common from Florida to Cape Cod and may be distinguished from the alewive in various ways. Perhaps the best distinction is that the alewife's eye is broader than the distance between the forward edge of the eye and the tip of the snout. With the blueback, the eye-to-snout distance is about equal to the eye's width.

The blueback also has a definitely green back while that of the alewife is lighter, a gray-green. This coloration fades rapidly after death, however. Also, the belly cavity of the blueback is dark while that of the alewife is pearly or pinkish gray. The scales of the alewife form a serrated edge along the bottom of the belly and this edge feels rough to the touch, hence the name "sawbelly."

The alewives, the blueback herring, the smelts, the striped bass and the salmons are all anadromous fishes, spawned in fresh water, reaching growth and maturity in the ocean and returning to the streams of their birth to repeat the cycle. The mystery of how they perform these journeys—the long-range navigation needed by those that wander far at sea and the mechanism involved in identifying home streams—are only partly understood. Also, of course, these fishes must adapt to fresh or salt water in a relatively short period of time, an experience that is fatal to many species.

The roes of alewives or bluebacks will usually be small—not much more than the diameter of a fountain pen—when they first arrive in a stream and the gatherer wanting more for his efforts should wait a week or two for those roes to develop more fully.

With practice, fully ripe females can be distinguished from males by their swollen bellies. The sex also can be ascertained by gently squeezing the belly toward the anal vent. If the white milt emerges and you are after roe fish only, toss your captive back.

There appears to be—although I know of no definitive research on this—something of a segregation of sexes in alewife and blueback spawning runs and you may sometimes discover that all the fish are males. (A few years ago on the aforementioned Popolopen Creek, some friends and I gave up our quest for roe when the first fifty alewives we netted proved to be males. At some point, of course, the two sexes have to mingle.)

The tasty flesh of the fresh-run alewife is incredibly bony and, unlike the larger shad, the fish is so small that laying the bones away leaves very little. If you have a methodical temperament you won't mind picking away around the bones of a baked alewife or blueback, but most people dislike this regimen.

The usual way to cook the roe is to fry it in butter, margarine or oil.

You might wish to experiment with pickling the fish. Scale and fillet them, ignoring the bones. Cut into small cross-section strips and immerse in a one-part vinegar, four-parts water solution to which a little salt has been added. After a few days in the refrigerator the vinegar will have softened the bones. When you are ready to eat the fish, remove as much of it as you want from the solution, pat dry on paper towels and mix with sour cream.

If the pieces of fish in the vinegar-water solution fall apart, you have used too much vinegar; if the bones are still too hard, you have used too little or you might try waiting another two days.

I have tried storing these little delicacies with the sour cream added beforehand, but that doesn't seem to work as well as the method outlined.

Deeply Involved in Thin-Water Fishing

Bonefish in thin water—water that barely comes to the knees—are as nervous as a teenager on his first date.

The fish move up current out of the deep, green channels, and across the shallow flats where they root for bottom-dwelling invertebrates. The angler often has only one or two chances to cast his bait, lure or fly to them. The presentation must be near-perfect or the prey will be spooked, will hurtle away across the flat, its departure marked by a lengthening furrow.

Working the flats, whether for bonefish, tarpon or permit, is a marvelous blend of hunting and fishing, for the prey must be seen before the cast is made. It is the wait between the time the fish is sighted and the time it gets within casting range that sets even a veteran angler trembling.

The classic way to go after bonefish is to stalk them on the flats, either on foot or from a boat poled by a guide or companion. A modification of this is to stake out the boat on a flat and chum the fish into casting range with bits of shrimp. This last-named technique produces the most fish, and one reason for this is that bonefish responding to chum lose most of their nervousness.

When the water is truly shallow—from less than a foot to a foot and a half—the large, deeply forked tail of a head-down, feeding bonefish may be seen waving above the water, a gleaming pennant that can be spotted for 100 yards or more under the right conditions. In deeper water, there is no flag, but the fish's digging produces a small, muddy cloud. Cruising bonefish can also be caught with properly placed lures, baits or flies.

The second phase of excitement in bonefishing comes when the banana-shaped creature is hooked. It takes off at astonishing speed and may go 125 to 150 yards before it is stopped. The velocity of this initial spurt for freedom makes it imperative that fly fishermen pay careful attention to the loose coils of line that were not expended in the cast.

A tropical and subtropical species, bonefish grow to 15 pounds and more, but along the East Coast of the United States—Biscayne Bay is generally considered the northern point beyond which any appreciable number of them go—a 10-pounder is truly large. They are commonly fished for with lines or tippets of 12-pound test or less.

Having angled for the species only half a dozen times in the past ten years and having caught only five of them—and only one on a fly rod—I was quick to disabuse Rob Killgore of Key Biscayne of any notion he might have that I was an expert bonefisherman.

My Key Biscayne hosts, Mr. and Mrs. Frank Mather 3d, had introduced me to Mr. Killgore, who is sales representative for the *Florida Sportsman* magazine. Mr. Killgore had asked if I'd like to go after bonefish with him.

"I'm not an expert, or even close to one," he said, "but I have a lot of fun at it, and I can show you fish."

We agreed to try the following afternoon. We also agreed that we would, that first time at least, cast live shrimp with spinning rods to tailing fish.

He took me to some flats a short distance south of the southern end of Key Biscayne and we had an abundance of tailing bonefish to importune.

We caught none on three separate afternoons, but it mattered very little, for sighting and casting to bonefish is as exciting as catching many other species. On our final day together we both spent a good time stalking tailing bonefish on foot with fly rods, an approach I find the most pleasurable. On two occasions when I did everything right, bonefish followed my fly for several feet but did not take.

That evening, I met Frank Garisto. He is one of Florida's top bonefishing guides, who can be reached at (305) 361-5040. He invited me to go with him and his wife, Joan, the following day.

We began by chumming. Mrs. Garisto, who has her own boat and has twice won the women's division of the Metropolitan Miami Fishing Tournament, quickly caught two bonefish, one on spinning gear, the other on bait casting (revolving spool).

The lure in each instance was a 4-inch plastic affair, slightly resembling a bloodworm.

"Bones go for it like gangbusters," Mr. Garisto said. "They make the lure in six-inch, too, but I have found the four-inch in root beer color the best."

It occurred to me that the hookworm—perhaps in a reddish hue if it is available—would make an excellent lure for small striped bass, and I intend to try that later this spring. A couple of split shot, or the conical lead head used by freshwater bass anglers when fishing with plastic worms, aids in casting.

Ben Franklin Talked Turkey, to No Avail

Those who sally forth May 1, shotgun in hand, for the opening of New York State's turkey season would not be doing so if Benjamin Franklin had gotten his way.

Mr. Franklin had sought to have the wild turkey declared this country's national bird, a classification that would have undoubtedly afforded it total protection.

A sagacious man, Mr. Franklin was not off base in his desire to have the turkey so honored, for it is a bird of the American wilderness, one that ranged over most of this country and whose populations—there are four major species native to this country—in pre-Columbian days have been estimated at more than ten million. Pursued insatiably both for home consumption and for sale, it was virtually extirpated from this country by the latter part of the last century. Destruction of mature hardwood forests—its preferred habitat—was also a factor in this. By 1850, there were no wild turkeys at all in New England and New York State and only a few scattered flocks in Pennsylvania.

A few decades ago, state fish and game departments began paying attention to the wild turkey. It has been restored to its former range and, in a few instances, to states outside its historical territory. The fundamental technique for this is live trapping with nets and transfer to a new area. New York began its turkey trapping and transfer program in 1959, using birds that had strayed into the southwestern part of the state from Pennsylvania.

It was not uncommon for a hunter to bag a couple of dozen birds in a day's hunt in the early part of the last century. In Arlie Schorger's *The Wild Turkey: Its History and Domestication,* there is an account of two men in Scotland County, Missouri, who killed 132 turkeys with their rifles in one day while husking corn. This could not happen today. The huge flocks—sometimes in the thousands— no longer exist, and the birds that now range our woodland are, for the most part, incredibly wary.

It is possible for a spring season turkey hunter with no previous experience to bag a gobbler, but this is a rare occurrence. To be assured of even a fair chance of success, one must learn how to locate the birds—in spring hunting, this means finding the places where gobblers roost—and how to call them in.

As in other states, New York's spring turkey hunt is aimed at the male birds, also called toms or gobblers. The most obvious difference between the sexes is the beard protruding from the chest of the male, although a few females are so adorned.

Hunters may take only bearded birds in spring. Shooting hours are from thirty minutes before sunrise to noon. This timing affords protection to the hens, most of which are on their nests during that period. .

Having the spring season coincide with the nesting and incubation period also aids the hunter. With most of the hens in his range impregnated, a gobbler—his procreative ardor still aflame— is hard-pressed to find a receptive female.

The typical hunter—wearing full camouflage—is in the woods long before dawn. Ensconcing himself in a likely spot—sometimes nothing more than a hollow on a mountainside—he begins to make the sounds of a lovelorn hen. There are a variety of commercially available calls one may use for this, and one of the most effective and easiest to master is the swinging-lid box call. Some accomplished hunters switch to a diaphragm—or mouth—call for the closing moments of the game because it leaves their hands free to handle their guns.

There are occasions when less than half an hour passes between the time a gobbler first responds to the hunter's blandishments and when he comes within shotgun range, but that is uncommon. More often than not, hours pass while the tom closes in, circling, pausing and even retreating. Turkeys have incredibly good eyesight and first-rate hearing, and it may be that a wary gobbler has seen something that troubles him or that the hunter has sounded a sour note.

During this approach period, the hunter must remain motionless except when he eases around to face the direction from which the bird is coming. In the final minutes, the gobbler can usually be heard strutting through the leaves.

A prolonged wait can be surprisingly difficult. On one turkey hunt more than a decade ago, my companion shot the gobbler, then lay writhing on the ground with a cramp in his leg shrieking for me to make sure the bird was dead.

The best way to learn how to go after spring turkeys is to go out with an experienced hunter, but one can teach oneself, or at least speed up the learning process, by reading books on the subject and by listening to records of turkey calling.

New York state also permits the use of decoys, either full-bodied or silhouette, and these often work very well.

Only shotguns may be used, and the shot size may be no larger than No. 2 and no smaller than No. 8. A more realistic shot size requirement would be from BB's through No. 6, but there are bizarre shot-size and caliber restrictions in the hunting regulations of almost every state.

Spring turkey hunting is allowed in all of New York state save Long Island. A map and description of the spring turkey hunting area is provided each hunter when he applies for his $2 turkey permit at license-issuing agencies or regional offices of the state's Department of Environmental Conservation. One must, of course, have a hunting license in order to obtain a permit.

Dave Harbour's *Advanced Wild Turkey Hunting & World Records* (Winchester Press) is one of the most recent texts on the subject, and it includes a list of sources for turkey calls and recordings of experts using them. Mr. Harbour's earlier work, *Hunting the American Wild Turkey,* was published by Stackpole in 1975. Other books on the subject are: *Modern Turkey Hunting,* by James Brady (Crown); *The Education of a Turkey Hunter,* by William Hanenkrat (Winchester Press); *Turkey Hunting with Charlie Elliott,* by Charles Elliott (David McKay), and *The Book of the Wild Turkey,* by Lovett Williams Jr. (Winchester Press). The last-named devotes considerable space to the history, habits and management of the bird.

Fishing for Memories

The Delaware River's shad were our quarry, but although Roger Kitchen of Stroudsburg, Pa., and I dutifully cast flies and lures at them, we were fishing other waters also.

We had served together in D Company of the 82d Airborne Division's 508th Parachute Infantry Regiment in World War II, had jumped into Normandy and the Netherlands, had fought in the Battle of the Bulge, and had not seen each other since a Liberty ship delivered us back to the United States in the fall of 1945.

As our guide Rich Hanson, who is also Roger's nephew and the one who arranged for our reunion, sat tending the two stern rods from which shad darts dangled in the current, we began to probe each other's memories.

Sometimes we agreed on the details of a specific battle or the name of a bar in Nottingham, England, where we had made asses of ourselves. But often we disagreed on where or how a buddy had died, or whether, in spite of alleged security, the people of the city had lined the streets to wish us well when we left our tent encampment below Nottingham Castle to go to the airport in preparation for the D-Day invasion.

Over more than forty years, we learned, each of us had often focused on a single aspect of some grim or ludicrous scene that the other no longer recalled.

So it was when Roger said that he had always wanted to apologize for reporting me dead a short while after I had taken a machine-gun bullet through the chest in Normandy.

I told him I hadn't known of his exaggerated assessment of my condition and added that no harm had been done. That didn't stop him.

"I looked at you when the rest of us were coming back from that combat patrol," he said. "You were lying on your back against what looked like an ant hill. I bent over you. Your mouth was open and for the life of me you weren't breathing."

My memory of that event was that I was lying on soft June grass, watching clouds go by, distressed that what I had hoped would be a meteoric, Sergeant York-type combat career had been so rudely interrupted. And, after a medic had given me a shot of morphine and taped condoms over the bullet's entrance and exit holes, I began to entertain the notions of survival.

Roger cast a few more times then put down his rod and reached for his wallet.

"Something else had been bothering me," he said, handing me a ten-dollar bill.

"Remember," he went on, "that tent city at Marseilles where we all were before getting on board ship for home?"

I told him that I remembered the place ablaze with lights from dusk to dawn while we who had lived gambled for a stake in civilian life.

"I lost everything," said Roger, "and when we got on board ship the crap games continued and I asked you for a loan of ten bucks. I turned it over to another guy who was good at the game. He added ten dollars of his own and won more than three thousand dollars and we split it."

I had no recollection of the loan, perhaps because I had made more than $3,000 myself shooting crap on that voyage. I'd have cleaned out the ship if I'd had the guts. I made nineteen straight rolls, but could not resist—after the fifth—from continually pulling half my winnings out of the game.

Not wishing Roger to remain burdened with a real or imagined obligation, I took his ten dollars. We went back to casting after the transaction and a few minutes later he hooked and landed a nice roe shad of about six pounds. This was a cause for rejoicing because it was our first fish of the day and one of the few taken by our group, most of whom were outdoor writers from the Northeast.

We had been invited there by the Big River Guide Service of Columbia, New Jersey—which is owned by Hanson and Alan South—and Shawnee Village, a resort community on the west bank of the Delaware near Stroudsburg that has sprung up around the venerable Shawnee Inn, once owned by the band leader Fred Waring.

Our sleepy-eyed band of anglers was in the minority at Shawnee, which is in the Poconos and on the southern edge of the Delaware Water Gap National Recreation Area. Most of the Village's guests seemed to be devoted to golf and tennis, although, on the second morning of our stay, vividly clad men and women were climbing into the gondolas of huge striped, hot air balloons on the Inn's front lawn at sunrise.

A little later in the season, the Village's Delaware canoe excursions are popular, and even as we were leaving an outdoor barbecue was being set up for an annual shad fishing tournament that offers over $5,000 in prizes.

Hanson's service—(201) 496-4688—also guides anglers to black bass, trout and muskellunge in the Delaware and to trout and salmon in Lake Ontario. The shad season is limited to April and May in much of the river.

Cold and sometimes rainy weather—the water temperature remained around 50 degrees—was the reason for the poor angling. The first morning, more than fifty boats in the short section of the river we fished caught about a dozen fish.

During a day and a half of angling I had no cooperation from any of the estimated 600,000 shad that swarm up the Delaware each spring to spawn even though I was using flies tied for me by two friends—Joe Purcell, clerk of Sullivan County, New York, and (Perk) Perkins of the Orvis Company—who had been having great success with the river's shad this season.

This troubled Hanson, but I assured him that over the decades I had become accustomed to blank days and had grown adept at chronicling my multitudinous failures with rod and gun.

Late in the afternoon Roger told me that he had invited another member of our unit, Abe Oybkhan of Wilmington, Delaware, to his home. It was a strangely moving gathering: Three aging comrades-in-arms—I with my paratrooper wings on my beret, Roger with a tiny sterling silver replica of them on his suit jacket and Abe with "508 Parachute Infantry" emblazoned on the back of his windbreaker—talking in bursts, then subsiding into silence as scenes from nearly a half century ago appeared then slid away as do dreams at dawn.

When we parted, Roger and I shook hands, Abe, less reserved than either of us, embraced me and I remembered a snow-filled valley in the Ardennes where, as the light was failing, we slogged side by side toward dark spruces on a distant hill.

Fly Casting
for Shad

Anglers have long known that the American shad does not feed during its spring spawning run, that it seizes lure or fly for some other reason, perhaps irritation at repeated intrusions into its procreative odyssey by small, shiny creatures from another world. If this be so, Joe Purcell and I were unable to irritate any of them during two-and-one-half days of fly fishing on the Delaware River.

Purcell, who lives in Grahamsville, New York, has long fished for shad, in the beginning with the standard gear for the species, light spinning rod and shad darts, and for the past few years with fly rod and bright flies—he ties them himself—with metal beads for eyes.

For a little more than a month each spring, the American shad can be caught on rod and reel in the Delaware and other northeastern rivers including the Hudson and the Connecticut. It is the brevity of this visit that helps make the shad so special. One cannot dawdle if one wishes to hook one of these gleaming acrobatic fish.

I did not dawdle when Purcell invited me to go on our recent trip. He fishes hard, is possessed by the Delaware and its shad and

has established, as every dedicated angler does in his own territory, a network of sources to keep himself informed of the species'
ascent of the river. The shad is an anadromous fish. Spawned in
fresh water, it descends to the ocean to attain growth and maturity,
returning after a few years to repeat the cycle.

Because of Purcell's reputation, I had lost no optimism at the
end of our first fishless evening even though I knew that, after
taking a few shad on flies earlier in the season, he had done nothing in a weeklong series of morning and evening sessions.

We might have doubted that our flies and the manner in which
we presented them were correct, but we had been joined by several
other anglers using the standard spinning rods and darts and
knew that would have experienced some action if the fish were
about and inclined to strike. This suggests that fly casting for shad
is more difficult than spinning for them, and that is the case. The
advantages of the latter technique are that one can reach out twice
as far and can also be more certain that the lure is just above the
bottom where the shad are wont to cruise. Continuous blind casting with a fly rod over big water also becomes fatiguing after an
hour or two.

Fly fishermen on the Connecticut River in the last quarter of
the nineteenth century were probably the first recreational anglers
to catch shad, and it wasn't until spinning gear, with which the tiny
lures favored by shad can be cast, arrived in this country after
World War II that fishing for the species became popular. Today's
angler who goes after shad with a fly rod is motivated by the
additional challenge such a technique provides.

For many years, fly fishermen were catching shad by design or
accident in the upper reaches of the Delaware—its East Branch
would be one such location—fish that were in relatively shallow
water and had lost some of the zip they possessed when fresh from
the salt. It was only in the past decade or so that Purcell and others
discovered that a sink-tip fly line, a leader with a short lead core
section and a bright, sparsely dressed fly with the aforementioned
metal beads for eyes was a good combination for getting near the
bottom and attracting shad in the deep pools and runs of the
river's midsection. The lines used for this are usually No. 6, 7 or 8.
Such a leader-heavy rig is an abomination to cast, although this

effect can be mitigated slightly by keeping the entire leader less than 6 feet long and using a heavy tippet, perhaps 10-pound test and no more than a foot long, to help turn over the metal-weighted fly.

So equipped, Purcell has taken at least two shad that would have established world fly fishing records had he chosen to submit them to the International Game Fish Association, one more than 8 pounds, the other 7½.

As with the striped bass, the American shad was not native to the West Coast. Taken from rivers of the Northeast, both species were introduced into California waters before the turn of the last century. Long after that, three anadromous West Coast salmonoids—the steelhead trout and the chinook and coho salmon—were transplanted in the East, most notably in the Great Lakes.

Purcell and I returned to the river the following dawn in the company of Melvin Eck of Liberty, New York. Eck, who operates a family sawmill that specializes in providing select hardwoods for musical instruments, proved to be a splendid fly caster as was only proper for a grandson of the late Herman Christian, a trapper, hunter, guide and one of the foremost Catskill fly fishermen and fly tiers of yesteryear.

Together we fished various sections of the river from Callicoon in the north to Barryville in the south, and caught nothing. All but one of the shore and boat anglers we encountered had done no better. That one man had taken two small fish, a buck and a roe, at a pool in Narrowsburg.

The river was high and cold, about 45 degrees, and the weather, as it had been the previous several days, was dark and chilly with intermittent showers. It is generally believed that shad are not disposed to strike at lures or flies until the water reaches at least 50 degrees.

Somewhat daunted, but still hopeful, Purcell and I were back on the Delaware the following morning. As on the previous day, we fished until eight then repaired to a diner in Narrowsburg for breakfast.

When we returned to the river it had dropped a few inches and this may have been what prompted my companion to edge out a few more feet into the pool. From my vantage point downstream, it looked to me as if there was less than an inch of freeboard between the top of his waders and the water. A short while later he went ashore and announced that he had waded too deep.

"No problem," he said. "I'll dry my things off at the laundromat in town." On our way to that establishment, he told me that he had gone through the same maneuver four years before.

"A woman was in there doing her laundry," he said, "and I asked her if she minded if I disrobed, including my undershorts— I had a shirt with long tails that I kept on—and she didn't panic."

The same woman was on hand the second time around, and, perhaps reassured by my presence, she eyed the soggy Purcell and told him to do his thing.

A Pigeon Drops
In on Anglers

Paddling our canoe out of the mouth of the Croton River against a stiff southwest wind, Dan North of Croton and I made for the tide rip off the south end of Croton Point, where we hoped we would find hungry striped bass.

A hundred yards short of the point, we put his two young sons, David and Sam, ashore, where they fished, swam and engaged in a prolonged rock-throwing contest.

The rip was churning and the deep water on the outside of it looked like ideal holding water for stripers, but we had no strikes in more than an hour of casting.

By 4 P.M., the tide in the Hudson had turned and was moving upriver and it was time for us to depart, for we wished to fish the last half of the flood in the Croton River itself.

Our return trip was delayed on two occasions. The first halt came when we spotted a Canada goose eying us from the marsh a few yards away. Its behavior was so strange, we investigated and found that it could not fly, being saturated with oil. The boys wanted us to take it home and clean it off, but we felt that without a net we would never succeed in catching it.

Then, as we passed under the highway

bridge over the mouth of the Croton, a young pigeon toppled from its nest above us and fell into the water. We rescued the bird, which was not yet ready to fly. We could not reach its nest, and there was no point in putting it on the shore where it would surely have died, so we made a place for it in a life jacket and the boys vowed they would take it home and rear it to maturity.

The incoming tide, which rises and falls about three feet in the area, had nearly neutralized the outgoing waters of the Croton by the time we reached the pool downstream of Paradise Island, which is just below Croton Gorge. A few alewives, on their way upstream for spring spawning, splashed about us; huge goldfish were in the shallows, and an occasional large carp broke water lazily.

A pair of great blue herons flew past us downriver, followed by a male and female mallard, then Dan, who had been casting toward shore as I paddled upstream, had a sharp strike and a few minutes later boated a striper of about four pounds.

In the next half-hour, four more stripers, all about the same size, were hooked and landed, all taken by the way, on a medium-sized, silver-scaled Rapala swimming plug.

Then the action stopped and we moved upstream planning to fish near the rapids at the other end of the islands, but shore anglers were already there and there was not room for us too.

The fish we caught were about average for the striped bass that are taken in the Croton in spring and early summer, although occasional fish of fifteen or twenty pounds or more are caught in the river itself or between it and Croton Point.

(The baby pigeon—to leave no loose ends—survived the night in my fishing creel in the dining room and by the evening of the next day was eating earthworms and cottage cheese. Feeding it was a two-person operation: one to hold the bird, the other to open its mouth and drop the food in. If one cannot return a young bird to its nest, one should feed it worms, cottage cheese, the yolk of hard-boiled eggs or one of the inexpensive brands of dog food that contains a great deal of cereal. Under no circumstances, should the bird be forced to drink water or milk.)

The Case for Handlines

The handline is to the saltwater angler as the cane pole is to the freshwater counterpart, an utterly simple item of equipage that for certain kinds of fishing is as efficient and as much fun to use as the most expensive rod and reel.

Watching a boat-owning summer visitor to the seacoast recently lay out more than $70 for a spinning outfit for his eight-year-old son that was to be used for catching scup (porgies), tautog, sea bass and flounder from an outboard runabout, I was tempted to suggest that a 100-yard hank of marline and assorted sinkers and hooks that could be had for about $10 would be more suitable. I remained silent, however, because the owner of the tackle shop is a friend of mine and would have, I thought, been upset by my suggestion. So, being something of a craven, I'll make it while removed from his premises.

Marline would be ideal for the occasional bottom-fishing angler or for those who fish from piers or docks. It cannot be used for casting any of the welter of lightweight spoons, jigs and plugs intended for more sophisticated gear, but it is also good for saltwater trolling, the most likely East Coast species for that approach being the bluefish.

Marline is often called "tarred line" because it is impregnated with what appears to be a substance akin to creosote—not enough to rub off on your hands, but enough to give it a faint but distinctive smell. It is a smell that to this day reminds me of the days when my father and I would run offshore for bluefish or Atlantic mackerel in his big skiff which was powered by a one-lung Lathrop engine. We had a rod or two on board, but when we located big schools of the fish we used the handlines, trolling feathered jigs for the blues and spoons fashioned by a local blacksmith from the chrome rings taken from the headlights of discarded automobiles. (Those were the days when chrome plating seemed to last forever.) The lines were stashed below in a half-bushel basket and when they were new the boat's tiny cuddy cabin had a mild and not unpleasant aroma of creosote. After they had been used for a year, they were bleached nearly white by the sun and salt water and lost all their smell.

The line, which came in 100-yard hanks, was wrapped around a shingle in a spiraling weave that speeded up the winding process, and today when I go aboard a small boat for a day of bluefishing and spend twenty minutes stashing rods, reels and tackle boxes away, I yearn for the simplicity of the older technique.

My first surf casting was done with marline, either by fishing bait held on the bottom with a pyramidal sinker, or by heaving heavy—at least 6 ounces—lead jigs to sea and retrieving them hand over hand. I haven't done the latter for nearly thirty-five years and in recent decades one would be hard put to find enough room on the beach to safely pursue such an endeavor. The lure or sinker and bait is whirled about one's head two or three times before letting go. I seem to remember some veteran "heave and haulers" making 100-yard casts with jigs, but I was elated if I reached half that distance.

There is little finesse in bringing a hand-lined fish to the beach and one's catch is out of the water in less than a minute if it weighs 10 pounds or less. The handline is ideal when fishing from boat or pier, although there is not, to be sure, any of the challenge one gets from playing a fish on light tackle.

More than a decade ago, one of the most pleasing angling evenings I ever spent was rocking on the moonwashed ocean off

Grand Cayman Island in the West Indies in the company of a marvelous gentleman, an angler in late middle age known as Sam the Fisherman. Sam was a master of handline bottom fishing. Reclining in the bow of the boat with a tattered straw hat hiding his eyes, he put his left leg on the gunwale and ran the line out between his big toe and the adjacent digit. When a fish nibbled, he hooked it by lifting his leg sharply. This offered a double advantage, giving him more leverage to set the hook, and allowing him what seemed to be total relaxation. I tried his technique, but the skin between my toes wasn't tough enough for some of the large grouper-like fish we were catching. Sam had gone barefoot most of his life.

Less than 100 years ago, handlines were widely used from Cape Cod to New Jersey by those fishing for blues with either bait or trolling lure and the angling literature of that time is replete with descriptions of sailing craft—most often the stable, beamy catboat—weaving back and forth past each other over a school of the ravenous fish. In some instances, short wooden poles were rigged at right angles to the stern, outriggers permitting four lines—two in addition to those leading straight back over the transom—to be kept in the water.

The handline is ideal for so-called jigs, whether all-metal or lead and bucktail, because they need not be cast, simply lowered to the proper depth and jigged—raised and lowered—up and down. Fishing for cod with huge diamond jigs in deep water is perhaps the handline's classic role.

I suggest that if you are at most a desultory angler and if your summer seacoast vacation involves a chance to be on the water in a small boat, you give handlines a try. At the very least, you will have a good supply of strong cord with which to lash scavenged lengths of driftwood to your car's luggage rack on your return home.

Modern nylon monofilament line—40-pound test or more—can be used when handlining, but it is not ideal. It tends to snarl and its relatively small diameter and smooth surface can result in painful cuts if you hook a decent-sized fish. The marline, which is made of twisted strands of cotton, is thicker and not slippery.

To make sure marline is still generally available, I called the first two Cape Cod tackle shops that came to mind, Gun and Tackle in Falmouth and the Red Top in Buzzard's Bay. Both had it in 15-, 21- and 30-thread—each thread tests 2 pounds—diameters, in the time-honored 100-yard lengths. They also had the little marline handlines that come on a square frame in 50- and 100-foot lengths. The latter would work well for pier fishing or from a boat for small, bottom-dwelling species such as scup and sea bass.

A final thought: there are some, this writer among them, who believe that the tremulous first nibble of a fish full fathom five beneath an anchored boat is best recognized and most enjoyed when it is transmitted directly from the depths to thumb and index finger, a marvelously intimate link with the unknown and unseen.

Casting Away Doubts

You will have heard—if you bother to listen—
anglers prating about how catching fish is
really less important than the quest itself, than
feeling the wind in their hair or listening to a
lovely stream's sweet song.

This romance with the natural world is not
make-believe, but its magic can be overstated.
There comes a time when even the most contemplative angler must catch fish if he is to
enjoy his outing and maintain confidence in
his piscatorial savvy.

Such a mood possessed me earlier this
month after returning empty-handed from
fly fishing for steelhead trout on New York
State's Salmon River and for shad on the Delaware. I decided to get back in the groove
with a mackerel excursion. If ravening mackerel are under the boat, there is no way to
avoid catching them.

With this in mind, I made a date with Bud
Beckley of Branford, Connecticut, a long-time
hunting and fishing friend. Mackerel hadn't
yet showed up along his area of the coast, he
said, but they should be there a day or two
before my arrival.

Driving west from Cape Cod on Interstate
95 on my way to Connecticut and the mack-

erel, I was assailed by doubts and, shortly after passing through Rhode Island, pulled into a rest area, called my friend and learned that the fish had not arrived.

"I'd like to stop and chat," I replied, "but I've got to go somewhere and catch something."

I pushed on for another three hours to Brewster, New York, which is situated between the east and west branches of the Croton River.

I had visited both streams April 1, opening day of New York's trout season, and had been reminded afresh of the beauty of the West Branch. It is more brook than river, perhaps one-quarter the size of the East Branch, and the 2½-mile stretch of it that I had in mind—between the West Branch and Croton Falls reservoirs—wanders through a forest of hardwoods interspersed with small stands of hemlocks and pines. Because one has access to it from either end only—from Route 6 between Carmel and Mahopac or, on the downstream end, from the parking area just off the Drewville Road—it is never crowded.

I reached the West Branch in early afternoon, chose the downstream access, and lumbered rapidly up the streamside path in my waders. I had no particular location in mind. I simply wanted to get the road and the sound of its occasional vehicles behind me, and I reached the lower Split Rock Pool, which is a short distance below the halfway point, before I began to fish. I saw no anglers in that hike—during which I put up a ruffed grouse and startled two pairs of mallards into flight—and the only fresh tracks in the trail had been made by deer.

The West Branch is tough to fly fish, there being few places where there is room to manage anything but a roll cast. I caught and released three small brown trout in two hours, all on dry flies, even though I saw no rising fish.

During the spring and summer, nearly all the browns in the West Branch—they are all wild fish—are small, and one may, if one wishes, keep five of them at least nine inches long. In the fall, big browns from the Croton Falls reservoir ascend the stream to spawn, but most of them arrive after the September 30 closing of the trout season.

The three little browns did not satisfy my hunger for success, and at six o'clock I was on the East Branch, parking near the Sodom Road bridge east of the center of Brewster. I headed downstream for the Phoebe Hole—stopping for brief conversations with three of the half-dozen anglers I encountered—having taken some good fish at that spot in years past.

In its meandering 2¼-mile course between the East Branch Reservoir and the diverting reservoir, the East Branch is always within sight or sound of civilization, but many of its trout, mostly browns and rainbows, are large. The creel limit on the East Branch is one fish daily, at least 14 inches long.

At the Phoebe Hole, I found a wading angler positioned exactly where I wanted to be, about 25 yards downstream from where Bog Brook enters the river, and as I watched he hooked and released two fish, one of which appeared to be a rainbow of about a pound and a half.

Trout were rising around the bend in the same pool, so I waded out and—using a small, floating version of the Gold-Ribbed Hare's ear—caught two browns, each about 10 inches long. I hooked another, but he shook loose and the rising fish moved upstream closer to the other angler.

Not wishing to crowd him, I hurried back through the greening woods to the fast, broken water at the upper end of the area known as The Bathtub that is a few hundred yards below the reservoir outlet. I had ended my fishless jinx, but needed reassurance.

There, as the sun went down, I tied on a size 12 Royal Wulff dry fly hoping that its white wings would enable me to spot it in the jumbled water, foam and failing light.

My location called for a long cast across the main current to an eddy against the far shore, and it was impossible, except for the first few seconds after it landed, to keep my fly from dragging. Happily, that made little difference. Trout were on the prowl, and although they sometimes weren't able to move rapidly enough to catch my fly at the peak of its downstream swing, the bursts of spray they created in the effort were a delight to see and four of them connected. All were browns about 11 inches long.

In what became an unseemly lust to hook as many trout as possible, I forgot about the bushes behind me and lost my fly in one of them on a sloppy back cast. Holding a new and similar fly silhouetted against the sky, I managed to tie it on and made one more cast. A trout much larger than all the others took my offering—I felt its weight for two or three seconds—then departed with my fly in its mouth.

I called it quits. A nearly full moon came up behind the Interstate 684 overpass above me and although I would have preferred to see it rising over cathedral spruces on some wild northern stream, preferred a coyote's quavering yelp from a distant mountainside to the wailing of truck and automobile tires on a superhighway, I was content.

Steps to Stargazing

Whether from beach or mountain, meadow or city park, scanning the night skies is among summer's sweet pastimes. And with a little study a beginner will soon be able to identify many of the major constellations or their more prominent members.

In a world in which change and chaos often seem the rule, the rhythmic and predictable wheeling of the stars is comforting. The stargazer is also responding, as does the bird watcher or naturalist, to the human hunger to identify that which he sees.

The equipage for stargazing is minimal: a blanket or sleeping bag, star maps or a planisphere. The last named, also called a star wheel, shows what stars are visible at any hour of the night for any day of the year. (A star wheel for the Northern Hemisphere costs only a few dollars.)

A small flashlight with red plastic or cellophane covering its lens will provide enough light for reading the star wheel or map without temporarily spoiling your night vision, and unless you know how to find the North Star, you'll need a compass. If you have binoculars, they can be helpful.

You can stargaze as you walk. But to get into the proper mood and to see as much of the heavens as possible, you should lie on your back and relax. When standing up, even those with limber necks will strain to see more than 40 degrees above the horizon.

Your ability to identify stars can be improved by attending "Stars, Constellations and Legends," one of the courses offered by the Hayden Planetarium in spring.

Other spring courses include those in using small amateur telescopes for sky watching, astronomy and celestial navigation and small boat piloting and navigation. There is also instruction for those planning to take the F.A.A. written examination for a private or commercial pilot's license.

"Stars, Constellations and Legends" is taught by Steven Beyer, whose book *The Star Guide* (Little, Brown & Company) is suggested reading for the course. Beyer is a disarmingly enthusiastic junior high school science teacher from Staten Island who is working toward a doctorate in science education at Columbia. A few days ago he invited me to a short preview of his course, and as he turned out the lights in the planetarium's Sky Theater, I was reminded of the hours I have spent flat on my back in the cricket-chirping night striving to direct a companion's eyes to a specific star.

Beyer accomplished that instantly with a hand-held device that projected a small arrow of light on the make-believe heavens.

Each star or constellation identified serves as a reference point for locating others. Because the North Star, Polaris and the Big Dipper, the constellation used to locate it, are always visible, they are ideal starting points.

An imaginary line extended bottom to top through the two stars that form the outermost edge of the dipper's cup will intersect Polaris, which is not a particularly bright star and which, in this latitude, remains about 40 degrees above the northern horizon all year. From Polaris and the Big Dipper, one could move on to Arcturus, the brightest star in late spring and summer evening skies.

Follow the curve of the Big Dipper's handle onward for approximately 30 degrees and you will come to Arcturus. The second evening of spring, Arcturus will be about 15 degrees above the horizon in the east-northeast. At midnight, it will be in the southeast about 40 degrees above the horizon.

Besides star lore and legend, Beyer weaves historic and current discoveries in astronomy and astrophysics into his lectures.

"I encourage students to get out as often as possible to look at the heavens," he said. "Unless they do this on a regular basis, the connection between a map and the real sky cannot be successfully bridged."

The glow of light that surrounds a city at night makes it difficult or impossible to see many of the fainter stars, but Beyer said that this was often of assistance to urban stargazers in that they weren't confused by hundreds of sparkling pinpoints of light.

Beyer's *Star Guide* is the best work of its kind I have ever encountered, a delightful blend of practical instruction and the history of astronomy and its legends.

At its core is a series of more than 100 "sky screens," each depicting small portions of the eastern sky in which a prominent star is about 30 degrees above the horizon early in the evening during various months of the year. This 30 degrees, one learns, is approximately the distance from the horizon toward the meridian that is covered by the width of three fists when the observer's arms are fully extended.

The eastern sky is chosen because the stars, like the Sun and the Moon, appear (because of the Earth's rotation) to rise in the east and set in the west. Another apparent shift of the stars' location is caused by the Earth's revolution round the Sun, which results in a different set of stars overhead during the various seasons of the year.

Beginning star watchers would do well to avoid trying to pick out the various shapes—whether human or animal—that the ancients saw in the constellations. One of the few constellations that appears (to this observer at least) to bear any resemblance to that for which it was named is the Northern Crown, whose seven stars do inscribe an almost-perfect semicircle. Tonight at nine, the Northern Crown will be slightly north of Arcturus and barely above the horizon.

In their wanderings through the constellations, the five planets that are visible to the unaided eye—Mercury, Mars, Venus, Jupiter and Saturn—sometimes confuse the amateur stargazer, who should remember that they, unlike the stars, shine with a steady light. Their movements are predicted, among other places, in the annual editions of *The Old Farmer's Almanac*.

The Sugar River Has Trout Again

The Sugar River in west-central New Hampshire is sweet once again for most of its length.

Fifty year ago, this good-sized stream, which runs from Lake Sunapee west to join the Connecticut River in Claremont, was a highly regarded rainbow-trout stream. Pollution, industrial and domestic, ended all that, but in recent years Newport and Sunapee, communities on the river's upper reaches, have installed sewage treatment plants, and the Sugar's water quality has improved markedly.

A few year ago, Victor Pomiecko of Claremont and I journeyed to the stretch of the Sugar that runs between the Claremont-Newport Highway and North Newport. Access to it is provided by the abandoned Claremont-Concord Railroad bed that runs along much of the river. The railroad's right of way in that area now belongs to the state, and because ties and tracks have been removed it is negotiable by automobile.

I had fished that stretch of the Sugar, about 2 miles long, now and then over the last three decades but had caught only a few dace, a species highly tolerant to pollution. This visit was different.

Looking down at the first major pool upstream of the highway, we saw rising trout. And in less than three hours of fly fishing, we had caught—though we released some—more than forty of them, mostly rainbows. Brown trout accounted for about a third of the catch, and there were also a few native brook trout.

The fish were not large, none over twelve inches. It was their presence rather than their size that was exciting. The state has been stocking the upper parts of the stream with brown and rainbow trout since Newport completed its sewage disposal plant, and some rainbows have been taken as far downstream as Claremont.

This section of the Sugar is unusually attractive. There are no dwellings along the shore, and the stream, about thirty yards wide in most places, tumbles down through a narrow valley.

On several occasions while we fished, woodcock fluttered away as they worked through the trees and the bushes down to the river. Wild honeysuckle grew in most of the open places, its scent as delicate as a woman's just-washed hair. In the shady, moist spots along the edge of the stream, a profusion of ferns swayed in the upriver breeze. At one point, while Vic was casting over rising trout in early evening, he saw another angler, a mink, come out onto the stones on the far shore.

Because of its width, the Sugar is a fly fisherman's dream, allowing one to lay out long casts with no fear of becoming hung up on bushes and trees.

To fish most of the good water properly, though, one must be prepared to wade, and a staff is absolutely essential for this. The river is fast and rocky in this area, and the footing is slippery. Felt-sole waders or shoes are a great help.

On our first visit to the stream, my companion left his wading staff behind and within five minutes was floundering about on his belly in a stretch of fast water. He fell four more times before the day was done but kept on fishing until sundown.

We visited the river three times in as many days, and each time streamer flies were the most effective. The fish feeding on the surface were after what appeared to be a small mayfly, but all my efforts with dry flies failed.

I also tried classic upstream fishing with weighted nymphs but caught only a few trout that way. Later a nymph fished downstream as a dropper fly produced one brook trout of about a pound and several rainbows.

Nearly all the trout we caught were in the tails of the large pools, but I rather imagine that as the water warms one will find many of them, the rainbows in particular, in the pocket water in the fat runs, where there will be more oxygen. Some will also hole up in deep pools that are cooled by springs.

Even this early in the season the river was not truly cold. I had forgotten my stream thermometer, but even after two or three hours of bare-legged wading on cloudy days, I did not become chilled until dark, so the water temperature was probably a little over 60 degrees. The Sugar becomes quite warm by midsummer, and one suspects that the brook trout, which need cold water, will have retreated to the mouths of cold feeder brooks by July.

Every trout stream has its legendary monster fish, and one Sugar River angler with whom we conversed said that the Sugar held some extraordinarily large brown trout and some rainbows of more than two pounds.

"Gotta use shiners for them, though," he said as he clambered down the bank from his pickup truck, with spinning rod and minnow bucket in hand. He's probably right, but some warm June evening before many years have passed, I would like to try for those Sugar River browns after dark with a big dry fly.

And then there is the stretch of the Sugar downstream of the highway. It has not been stocked, but rainbow trout are notorious wanderers.

Truthfully, however, it would take an angler an entire season to probe thoroughly the 2-mile section Vic and I visited. And what one learns in May and June on such a stream may not apply in midsummer or fall. Trout, unlike man, cannot manipulate their environment and must make constant adjustments, however subtle, to find food and suitable water temperatures.

There are times, when a stream grows too warm, that trout simply lie about during the day, doing all their feeding in early evening, night and early morning, when the heat of the sun is gone. I recall fishing a big pool on the upper Delaware River in early summer several years ago. It was useless during the day to try for the rainbows we knew were before us, some of them more than twenty inches long, but just before all the after-light of the sun had gone, the fish began to rise. They provided us an hour of splendid action. I am certain that something like this will occur on the Sugar in the middle and late summer.

The river flows cleanly enough for trout all the way to Clare-mont, but from Claremont to the Connecticut River, about a mile, it becomes again corrupted. Claremont has an outdated primary sewage system, which means, essentially, that only solid wastes are removed and that the remaining effluvium is discharged into the stream. The worst source of pollution in Claremont is probably two industries—a paper company and a wool mill—that empty wastes directly into the stream. Claremont was scheduled to com-plete construction on a multimillion dollar sewage disposal system by 1985.

Those fishing the Sugar River would do well to obtain a map of the section of the stream described in the accompanying article. The Sunapee quadrangle of the United States Topographic Map System (scale 1:62,500) is a good choice and includes the north and south branches of the Sugar, which also hold trout.

This map covers the main stream to within a mile of the Claremont-Newport line. From that point on to where the river enters the Connecticut, one needs the Claremont, New Hampshire–Vermont quadrangle.

My brief encounter with the Sugar suggests that streamer flies such as the Queen of the Waters, the Muddler Minnow, the Horn-berg, the Black-Nose Dace or the Gray Ghost in sizes 10 or 12 are most effective at this time of year.

It is possible that sometime soon there will be a gate on either end of the abandoned railroad bed that follows the river in the section between the Claremont-Newport Highway and North Newport. If so, the 2-mile stretch will have to be walked. The proposal for a gate, mentioned to me by Clayton Phillips, a re-gional state conservation officer who loves the Sugar dearly, has great merit. Keeping vehicles out of the area will serve to preserve the stream's wild quality and will also limit the numbers of casual anglers visiting it.

Parlaying Trout Fishing with a Very Scenic Trip

Somewhere in the greening woods a ruffed grouse drummed his message of love and territoriality, a distant throbbing as much felt as heard and nearly lost in the tumultuous descent of Eagle Creek to Fontana Lake.

When the grouse's strangely ventriloquistic sound ceased, a kingfisher flashed across the stream and I sat watching rainbow trout rise in the pool before me. I was soon joined by large butterflies, their yellow-and-black-spotted wings bright against the dark green of rhododendron bushes, and before long a dozen of them, crowded on a small rock ten feet away, engaged in a ritual I couldn't fathom.

The mountains of North Carolina are graced with a handful of wild trout streams, and none are lovelier than Eagle Creek, which flows south out of the Great Smoky Mountains National Park in the northwest corner of the state.

In bygone years, these streams held only native fish, the brook trout. Brookies still survive in some of these waters but rainbows and browns have been introduced.

Today the fish in these streams maintain their populations; there are no pale-fleshed hatchery trout among them.

Before World War II, Eagle Creek flowed into the Little Tennessee River, but the Fontana Dam, a Tennessee Valley Authority hydroelectric project, created 30-mile-long Fontana Lake where the river once ran.

On arriving at Eagle Creek—a twenty-minute ride in an outboard-powered skiff from the Fontana Village Resort Marina at the west end of the lake—Joel Arrington of Raleigh, North Carolina, and I beached our craft at the Lost Cove Creek campsite at the mouth of Eagle. I immediately moved upstream past the white blossoms of dogwood and trillium and the lavender petals of dwarf iris, until I found the dark, oval-shaped pool where the butterflies danced.

There were three other first-rate pools up to that point, but none—including the pocket water in the fast runs between them—had any trout feeding on the surface. Casting blind with a small, No. 16 floating imitation of a mayfly, I had caught three rainbows, each about 8 inches long, but returned them to the water.

Within the park, which contains most of Eagle Creek, one may keep four trout but the fish must be 9 inches long or more.

I reached the butterfly pool shortly after noon and decided to have a pipe before fishing. A cloud of tiny midges hovered over the water, but no fish were coming up. A short while later, a hatch of small mayflies began, and in the fast, dark water against a ledge at the head of the pool a trout rose. Another came completely out of water in a vain effort to catch a mayfly and in five more minutes at least a dozen trout were breaking water.

It was then that Mr. Arrington pushed through the streamside rhododendron jungle and spotted the rising trout.

"Oh Lord, look at them!" he said. "Beautiful, beautiful. What are you using?"

I still had on the mayfly imitation.

"Go ahead and try it if you want to," he said. "They'll probably hit it, but you won't be able to follow it in that fast, broken water."

He was right, and after two dozen casts I had missed four fish and hooked one, another 8-incher that was released.

By that time the flies were still hatching but the rises were sporadic.

"You're going to have to give the pool a rest," he said. "These North Carolina wild trout are sensitive to disturbance. Usually you have to do it all in the first three or four casts."

Bowing to a native's knowledge, I put my rod down and we whiled away an hour drinking coffee and eating crackers and cheese.

"When you are ready to try again," my companion said, "try something bigger and brighter that you can see on the water."

He handed me a Royal Wulff, a Blonde Wulff, and an Ausable Wulff, all tied with wings of calf tail and all size 10.

These relatively large and highly visible flies made all the difference, and I quickly caught two trout about 11 inches long. There are larger trout in Eagle Creek, but they are uncommon.

That evening when we returned to the boat we found three young hikers at the Lost Cove campsite, the brothers Kovacevich, Robert and Peter, and Denise Woods, all of Kalamazoo, Michigan. They were walking a section of the Appalachian Trail and had detoured to visit the Lost Cove area.

I had kept two trout because the people at the Fontana Village Resort where we were staying had said they would be happy to cook our fish for us, but I decided that the trout would be a treat for the hikers.

"Bob loves trout, and it's his birthday," Miss Woods said delightedly. He responded with a gift of his own, a shot of Southern Comfort in a tin cup.

Our second day on Eagle was much like the first except that I went upstream a mile farther. On one occasion, three backpacking anglers passed by, but they were the only of my ilk that I encountered.

Here and there along the shore I found sticks cut by beavers, and I knew that somewhere in the valley ahead the stream grew less tumultuous, because a beaver would have to be demented to try to dam the portion of the stream I visited. In relatively flat water where the beavers were working, I reasoned, there might be larger trout.

I failed to pursue this concept, however, because there was simply too much good water to fish where I was.

Although I used rubber, stocking-foot waders on my first day on Eagle Creek, I soon discovered that they weren't necessary and were an encumbrance in climbing. The water temperature was perhaps 58 degrees, and all that was needed was a pair of wading shoes and a wading staff plucked from the shore.

A Versatile Resort Area in the Smoky Mountains Region

Four first-rate wild trout streams flow into the northside of Fontana Lake, Eagle and Hazel in the west, and Forney and Noland in the east of North Carolina.

If one is staying at the Fontana Village Resort, one may rent a boat from the marina there to get to the creeks. The resort, whose address is Fontana Dam, North Carolina 28733, also will take fishermen or fishermen-campers to and from the creeks. If one wishes to camp within the park, a permit must be obtained. One is limited to three days at any one location. For information, write to Great Smoky Mountains National Park, Gatlinburg, Tennessee 37738.

The resort complex, tucked away on wooded hillsides, is not for the jet set, but for those who enjoy hiking, camping, birdwatching, fishing (the lake itself has smallmouth and largemouth bass, walleyes, rainbow trout and white bass), square dancing (the village informally bills itself as the square dance capital of the world), tennis and horseback riding. The food is good, the service excellent and the surrounding country magnificent.

Fontana Village is in a dry country so one must bring his own alcohol beverages.

The Nantahala National Forest is on one side of the Village and the Great Smoky Mountains National Park on the other, and the Appalachian Trail passes through it. The post office at the village is a much-used place—for mail and goodies—for those hiking the trail, and a shelter and tables have been provided for them to repack their gear. There is also a cafeteria, laundromat and a store well stocked with hiking foods.

Fontana Village grew up around the community that was established for those who built the dam, and the original cottages are available for rent, as well as rooms in the new Fontana Inn and the older Fontana Lodge.

To be fully prepared for all fishing, an angler should bring bait-casting or spinning gear for the lake and a flyfishing outfit (a No. 4, 5 or 6) for the streams. Within the Great Smoky National Park, one may use single hook lures and a spinning outfit, but flyfishing is the classic approach.

For trout fishing in the park, one needs a regular angling license plus a special trout license.

Tongue-in-Cheek Opinions

Often, after I start telling someone of a big fish that didn't get away, or of how I faced death with equanimity at some disputed barricade, his eyes go out of focus, made so by boredom and disbelief.

This has happened all my adult life. Boredom I could understand—there are many insensitive clods who cannot appreciate the nuances of a finely crafted yarn—but, until yesterday, I couldn't comprehend my lack of credibility. How could a pipe smoker who thought that he oozed sincerity be doubted?

Yesterday, I received the answer in a bulletin from Communications Briefings, a Blackwood, New Jersey, firm that asks if I am worth $1 a week, the cost of subscribing to its monthly eight-page newsletter that will inform me of the "latest and most useful communications techniques available today."

Being worth more than a dollar a week— even fifty years ago, I earned ten times that amount hoeing corn—I read on.

The first item in the newsletter laid bare my communications problem. "Talk faster," it said, "if you want to increase your credibility. People who speak rapidly (as fast as 190 words a minute) are perceived to be more trustworthy than slower talkers. They are seen as having honest enthusiasm."

To test what it takes to give the impression of honest enthusiasm, try reading aloud the five paragraphs above as fast as you can. Going at the aforementioned clip, it should take a minute and six seconds. talking at my usual speed—with only one stop for a puff on my pipe—it took me a minute and forty-five seconds.

During the days when I was hoeing corn and hanging out on the edge of the group of old-timers that gathered at the general store, I came to believe that a measured delivery denoted integrity rather than indecision, an earnest effort to be accurate. With the same deliberateness they showed in plucking coins from little leather purses with their gnarled, horny fingers, those men searched for the exact word, and a ten-second pause was not unusual. A pipe was often part of the ritual, and except for a brief period when I sat on the steps of the same store in summer and puffed Benson and Hedges cigarettes in an unsuccessful effort to persuade the passing golden girls of summer that I was a sophisticate, a corncob has been part of my own story-telling since high school days.

While inserting a fresh charge of tobacco, an accomplished pipe smoker can count on at least a half-minute break to organize his thoughts, and scraping a pipe clean with a jackknife and searching for a suitable receptacle for the dottle will triple that hiatus. Additional times can be gained in stomping out sparks on his host's rug.

Fast-talk has swept the reason for these ruses aside, and I reveal them only to provide an insight into the challenges I now face. For more than forty years in drawing room and bar, in duck blind and grouse butt, in log cabin and fishing shack, in canoe or bonefish skiff, in tent or lodge or castle, hunkered beside campfire or circling a smoking backyard barbecue with streaming eyes, deliberateness has tarnished my credibility.

Reminding myself that I am not altogether resistant to change—I learned to use word processors the year before I became eligible to ride downtown in the senior citizen van or to purchase rutabaga seeds at a ten percent discount—I have begun a campaign to become believable.

Today, when I went to the general store for my mail, I encountered Lisha Jones in the parking lot.

Lisha is not known for his eloquence, but he was clearly dealing with a burning issue, and words tumbled from him.

"You got squash blight?" he asked.

In recent years, few things have troubled me as deeply as the yellowing—even as the blossoms are forming—of squash and cucumber leaves in my garden, and my friend's questions sent half-formed phrases whirling through my head.

Faster than the eye could follow, my right hand went toward my hip pocket, where I keep my corncob. I use the hip pocket because at least once a week a still-smoldering pipe burns holes in it, and better there than the side pocket which holds my jackknife and my change. The pipe was clenched in my teeth, and I had loaded it and was searching for a match before I realized what had happened. Lisha rested his forearms on the tailgate of my truck and gazed into the middle distance, halfway between there and the salt marsh at the head of Town Cove.

I wrenched the pipe from my mouth and, at a conservatively estimated 180 w.p.m., responded to his question.

"I live with squash blight, it is inevitable, rotate your crops they say but that doesn't amount to a damn, the blight is a heaven-sent penance whose duration is unknown nor can it be cured by sprays or dusts, the best thing to do is hoe the plants up and plant ruta bagas or turnips, you can do that as late as the second week in August, I like rutabagas better and they'll keep most of the winter in your root cellar, if you haven't got a root cellar dig a hole in sandy soil, and how many places on this island are without sandy soil and store them in it with hay to keep them from freezing in the winter and a cover to keep out the snow and rain, that's the best way to deal with squash blight."

Before I was halfway through my response, Lisha's eyes had left the middle distance and were fixed hungrily on mine.

"I'll do it!" he cried and raced toward his pickup.

Intoxicated by my success, I turned to enter the store and was not sufficiently quick to avoid being struck in the thigh by a bicycle-riding lad of thirteen. I felt an affinity for him because it was only fifty years ago in that same spot that I had driven my new Sears, Roebuck bike into Evan Allan's pony cart, but it seemed to me that a little fast-talk was in order.

"Where's the fire, slow down, better learn now for when you'll be driving a car and that isn't far off, you'll be astonished at how swiftly the seasons flee and the athletic yearnings of youth become arthritic and desire's fury is spent or corrupted and it is then that you'll wince at yesteryear's callow conduct."

Obviously distraught, the boy dropped his bike and seized my hand.

"Take it easy, sir," he said. "You don't have to talk. Let me help you over to the steps where you can sit down."

SUMMER

Big Catch, Revisited

After more than fifty-five years of catching everything from giant bluefin tuna to tiny brook trout, I know that I will never become a consistently successful angler.

I am adept with fly rod, surf rod and bait-casting and spinning gear, have read hundreds of volumes devoted to the wooing of various fresh- and saltwater fishes, and have picked the brains of experts from Atlantic salmon guides in Canada or Scotland to tarpon guides in Costa Rica or Key West. I know what to do and when to do it, but various personality quirks subvert that knowledge and those decades of experience. A sudden yearning to recreate a delightful fishing experience of years past is one of them and I yield to it even though the time of year of the conditions may be wrong.

Early last summer, I began thinking of the 3-pound brook trout that a boyhood chum pulled from beneath a stump on the west shore of Mill Pond brook nearly fifty years ago. I became possessed by the notion that another such fish was waiting there for me. I knew that the brook had been altered by a series of ponds on its upper reaches, ponds that had reduced its flow and warmed its water. Such an alteration might have made the brook untenable for its wild brook trout population, but logic fled before the image of that fat, silvery fish writhing on a gravel bar.

I walked across the meadow to the brook to discover that pools that were once waist-deep reached only to my knees, and, even more critical, the water was no longer cold enough to make my legs ache. A raft of watercress was where it had always been, however, and I tarried beside it as I had done in days of yore, savoring its peppery leaves and stems and reassuring myself that all was well. Moving downstream to where the brook empties into the long, narrow cove of a salt pond and to where that lovely sea-run trout had lurked, I discovered that the stump was gone as was the flow of water that had once cut a resting place for trout against that shore.

I left the place in discontent, not even bothering to fish. That was a mistake, I learned a week later when one of my sons took his son there. Although distressed by the brook's degradation, my son was not enslaved by a vision of what ought to have been. He tarried at the brook's mouth until after sunset. As the shadows deepened, trout began rising in less than two feet of water against the wooded, steep-sided eastern shore of the cove's upper end. They had forsaken the overheated brook itself for a spot into which the cold water from a dozen small springs flows.

A few trout fishermen become so enamored of tying flies that they forsake the water. Gathering or refurbishing rods and reels or fashioning fishing lures sometimes keeps me from the sport itself and I am buried in gear, most of which remains unused season after season. Several mornings ago, my other son told me of raising—but not hooking—dozens of large striped bass while casting from his boat along the north shore of the island on which we live. When his surface-swimming plug went over the fish, he said, sometimes as many as six or eight of them, all over 30 pounds, would rise from the bottom as one, but at the last second they would refuse his offering, flail the water with their broad tails and return to the bottom. After many casts and after switching to a one-handed spinning rod and a small needlefish plug, he managed to catch and release a twelve-pound bass that raced in from the side.

He was going out again after work, he said, and asked if I wanted to come along. I should have said yes, because the fish proved to be more cooperative on his second trip, but I had already begun to believe that a small, surface-riding fly rod lure would be just the ticket for those recalcitrant stripers. I devoted the last two hours of that day to making several of them. They are shaped out of the light, dense-celled stuff that provides the flotation for the "boards" used by wind surfers—the cellular plastic of which lobster pot buoys are made also works—and are about 4 inches long, tapering from five-eighths of an inch thick at the front end to less than a quarter of an inch at the other. The side and top are rounded, the bottom is flat and the head end is cut on a bevel from top to bottom, angling back toward the rear. A single long-shanked hook is secured with epoxy in a slit cut into the bottom.

Twilight was nigh before the black spray paint on the lures was dry. Wanting to try them out and perhaps prodded by the nearly full moon, I hearkened back to a similar night more than three decades before when I took my first fly rod stripers, several fish between 12 and 18 pounds. I had landed them while casting from the rocky rough and tumble terminal moraine on the island's North Shore, and lost one over 30 pounds right at the beach, a fish that would have broken the fly rod record for the species at that time. The tide was wrong, falling instead of rising, but the moon was right and I succumbed.

I hadn't visited that spot in twenty-five years and as I walked along the beach in the premoonrise darkness, the lights of houses built since that time were intrusive, but all the landmark boulders remained unchanged, including the one that marked where I would begin to fish.

Sitting beside the boulder savoring the sea-smell on the southwest breeze, swatting mosquitoes and enjoying a pipe, I was amused to recall that those first fish had been caught on a $10 fly rod and a cheap trout reel, using one of the three simple bucktail flies I possessed. By contrast, the graphite rod leaning against the boulder was worth more than $300, its reel $150 and in the shoulder tackle bag a friend had bought for me in Paris reposed dozens of saltwater flies—some tied by such angling notables as Lee Wulff and Lefty Kreh—as well as my own just-completed slider lures.

The moon rose, sometimes gleaming, sometimes a dull yellow disk half-obscured by swirling fog, but always providing enough light for me to watch the wake of my new lure on the barely ruffled water. It looked good to me, but no fish were there to confirm my observation. I walked up and down a quarter of a mile of beach, and, with intermittent breaks for pipe and coffee, kept it up, without a hit, until midnight and slack low water. The same thing had happened that night long ago, after which I had dozed beside the boulder as the tide came in, resuming casting at 3 A.M. and catching my first bass two hours before dawn. I thought of attempting to duplicate that scenario, but being somewhat older and also less intent on catching fish, I declined the gambit and strolled back whence I had come, past the familiar night shapes of boulders and headlands and past the salt pond creek where black-crowned night herons yapped above me unseen in the fog.

Surf Fishing: The Nighttime Provides an Edge

Surf fishermen who cherish the evening cock-tail hour or who feel they must eat every sup-per with family or friends should turn to tennis. With striped bass—and, to a lesser de-gree, bluefish—the very best time to be abroad is at sundown and thereafter.

Indeed, it is this urge to leave the beach for familial bliss or the tinkling of ice in tall glasses evinced by so many that makes it pos-sible for me to keep visiting the increasingly crowded beaches of the Northeast for a bit of angling. God bless gin and tonic, inane chat-ter and, though I risk sounding like an ogre, togetherness. Again and again, after virtually all the four-wheel-drive vehicles have ground their way into the sunset, and the bright boats off shore are cutting their full-throttle wakes for the dock, the fish arrive.

Although I have fished the salt water off every state from Maine to Florida, my surf angling south of Long Island has not been sufficiently intensive to permit me to extend my generalizations to areas beyond. I know only that on Cape Cod and its outlying islands, and on the south side of Long Island, my re-marks about surf fishing are valid.

Stripers in particular do a great deal of

feeding after dark. Bluefish forage at night also—witness the success of party boats out of New Jersey that chum for them off shore on summer evenings. One can usually, if they are running in any significant numbers at all, catch all the blues one wants during the day. Still, dusk can be the most productive time.

Some years ago, as I angled a stretch of Sound shore where I could consistently catch striped bass at night but not in the daytime, it occurred to me that the fish might be there in the day but simply not feeding.

For three straight days, I snorkled up and down the beach, covering more than a mile each time and ranging from 20 yards off shore to more than 150. I saw fewer than half a dozen stripers during those swims, but each evening after sunset the fish were responding to my surface swimming plugs.

I have a theory, though no way to substantiate it, that the striped bass's dislike of shallow water—by this I mean anything from 2 to 10 feet deep—is born of his days as a juvenile, when, only a few inches long, he was pursued by predatory fish, from which he tried to escape in the shallows, only to be harried from above by terns and gulls. At night, there was no danger of attack from above. At night, the striper can move, without this residual fear, in shore, in search of two of his favorite food fish—the sand eel and the silverside minnow. Also, of course, certain marine worms upon which the stripers feed are nocturnal.

Whatever the reason for this behavior, you will often find the stripers at night in areas they totally eschew during the daytime.

I know, for example, of two extensive sand bars off Chappaquiddick Island where, during a very low tide, a big bass would have trouble keeping wet. Yet large fish frequent these places at night, making them ideal for wading fishermen, including the fly rodder.

And, just to make this situation a bit more complicated, I have often been able to raise, but not hook, striped bass along a rocky beach during the daylight, and then, at dusk or dark, to catch all I wanted in the same spot.

For years, I thought that a rising tide at night was the best situation for shore fishing for striped bass, but in the past decade this theory has proved a bit wobbly. Movements of fish and baitfish change, and one must be constantly on guard against a rote approach. Experiment constantly with timing and technique, and remember to glean whatever information you can from fellow anglers. There is no substitute for local knowledge of an area.

Night surf-casting requires a reasonable level of expertise. If you are a beginner, practice during the daylight until you know precisely where your lure is going each time you cast it. If—though it isn't likely—you are trying to master casting with a conventional revolving spool reel rather than a spinning reel, you must, before you venture forth in the dark, have reached the point where backlashes are virtually a thing of the past.

And if there are other anglers nearby at night, keep an eye open for them and make sure you don't hook them on your backcast. This is particularly true when you're fly fishing, for 60 or 70 feet of line may be unrolling behind you.

Also, carry a light so that you can change lures, inspect lures for weed and remove lures from fish.

Someday I'm going to purchase one of those little penlights with a flexible neck and clip for a pocket I see advertised in fly-fishing magazines, but until I do I'll get by with a tiny disposable light, the kind a lady drops into her purse. It throws enough of a beam to do the jobs mentioned above and is small enough so I can hold it in my mouth and work with both hands. I dislike anything that is disposable, because in using it I am lending impetus to a waste-oriented culture. But total consistency is boring.

During the summer in the Northeast, I am quite comfortable at night in nothing but sneakers, shorts and shirt, but some anglers dislike remaining wet for long periods and use waders.

Your tackle box need be nothing more than a musette bag with half a dozen lures and a small hand gaff, although there are little over-the-shoulder bags with separate plastic-lined compartments designed for the surf fishermen.

The popping plug is a splendid lure to use on both stripers and bluefish. It is particularly effective with the latter, because—as with the fly fisherman's floating fly—one can see the strike. It is my belief that one has better luck with a surface or a subsurface swimmer after dark.

One sometimes hears surf fishermen discussing whether a

bright moon hinders angling success. I have no strong feelings on this, even though many years ago I read something by Jacques Cousteau, which was, I think, attributed to Mediterranean commercial fishermen, to the effect that when the moon is full, the sea is empty of fish.

I have taken more striped bass on dark nights than on bright ones but have also done more fishing on such evenings. I have also caught stripers on the full of the moon, when I could see the wakes of the big fish as they moved up behind the plug in the shallow waters of a bay.

If you have the bent for it—I have tried, but failed miserably—keep a log of your night fishing endeavors. List the time, the tide and the phase of the moon, an add solid information of a similar nature from reputable anglers. If you could do this for several years, you might discover something of value, but don't be distressed if the fish don't cooperate. Their world is one of raw survival—of opportunistic behavior, of endeavoring to find the most food with the least energy expended—and it is constantly changing, however subtly.

And, as an addendum to the Mediterranean quotation, remember that when a surf fisherman's glass and stomach are full, his freezer will be empty.

Sporting in the
Thousand Islands

We had waited until late afternoon to try for small-mouth bass off the upper end of Grindstone Island, because my host and companion, Harold Herrick, Jr., of Cape Vincent, knew that I preferred to catch them with top-water lures.

"We could get them any time with minnows," he had said that morning, "but by midsummer I find that I do best on top either early in the morning or in late afternoon and evening."

Early morning was ruled out, because we had risen late, a result of having spent all the previous evening talking of the superlative waterfowl hunting the area offers and discussing antique duck decoys, of which Herrick has an excellent collection.

We left Herrick's waterfront home at five o'clock, and, after fewer than half a dozen casts toward some giant boulders in a small cove, a lovely bass of about 3 pounds hit my popping plug and jumped three times before being brought to the boat. Another, of similar size, grabbed a little swimming plug Herrick was using, and in the next hour we caught and released about eight fish.

The Thousand Islands region of the St.

Lawrence River—which is split by the Canadian-American boundary—offers some of the most extensive and productive small-mouth angling in the country. It also has some first-class large-mouth bass fishing, most notably in Lake of the Isles, a long, shallow lake on the lower end of Wellesley Island, just downstream of the Thousand Islands Bridge to Canada.

And if one wishes a change of pace, one can also cast or troll for muskellunge, an endeavor that often produces big Northern pike as well.

In recent years, the Thousand Islands area has attracted the attention of anglers who participate in professional bass tournaments, and this June the 233 contestants in the three-day New York State Invitational Bass Tournament registered nearly 2,000 bass. The number of fish caught was actually much higher; the anglers returned many smaller fish to the water instantly, rather than putting them in live wells for measurement and release at the end of the day. This year's winner, Robert Murray of Nashville, for example, brought at least thirty legal-size bass (12 inches long or more) to the boat each day.

After we had fished most of the aforementioned cove on Grindstone, Herrick elected to move. But before we resumed our efforts, he put in at a boathouse in front of a summer home on the island's Rum Point, and from the tree-surrounded lawn came laughter and an occasional strange rattling sound.

"They've got a game going," Herrick said as he moved some tackle boxes out of the way to get at a framed and mounted print of muskellunge fishing by Frank H. Taylor a summer resident of the area in the late nineteenth century, whose work often appeared in *Harper's Weekly*.

The print was for Michael White of Boston, whom we soon spotted dashing about under the eaves of his house with a tambourine in hand. Three others present also had tambourines, and there was much merriment.

I wondered if I had stumbled upon some esoteric rite that the isolation of island living—the residents of Grindstone and many of the islands in the area must use skiffs and launches to reach the mainland—had engendered.

Noting my expression, which I am sure was both wary and

intrigued, Herrick, who spent his summers as a lad in a nearby home on Grindstone, said, "It's roof ball, but let Michael tell you about it."

The introductions over, White, a tall, ebullient fellow, said: "You're just in time. Why don't you join us for a set?"

I declined, pleading a flare-up of pain in one leg caused by an old shrapnel wound, but pressed White for an explanation of the endeavor.

"My grandfather, Lewis H. Morton of New York City," White said, "started it early in this century. He studied abroad for a time, and, although I am not sure he excelled in his studies, he did return with a penchant for bat-and-ball games and tambourines. Roof ball at this place, then his summer place, was a logical outcome of that interest.

"It is played with a doubles squash ball and tambourines. The scoring is one to twenty-one. The serve, underhanded, must land on the roof over the center window, and the ball must bounce twice on the roof before leaving it."

I asked White, a foreign investment specialist, if the game was played on only that one roof.

"Yes," he replied. "One must have a proper roof with the eaves the correct distance above the ground. One cannot overstate the importance of this.

"About a decade ago this place was razed by fire. I instructed the architect to rebuild it as before, but he made the foundation higher. It was a disaster, and I had to spend a small fortune, which I didn't possess, filling and grading to bring the lawn up to the correct level for roof ball."

I asked White if one should bring his own tambourine to a roof-ball match.

"It's not necessary, but if you have a tambourine of which you're inordinately fond—one, perhaps, that some dark-eyed gypsy lady gave you—but all means bring it along.

"I do wish you'd have a game with us. A shandygaff [a mixture of beer or ale and ginger beer, ginger ale or lemonade] is the appropriate roof-ball drink, but I wouldn't hold you to that."

Later we casted to more smallmouths in shoal areas around Grindstone as night came on, and it was singularly pleasing to reflect on the variety of simple pleasures the Thousand Islands offer.

Fishing, of course, is one of the main attractions and, if one wishes to be shown the ropes by an expert, that is easily arranged. The fishing guides of the region—there are more than thirty-five of them in Cape Vincent, Clayton and Alexandria Bay—will also, upon arrangement, follow the old tradition of cooking a shore lunch for their clients, a meal of which some of the fish caught that morning are the pièce de résistance.

One Cape Vincent guide, Bob Eveleigh, took Herrick and me bass fishing for a few hours one morning off Grenadier Island, which is in Lake Ontario at the western end of the Thousand Islands area.

"If you think you had good fishing with lures," Eveleigh said, "wait until you try minnows on the bottom off Grenadier."

"I'd like to try bucktail jigs and plastic worms first," I said when we arrived at the spot and began drifting over a vast shoal that was about 10 feet deep.

"Try what you want," Eveleigh said, "but you will find that minnows are best."

He was right. After fooling around with my lures for half an hour and getting no strikes at all, I switched to minnows out of self-defense because my companions had all but four of our three-man limit of fifteen bass on the boat. In less than an hour of actual fishing, we were heading back to the dock.

Difficulty Is the Lure of Saltwater Fly Fishing

Saltwater fly fishing isn't wildly popular in the Northeast, but some of those who do turn to it lose interest in all other forms of angling.

The fascination of what is difficult accounts for most of the sport's appeal, and its greatest challenge is putting the fly in front of the fish. Once the quarry is hooked—be it a 10-pound blue or a 30-pound striped bass—bringing it to shore is a relatively simple matter. For the resilient fly rod—if it and its reel are of suitable size and quality—is a marvelously efficient fish-fighting tool.

I was reminded of this a few years ago when fly fishing for tarpon off Key West, Florida. The tarpon were averaging about 90 pounds. After having experienced the excitement of the strike, the several jumps and the first long run, I experimented with putting extreme pressure on those fish (they were always released anyhow). It was, I discovered, almost impossible to break them off if the rod was held high and a 14- or 16-pound test tippet was being used.

When venturing on salt water for the first time, the fly fisherman who learned his craft on intimate trout streams is immediately aware that he is involved in a different ball game in which long casts, rather than delicate presentation, are often all-important. In southern waters when one is after tarpon or bonefish on vast and shimmering flats, fast and accurate casting is also called for because the fly is being offered to cruising fish that have been spotted in the shallow water. North or South, one of the most formidable obstacles to consistent saltwater fly-fishing success is the wind; if you can't reach feeding fish, you won't catch them.

From Cape Cod to New Jersey, the prevailing summer breezes are off the ocean and the land-based fly fisherman who is truly serious memorizes all of the twists and turns of the shoreline within his bailiwick so that he can often fish with the wind at his back or (just as good) blowing across his body and away from his casting arm; the reverse of the last-named wind direction creates an almost-impossible situation, one in which a fly driven into the back of one's head is a common occurrence.

Wind is less of a problem when fishing from a boat because it is usually possible to approach breaking fish or a likely looking spot from the best direction for casting. Not every boat is suitable for fly casting, and in the Northeast one finds very few craft with an uncluttered casting platform or deck. Loose coils of fly line inevitably catch on any protuberance, including cleats, hatch covers and even slightly protruding screws or bolts.

There will also be days when the wind is strong enough to blow the fly line off the deck. If your boat has low railings up forward, you can lash a large plastic garbage container in the bow and strip your line into that, or you can hang a so-called stripping basket, a wide-mouthed canvas container with a wire frame, from your belt. The last-named is probably the best solution because you have to learn to use it in most beach-fishing situations, particularly when you are wading.

The nagging onshore wind usually dies with the sun, which is why many fly-rod devotees do most of their fishing—particularly for striped bass—at dusk and thereafter. After-dark fly fishing requires greater casting skill because you are relying on feel rather than sight.

Another advantage of night angling is that many species, stripers among them, forage closer to shore at dusk and thereafter.

When fish are feeding selectively on sand eels, juvenile sand worms or shrimp, fly fishermen actually have an advantage over anglers using plugs, jigs and spoons because a fly can be tied to closely resemble, in both size and coloration, such small creatures. This is particularly true with the Atlantic bonito, a marvelous fast-swimming food and game fish that often displays an aversion for spinning or bait-casting lures.

In the Northeast, the bluefish is undoubtedly the ideal species for the neophyte fly fisherman to pursue. With rare exceptions, it will hit anything bearing even a vague resemblance to a forage fish, and its propensity for smashing at topwater plugs makes it an ideal candidate for a fly-rod popping bug. Any white bucktail fly with a gold or silver body will take bluefish, and if you tie your own, make them as simple as possible because the blues will destroy them in short order.

Although some might regard this maneuver as poor form, one can, from shore or boat, tease surface-feeding blues into fly-rod range with a hookless popping plug and a spinning rod. This is a two-man operation. One man throws the plug to the distant fish and begins a rapid retrieve, while the fly fisherman delays his cast until the rampaging fish are only a few yards away.

Any decent fiberglass, graphite or graphite-boron fly rod capable of handling a No. 9 or No. 10 line is suitable for blues and stripers. The reel for these species need not be a costly custom-made job, but it should have room for at least 150 yards of backing plus the fly line. The venerable Model 1498 Pfleuger will do the job, as will the Martin Reel Company's new and similarly inexpensive MG-9 reel. The Martin reel has an excellent drag and will hold a 10-weight line and 300 yards of 18-pound test dacron backing.

Unless saltwater fly fishing consumes you utterly, a good compromise is to include a fly rod in your surf fishing or boat fishing equipage, using it when the conditions are right. Unless you seek fly rod records, a short, simple leader dropping down in three stages—30-, 20-, and 10- or 12-pound test—will suffice. Some saltwater fly fishermen use a 6- or 7-inch light wire leader ahead of the fly when going after bluefish, but this really isn't necessary.

Blues are plentiful. If one cuts you off, it only takes a few seconds to tie on another fly. If you would like to try for an International Game Fish Association record in saltwater fly fishing, the organization has categories for 1-, 4-, 8-, 12- and 16-pound test tippets, the tippet being the weakest part of the leader. But to try for a record, you will have to, in order to get the most out of your leader, learn to master certain knots. These include the Surgeon's, Blood and Albright, plus the Bimini Twist. The records for the aforementioned species won't be easy to surpass. For 9-pound test tippets, for example, the record striper is 42 pounds and the record blue 18 pounds 6 ounces.

One way to hasten your mastery of saltwater fly fishing is to become a member of a club devoted to the sport. One such group in the metropolitan area is the Salty Flyrodders of New York, 559 Hollywood Avenue, Bronx 10465. If you choose to go it alone, the revised edition of *Lefty Kreh's Fly Fishing in Salt Water* (Nick Lyons Books/Winchester Press, 1986) is the best book on the subject.

A Lesson on Cooking Fish

The increasing popularity of fish in the American diet has helped push the price of highly prized species—including Atlantic and Pacific salmon, various flatfishes and tunas, and Atlantic cod—beyond the cost of a first-rate cut of beef, and this, if nothing else, should inspire treating such fare with more respect than that accorded the thigh of a chicken.

What follows is not a list of recipes—although there will be a few of them—but some guidelines for dealing with provender from stream, lake and ocean.

The greatest sin in preparing fish for the table, which no sauces or spices will mitigate, is overcooking. Many recipes specify a certain number of minutes for a fish of a certain weight, or a fish steak of a certain thickness, but the only sure test—long before the suggested time is up—is to prod them with a fork. They are done when the meat readily flakes apart under gentle pressure. Unlike red meat or poultry, which can stand a few minutes of overcooking without being ruined, fish that is baked, broiled or fried can become overdone, which renders it dry and tasteless, in a matter of seconds.

If one is broiling fish in a gas or electric

oven, the fillet is sometimes nicely browned a minute or two before it is thoroughly cooked. If that happens, turn the broiler off and let the ambient heat finish the job.

Broiling fish over an open fire is tricky because the heat is inconsistent. There is also the problem of turning the fillet, which isn't required when it is broiled in an oven, without its falling apart. An easy way around this is to put the fish in a separate, hinged grill. Separate grill or not, fish cooked over coals must be constantly attended.

Fish steaks lend themselves to outdoor barbecue cooking, but if you use fillets leave the skin on them; this helps keep the meat in one piece.

If you are ever moved to cook fish for a large group at lakeside or seashore over an open wood fire, you can arrange the fish—which should be split or in steaks or fillets—on a grill measuring about 2 by 3 feet. Wire another grill of similar size over the fish and fasten 6-foot (total length) loops of chain or wire to each of the grill's long ends. These loops will enable two of your helpers to suspend the fish at varying distances above the fire. Fish broiled in this manner, and over a barbecue as well, should be brushed with melted butter, or vegetable oil, seasoned with salt and pepper, and basted often during cooking.

Many years ago during an all-night shore-fishing trip for striped bass on which I had ventured without eating supper, I was beset by hunger pangs shortly before dawn. I had brought no food with me, but I did have two medium-size bass on the beach. I dug a shallow hole in the sand, lined it with round rocks the size of oranges, cut a one-pound steak from one of the fish, wrapped it in a thick layer of rockweed, and, when the fire died down, placed it on the coals and hot rocks.

I piled additional rockweed on top and less than an hour later—my table a boulder—reveled in what at the time seemed the sweetest fish I had ever enjoyed. The setting—a crisp, early October dawn, the murmur of small waves on a wild and rocky shore—and the simplicity of my repast undoubtedly contributed to my pleasure, but the steaming rockweed had imparted a marvelously delicate flavor to the bass. It was as if I had seasoned the fish with a gentle sea breeze.

A few years later—wondering if hunger and an overweening romanticism had completely misled my palate—I repeated the maneuver at home, the only difference being that the bass, again nesting in rockweed, was wrapped in aluminum foil and placed on white oak embers in the fireplace. This was highly successful also, but it lacked some of the impact of the original endeavor.

Steaks of cod, halibut, haddock, salmon, yellowfin tuna and striped bass surrounded by rockweed can also be cooked in a traditional two-part steamer. The water should be salted and boiling vigorously before setting the fish-containing upper half, which has a perforated bottom. Cooking time—with the lid on, of course—is usually ten to twelve minutes for steaks an inch thick.

Very small fish—trout or yellow perch less than 8 inches long would be two examples—can be pan fried whole after dusting with seasoned flour or corn meal. Because this can be done over low heat and the cooking takes only a few minutes, butter can be used. Larger fish or fish steaks, or fillets more than a half-inch thick, need more heat and more time, and oil must be used because butter will burn before the fish is done. Never put a lid on the pan. This will result in the fish being partially steamed, and not browned. Never, by the way, try to pan fry fish that has been dipped in batter.

Batters are used for deep-frying fish. A deep-fryer with a thermostat is ideal for this, but it can be accomplished in a simple iron or aluminum pot if one has a thermometer. In general, oil should be heated to about 370 degrees for deep-frying. Small fish, such as smelt, whitebait (silverside minnows and sand eels), or small pieces of fish require more heat so that the batter will be brown when—after about two minutes—the fish is done. Lower temperatures are needed to cook larger pieces of fish thoroughly without burning the batter.

When cut into steaks no more than an 1½ inches thick, certain mild-flavored white-fleshed fish—among them cod, haddock and striped bass—lend themselves to a marinade and pan frying. One such recipe comes to me from my mother who got it from a Martha's Vineyard dentist fifty years ago. It calls for steeping striper steaks in a fifty-fifty mixture of water and vinegar, to which a large sliced onion, several chopped garlic cloves and salt and pepper have been added, for an hour or two. The steaks, which should be covered by the liquid, are then drained, patted dry with a paper towel, dusted with flour and fried over low heat.

One of the best fish cookbooks published in the last fifteen years is A. J. McClane's richly illustrated *Encyclopedia of Fish Cookery* (Holt, Rinehart and Winston).

Casting for Tarpon

Fly fishing for tarpon is not for those who seek to blend angling with sweet sessions of silent thought. It is, if done properly, an intense hunt culminating in the few seconds when one's offering must be properly presented to the gray shapes moving past. Often there is only time for one cast and if that is botched the fish will either not see one's fly or hurtle away in terror if it lands too close.

And when, as often happens, not many fish are seen, one must also battle boredom, hour after hour of inactivity while standing in the bow of a shallow-draft, outboard-powered skiff, flyrod in hand as the guide on his elevated platform in the stern poles across miles of shallow, shimmering flats. It may also involve a stakeout on the edge of a deep channel in the flats that tarpon are wont to use.

When the intervals between tarpon sightings last an hour or more, an angler's self-discipline is sorely tested. The sun and the motion of the boat are soporific and he looks ahead but does not see, and at such a time the guide's shout that he has spotted a fish may find the angler totally unprepared to go swiftly into action. He will discover that he is standing on one of the loose coils of his flyline or, in a frenetic response to the guide's exhortation to "Cast! For God's sake, cast!" he may deliver the fly to the wrong end of the fish.

It is a highly specialized form of angling for those who wish to go after one of the world's most highly prized game fishes in the most difficult manner possible.

For the first three hours after Roger Donald of Brooklyn and I set forth from Key West, we saw no tarpon even though Captain Harry Spear, our intense and accomplished light tackle guide who is particularly fond of fly fishing, had poled steadily most of that time.

Our captain was not depressed, however, for he had been saving what he felt would be the most promising area—the Marquesas Keys, which are a few miles west of Key West—for late in the afternoon. He had delayed taking us there because many of the anglers and guides involved in a Florida Keys tarpon-fishing tournament would be working the area until the competition's 4 P.M. curfew.

The last tournament boat was leaving when we arrived. I was admiring a lone coconut palm towering above the green mangroves on the strangely desolate beach before me when Captain Spear shouted that four tarpon were swimming directly at me. I began my cast before I saw them—most occasional tarpon anglers, and I am no exception, have trouble spotting tarpon—but the fly was on the mark. I had made only two 6-inch retrieves when one of the fish hit. I struck back hard, three times, and a glorious silvery shape erupted from the pale green water. I remembered to "bow," to lower the rod and shove it toward the fish, thus creating as much slack line as possible, a maneuver that lessens the chance of a broken leader.

The next critical phase of fly fishing for tarpon—"getting the fish on the reel"—was accomplished without mishap. The loose coils of flyline lying on the deck must go through the rod's guides without snarling as the fish makes its initial run.

Although what follows is hard work, it is marvelously satisfying. The fish, which, will probably jump three or four more times, are linked with the angler, and all the latter has to do is to constantly maintain all the pressure his tackle can stand.

Ten minutes and four more jumps after my tarpon was hooked, Captain Spear announced that I would have to put more heat on the fish—we estimated its weight at 80 to 90 pounds—if we were to have time to try for another.

Fifteen minutes after the struggle began, when I had the tarpon wallowing about the boat less than two rod lengths away, the leader—which had been frayed by contact with the fish—parted.

That—and it is one of the peculiar charms of tarpon angling—was of no concern to any of us. Had the fish been brought to the boat it would have been released. Very few of today's anglers—fly fishermen in particular—kill a tarpon unless there is a possibility it is a record catch. The largest tarpon taken on a fly rod—caught in 1982 off Homosassa, Florida—weighed 188 pounds.

We saw several more tarpon among the Marquesas but none were within casting range.

That night a nasty east wind was born, making it impossible to revisit—in the two days of angling remaining to Mr. Donald and me—the Marquesas and fruitless to attempt any extensive poling of the flats.

We spent those two days staked out on the edge of a lovely green hole in the oceanside flats a few miles east of Key West. Our guide chose the spot because he knew that tarpon were wont to visit it and because its white sand bottom would make it easier for my companion and me to see the fish approaching. We did rather well in that location, hooking and jumping four more tarpon, all between 70 and 90 pounds, and bringing one to the boat.

The last-mentioned fish was caught by Captain Spear under rather bizarre circumstances. No tarpon had been spotted for an hour and just for something to do I asked him if I could see how one of his big fly rods performed. I made a long cast out into a deep portion of the aforementioned hole, remarked that I liked the way the rod handled and passed it to him with the fly still in the water. He had retrieved the fly no more than 3 feet when a tarpon hit, jumped and raced 150 yards out into the ocean before again launching high above the whitecaps in a shower of wind-torn spray.

Tarpon are unpredictable creatures. Earlier in the day, after a series of them had refused—even fled from—our flies, one took a shrimp-baited hook and then went on to pick up a fly. For a moment, he was on two rods simultaneously.

The morning Mr. Donald and I left the Keys, the harassing wind had died to a whisper, which is why, if one had the time and the money, one should set aside more time than we did for pursuing Megalops Atlanticus.

Skin-Plugging Bass

The first day of no fog in two weeks prompted Lou Palma, a visitor to Martha's Vineyard from Douglaston, Queens, to suggest that we throw skin plugs to striped bass along the Vineyard's north shore.

Skin-plug devotees are relatively rare on the Eastern Seaboard for a variety of reasons. One is that finding eel skins of proper size to slip over the plugs is often a major undertaking.

A skin plug is generally an Atom swimming plug, either large or junior size, dressed in the skin of an eel. Having procured the eels and skinned them, or the eel skins themselves, one removes the hooks from the plug and slides a snugly fitted skin over it, fastening the skin at the head of the plug, behind the metal diving lip, with elastic bands.

The hooks are then replaced and the entire plug is kept in a large jar of brine in order that the skin will not dry out or spoil. It is wise to make up at least half a dozen of these plugs, for if a bluefish grabs one, the skin will be ruined.

An inch or two of the eel's tail should hang beyond the plug, and the skin is actually on the plug inside out, for that is the way it comes off the eel.

A skin plug is retrieved very slowly on the surface, and the overhanging tail helps to create a wide and erratic wake.

Skin-plugging for stripers is much like dry-fly fishing for trout: one sees the fish when it strikes. It is obvious that the skin makes the plug's action more enticing, but Palma also feels that a striper will often come back for a second try if his mouth meets the skin of an eel rather than the wood or plastic body of the lure.

On my second cast a few miles north up the beach from Menemsha, a striper struck at my plug and missed. I let it rest for a few seconds, then gave it a twitch and the fish was fast, a 14-pounder.

A short while later we took another slightly smaller striper, which also was hooked the second time around, and we were confident that we would soon be into fish of 20 to 30 pounds, for the area we were fishing is known for its large stripers.

An hour later, having had no more strikes or follows, we were not so confident, and two hours later we decided to try again another day.

This decision was made after we had cast to several choice locations along 2 miles of rocky shore in water from 6 to 25 feet deep. Skin plugs, even though they run on the surface, have been known to bring stripers up from the bottom in 30 feet of water or more.

An Appetite for Bass

When we arrived at the opening that links one of Martha's Vineyard's salt ponds to the sea, a large school of menhaden hovered just below the surface where the onrushing current met the surf.

Until that evening—it was after seven—I had not fished for striped bass in nearly four years. The species' reproductive difficulties in its major East Coast spawning grounds, the Chesapeake Bay, had dissuaded me from adding my depredations, however slight.

The striper's problems have not been precisely identified let alone cured, but ever-increasing restrictions on the harvesting of them both by sport and commercial interests have improved their lot, and it seemed reasonable that I might try after such a long hiatus to take one fish. And, lest I seem overwhelmingly altruistic, other factors were involved. In recent weeks I had dined heavily on bluefish and wished to change my diet. More important, perhaps, were the reports from my oldest son, Steve, and my brother Dan that they were catching big stripers—30 pounds and over—with great regularity at the opening.

Dan had followed up his report by

dropping off a 33-inch, 25-pound bass at my house one misty dawn, and the fish's size and the pleasure I gained from eating it made me lust for more. I used a Portuguese recipe that calls for steeping inch-thick steaks in a 50-50 mixture of water and vinegar, a chopped onion, garlic cloves, salt, pepper and pickling spices for a few hours, dusting them with flour and pan-frying.

The technique they were using to catch those fish also appealed: 14-pound test line, revolving-spool reels and rods that were not much larger than conventional one-handed bait-casting outfits.

"You won't need any more than that," Dan had said as we drove to the beach. "The fish—particularly after the sun goes down—are usually right at your feet. The opening has cut a long channel right against the shore."

The school of menhaden we spotted on our arrival raised our expectations, because they are one of the striper's favorite foods, but my brother's hopes fell after our first two casts resulted in two bluefish. I unhooked mine and threw it up on the beach behind me, resolving, if I caught several more, to smoke a batch of them.

My brother cursed and flung his fish back into the ocean. "Blue-fish," he said. "They screw up everything. If there is a school of them chasing those menhaden we won't catch any stripers unless they leave."

His curses became more frequent as the evening progressed because the bluefish were everywhere. "I wish I could banish them from the ocean!" Dan said. He shrieked as he struggled to disengage his tenth blue from his swimming plug's treble hooks. "They ruin your plugs, they fray your leader, they cut your line, they keep good fish away and they taste like manure."

I mildly suggested that the blues might leave in an hour or so—it was then ten o'clock—but they simply came closer to shore. A dense fog moved in from the sea, nearly obscuring the first-quarter moon and making it impossible to see more than thirty feet. That made no difference in the fishing, however, for by that time—and just before we left without having seen a bass—the blues were often hitting my plug as it was emerging from the dropoff less than 10 feet away. We were using the smallest of the so-called Danny plugs—no relation to my brother—surface swimmers that must be retrieved at a snail's pace to obtain the proper action from them.

Two nights later we returned with Mike Lynch, Dan's neighbor, and my brother went into a rage when a bluefish made a swipe at Mike's lure. His mood improved in the next hour, however. The blues were not as numerous as they had been on our previous visit and there was a good chance that stripers would move in. By ten o'clock, Mike had three blues, and I had six on the beach and Dan had released seven. The skies had been scrubbed nearly clean by a northerly wind and the rapidly waxing moon made it possible for us to see what appeared to be large bass breaking on the surface 50 yards offshore. Two other anglers arrived, and the five of us cast for another half hour before my brother hooked a fish that he had trouble handling.

"Either I've got a record striper, or it's hooked in the tail," he said, and fifteen minutes later he brought a tail-hooked 33-inch bass ashore. (Massachusetts allows anglers who do not possess a commercial license one striper, at least 33 inches long, daily.)

Mike caught and released two bass in ten minutes, both a few inches under the 33-inch minimum, then lost a truly heavy fish that parted his 20-pound test line.

I was becoming fearful that it was not my night when, at the end of my retrieve when the plug was only a few feet away, the water erupted, providing me a glimpse of a broad tail. The fish ran straight offshore for 100 yards with me applying all the pressure I dared. It rested for a few minutes, then started offshore again, running straight into the moon's path over the tumult of smaller waves beyond the unrolling white scrolls of surf. It was a wild scene that reminded me, even as I was going through the mechanics of playing the fish, of Albert Ryder's lyrical, swirling paintings in which the open sea is the background.

I realized ten minutes later that I wanted that fish more than I should have. When I eased it through the surf where it lay gleaming and motionless on the wet sand as lightning flickered in the west, I felt none of the sadness that sometimes touches me when I have caught a bass—with intent to kill it—that has been swimming up and down the coast for more than a decade. It was 45 inches long, weighed 45 pounds and was 12 years old (I counted the annual rings on its scales).

Shortly after midnight, as lightning flared and cracked about me and torrents of rain descended, I laid the bass on the grass behind my workshop and scaled it with a small garden hoe, and was sodden and shivering before it and the bluefish were filleted, packaged, and placed in the refrigerator. Only on cold October nights—when there is no possibility of spoilage—do I feel free to leave the ocean's provender untouched until dawn.

Shark Bait

Shark fishing is often a blend of boredom and intense excitement.

The boredom comes during hours spent on the deck of a boat that is wallowing in giant swells far offshore while you wait for something to happen. The excitement when the sharks do appear is borne of the average man's instinctive fear of them and the knowledge that his quarry could weigh 200, 500 or 1,000 pounds. Also, many sharks are superlative fighters and none is so spectacular as the powerful, leaping mako.

Nearly all shark fishing is done from boats because most of the species do not normally range within reach of an angler casting from pier, jetty or surf. My sons and I and many others have caught sand sharks and brown sharks in the surf of the Northeast, but there is really no way of anticipating when this will happen.

Although sharks are occasionally taken on lures, bait is virtually essential to success.

The tackle one uses in going after sharks is really a matter of preference, skill, size of boat and the specific species sought, but those setting forth for the first time would do well to equip themselves with tackle that is classified as medium—a rod and revolving spool reel made to handle line no heavier than 60-pound test and no lighter than 45-pound test. It is for this reason that the novice should shy away from spinning gear which is, for all practical purposes, not made for line heavier than 30-pound test.

The reel should have a good drag, whether the familiar star drag or the lever-type drag that appears on more expensive outfits, and it should extend a minimum of 250 yards of the line being used—300 yards or more is much better.

Fiberglass rods are ideal for shark fishing, and the roller tips and roller guides are the best.

Any competent boatman and angler who has a craft large enough to run offshore can catch sharks if he persists, but if you don't wish to waste a lot of time in learning, the best approach would be to go out with someone who specializes in shark fishing.

It would also be good to read a book or two on shark fishing. One of the best is *Sportfishing for Sharks* (Macmillan), by Captain Frank Mundus and Bill Wisner. Mr. Wisner is a knowledgeable writer-angler and Mr. Mundus is a Montauk charter-boat skipper who began sportfishing for sharks before many of his present clients were born.

One can catch big sharks on tackle of 20-pound test or less, but such efforts, if they are carried to fruition with any consistency, will be undertaken by highly skilled anglers who usually began with much heavier equipment.

Some remarkable shark catches have been made on ultralight line. The International Game Fish Association's 1981 record book contains the following sharks caught on 6-pound test line: a 242-pound, 8-ounce blue; a 101-pound, 13-ounce hammerhead; and a 342-pound mako.

A problem that sometimes arises when light or ultralight tackle is used is that when a fish is hooked on such an outfit the other angler or anglers aboard may have to wait for several hours without fishing while the rodman fights his fish.

It is possible to catch an occasional shark by trolling a strip of bait in front of the fish when it is cruising on the surface, but if you want more action a good supply of chum (ground-up fish such as menhaden, herring, whiting or butterfish) is essential, as are plenty of whole fish, whether fresh or frozen, to be used as bait and to augment the chumming endeavor.

Chumming involves ladling small amounts of the oily, ground-up fish overboard at regular intervals as the boat is drifting. If tide and wind cooperate, a long slick will develop, leading upwind from the boat. This slick attracts sharks and other fish and should be kept unbroken to maintain a continuous scent trail for the sharks.

Seventy-five pounds of chum will suffice for a full day of offshore shark fishing and one should also have perhaps 30 pounds (or five fish for each rod) of the whole fish, such as mackerel, for bait.

Bait should be properly rigged and this, as well as the critical business of knots and leader to swivel or hook unions, is explained in the Mundus-Wisner book.

In some areas, including Long Island, one would have little trouble in buying frozen chum, but there are many places up and down the coast where shark fishing is so sporadic that no chum is available. In such a situation, one has to improvise. When hand-lining for bluefish from a boat with my father many years ago, we often used chum to attract the fish and my job was to turn the handle of a huge meat grinder mounted on the stern of the boat into which we tossed various so-called trash fish obtained from commercial pound-net operators.

One can also catch mackerel and bluefish for live bait. The shark hook is generally run through the back of the bait fish and sometimes the bait fish's tail is partially severed to limit its swimming ability. Hooks ranging from 6/o through 12/o will deal with any situation, and they must have long wire leaders.

There are times when only a few sharks will respond to the chum, but on others they will be whirling about the boat in a feeding frenzy.

No live shark should be brought on board and don't—even hours later—come within reach of its teeth. Sharks that have been out of water for hours and seemingly dead have inflicted nasty wounds. If you want to keep a shark that is of any size at all, try to sink a flying gaff into its back between dorsal fin and tail, get a tail rope on it and make it fast alongside. If your boat is large enough and you wish to go to the expense, a gin pole is an excellent device for lifting a big fish out of the water and keeping him immobilized.

It is good to use three rods when shark fishing. Two of the bait are drifted out into the chum slick 30 or 40 yards from the boat and held at the proper depths by floats. The shallow bait should be 20 to 30 feet down, the other about twice that depth. The third bait, with proper sinker, is fished near the bottom below the boat.

Pieces of Styrofoam or bulk cork make excellent floats and small balloons may also be used.

In general, there is no rush to set the hook after a shark takes the bait. Give him time to move out 20, 30 or 40 yards. When he slows down or stops, set back hard. An exception to this is when a shark takes a bait at high speed. Then there's nothing to do but to strike immediately.

It is a good idea, if your crew is inexperienced, to rehearse what will be done after a shark takes a bait. There is a flurry of activity at the outset, including getting the other lines in and out of the way. When the fish is ready for gaffing and tailing, the decks should be cleared for action. The man handling the leader, or wire, should wear gloves, and with blue sharks in particular there should be as little time as possible between the "wiring" operating and the gaffing, for blues have a nasty habit of rolling themselves up the leader.

Fighting chairs in which the angler sits to play his fish are often permanent affairs in larger sportfishing boats and there are portable versions as well. All have a gimbal in which the rod butt is inserted. This is an essential item in fighting a truly large fish. Some anglers prefer to fight smaller fish standing up and for this a fighting belt, which has a socket or gimbal for the rod butt, is needed.

Serious shark anglers believe that a flag buoy—they can either be made or bought—is an essential piece of equipment. The buoy is used to mark the location of the chum slick if, while a fish is being fought, the boat has to be moved.

Many sharks are good eating, and among the best are the mako and the thresher. The blue is also good but it is the impression of this writer and others that its flesh seems to deteriorate quite rapidly.

Blue sharks are numerous along the Atlantic Seaboard and are logical prey for the beginner. In summer Northeast waters, blue sharks come in many sizes, from less than 50 pounds to more than 400, although 400 pounds are rare. They are found in water 30 feet deep and on out to a depth of 800 feet.

When deciding where and when to go shark fishing, haunt the waterfront and talk to the men who are successful shark fishermen.

Those interested in catching sharks for possible inclusion in the International Game Fish Association's record book should remember that the maximum acceptable length of the wire leader is 15 feet for all line classes up to and including 50-pound test, and 30 feet for all heavier tackle. The double-line limitations for the above are the same as for the leaders. The association is the only internationally recognized keeper of records for fresh- and saltwater game fish. For information on the organization's other regulations and the benefits of membership, write to it at 3000 East Las Olas Boulevard, Fort Lauderdale, Florida 33316.

Every shark angler should be able to identify the various species known to frequent the waters he plans to fish. For the region from Maine to Chesapeake Bay, John Casey's *Anglers' Guide to Sharks of the Northeastern United States* is ideal. It may be obtained for a small fee from the American Littoral Society, Highlands, New Jersey 07732.

Harpoon Fishing: Hunting Afloat

Harpooning swordfish is more like hunting than fishing, and although those who go after the species with rod and reel may shudder, it is an exciting endeavor.

One day not long ago, when the sun blazed down on a smooth sea, five of us went out from Menemsha on Martha's Vineyard Island to harpoon—or, in the commercial fisherman's vernacular, "iron"—swordfish.

We—the others were David Tilton, my brother Dan, my son Steve and Whit Manter—were aboard David's fast-moving 26-foot Mako, the *Super Sea Saw.*

A little more than an hour after leaving the dock we were 40 miles south of the Vineyard among surface-swimming blue sharks and one white shark. Whales spouted in the distance, and alongside us shearwaters skimmed the tops of the long, slick swells with consummate grace.

Arriving at the depth of water where we were to begin our search, we cruised slowly with all hands keeping a sharp lookout for swordfish, also known as broadbill, swimming or basking on the surface.

David, as harpooner, or "striker," maintained his post in a stand that projects from the bow of the boat. My brother was at the controls in the fly-ing bridge, and the rest of us took turns standing up there with him.

Those after swordfish for the first time will often mistake sharks for their intended prey, but they will soon learn that the curved dorsal fin of the swordfish is distinctive. A shark's dorsal is triangular.

Once a fish is sighted, the job of the man at the wheel is to put the swordfishing stand directly over the quarry.

Shortly after the hunt began, we spotted our first fish. It re-mained on top until we were nearly within striking range, then dived, and David had a difficult shot at it.

He struck his mark, and the line to the iron-shod pole's lily iron sizzled overboard as the fish sounded.

The arrowhead-shaped, bronze lily iron, with the line attached to it, disengages from the pole after the fish is struck and is de-signed to flip sideways in the fish's flesh when pressure is put on the line, thereby giving more holding power.

We were in more than 150 feet of water, and the line was more than twice that length.

Eventually the fish ran all of the line out, and the large plastic ball attached to its end went overboard. Wooden kegs once were used for this, but plastic is more durable. There were also occa-sions when a large, fast-swimming fish in deep water pulled a keg so far under that it burst.

With the ball overboard, David immediately rigged up another lily iron and line on his 12-foot striking pole and we went after more fish.

There is little advantage in immediately trying to haul a just-ironed fish aboard; it is much better to let him tire himself out. This is particularly true if the striker feels that the fish may be only lightly ironed.

There is also the problem of time. If many fish are about, veteran swordfishermen simply leave the ironed fish alone and go after more. The Vineyard's Louis Larsen, a longtime swordfish-erman, recalls one incredible day when his boat had sixty-three fish ironed before the crew started to retrieve them.

In years gone by, the traditional procedure was to put men

overboard in dories to fight and land the fish, while the mother ship kept on hunting, but that practice is no longer followed.

David believed that he had hit our fish solidly in the back, a good spot, but he nonetheless handled it gently when we returned to the ball a half-hour later. We never did find out where the lily iron was implanted, for in the closing minutes of the struggle the fish tore free.

In his forties, David fished commercially for swordfish out of the Vineyard with his father, Alton, but now he no longer relies on it for a living. His firm, the Tilton Equipment company, deals in the importation and distribution of chainsaws from Sweden and Italy. His home is in Rye, New Hampshire, but he spends all the time he can on the Vineyard, chasing striped bass and bluefish, and, above all, the mighty broadbill.

One can, as noted, catch swordfish with rod and reel, but David prefers to harpoon them, one of the two usual techniques employed by commercial fishermen to capture the species, the other being longlining.

Longlining involves setting a buoyed line several miles long in the ocean with shorter, baited dropper lines hanging from it. This is highly effective, but its drawback is that small, unmarketable fish are often caught and drowned.

Harpooning, or ironing, swordfish is obviously more selective than longlining.

Two hours after losing his first fish, David had a shot at another. That one was 6 or 8 feet down when struck, but an hour later it was beside the boat with a tail rope fast to it, and we guessed that it weighed well over 300 pounds. David leaned overboard and slashed its gills with a knife, and then the resulting cloud of blood soon attracted two small sharks. The next step was to saw off its sword while it was partially overboard to make its carcass easier to handle. On the deck a few minutes later, the great fish shuddered and died, and in a manner of seconds the blue of its body changed to silver.

After removing its tail and fins and gutting and beheading it, David scrubbed and scraped the fish's body cavity clean, then covered it with a water-soaked tarpaulin to keep it out of the sun and as cool as possible.

We saw no more fish in the next hour. David called on the two-way radio to see if the spotter plane, being shared that day by him and his brother, who was also swordfishing, could come our way.

The plane was soon circling us. It is much easier to spot a fish from a few hundred feet above the water, but soon after the plane arrived, a southwesterly breeze picked up, bringing dense fog with it, and we ran for home.

Technology
and the
Graybeards

Perhaps because my first saltwater angling was
done from my father's open skiff, which—
powered by a one-lung Lathrop engine—
moved twice as fast as a man can row a dory,
I have never been either emotionally or phys-
ically comfortable in one of today's modern
sport fishing boats that can hurtle over choppy
seas at 30 or 40 knots.

Ten knots is fast enough for me, and always has been providing decent headway
against the strongest tide I will encounter. At
such a pace, one can relax and smoke a pipe
while underway, rather than standing with
half-flexed knees to absorb the jolts of the
craft's hammering, lunging passage. High-
speed fishing boats—one sometimes hears
them called "fishing machines"—have helped
blur the once-traditional image of the angler
as a contemplative, deliberate, tenacious fellow. If half-a-dozen casts in one spot produce
nothing, one simply stows the rods away—and
they'd better be stowed or they'll be lost overboard or smashed—and hits the ignition key,
leans on the throttle and heads for another
location.

And hand-in-hand with increasing speed
has come a flood of electronic gear that is un-

dermining the myth of the graybeard angler who seemed to sense where fish could be found. In a fast boat so equipped, one no longer makes a leisurely run to a potentially productive area, cuts the engine, squints at the sky and the water, looks wise and announces, "It looks fishy to me," because all your companions have to do is glance at the depth recorder to see that nothing, not even a minnow, is swimming beneath the boat.

Even if you, the graybeard, believe that fish will be there shortly or that they are only a short cast away but out of reach of the device's scanning cone, the electronic pronouncement cools your zest and the inclination is to move on. Running from place to place has one fundamental flaw: the more you move, the less time your line is in the water.

In addition to "marking" fish, such sonar recorders inform you of the water's depth and "draw" a picture of the bottom over which you are passing. There are other devices that give you the water temperature at the surface or at any chosen depth, inform you of your lure's speed through the water, and of the depth at which you are trolling, and even pinpoint your position within a few feet when you are 20 miles at sea.

If you equip a high-speed hull with such gear and take the time to master it, there's little question that you will burn more gas, run less chance of running aground and also catch more fish, but you may discover that constant attention to knobs, dials, flashing lights, miniature television screens and unscrolling rolls of paper brings too much science to what was once generally regarded as a contemplative, relaxing endeavor in which native cunning played a substantial role in fishing success.

My lack of enthusiasm for modern boat fishing techniques is triggered by a longing for those still mornings in the fog-filled harbor when the steady thumping of the Lathrop bounced back from the gray, weathered, cedar-shingled boathouses as we approached the gas dock. My father being at the tiller, my job was to disconnect the ignition wire on the engine and to put it back on when the big fly-wheel slowed and kicked in the opposite direction, thus providing a reverse so we could ease up to the wharf's white oak pilings.

I also enjoyed running by compass courses and a watch, even

though—in fog or at night—there was always an element of danger created by human error in timing, failing to hold a steady course, or in not accurately estimating the boat's speed or the effect of tidal currents. The most accurate night compass course I ever ran was from a channel buoy off the harbor entrance in Woods Hole, Massachusetts, to another one—across Vineyard Sound—off West Chop on the island of Martha's Vineyard. All of us aboard were Vineyarders commuting home in a refurbished lobster boat from our work at the Oceanographic Institution, and it was my turn for a trick at the wheel.

About an hour after leaving the mainland, I glanced at my pocket watch and announced to those in the wheelhouse with me that we should be able to spot the West Chop buoy in ten or fifteen seconds. An instant later, I hit the buoy a little to the port of dead center. Although the impact did nothing more than crack a plank above the waterline—I had eased off on the throttle and we were moving at about three knots—it seriously damaged my shipmates' confidence in my piloting.

One of the pitfalls of electronic equipment is that one can become unduly fascinated with it, even to the total exclusion of fishing.

Many summers ago, I took a prototype flasher depth finder to a remote trout lake in Maine. Such a device signals what it sees—including fish—with a series of flashes, and because there is no printout, one must watch it all the time.

My companion, a professional guide, had spent most of his life in the region and knew how to take trout from the lake even in the sweltering days of August. We were picking up an occasional fat brook trout from various spring holes along the shore until I foolishly took the flasher from my kit bag, turned it on and stuck its transducer on the canoe's side. For the remainder of the afternoon, my guide cruised back and forth—trout forgotten—never taking his eyes from the machine, marveling at its corroboration of what he already knew.

That flasher was the only depth-measuring, fish-finding device I ever owned. Whenever I've weakened and contemplated purchasing another—I traded the first for a second-hand chain saw—I've reminded myself of that day in Maine. I am weakening again, however, because of a recent invention by Robert Tendler, a Boston patent attorney, who has formed his own company—Depth Talker Corporation, 19 Lawrence Ave., Newton, Massachusetts 02167—to manufacture it. The Depth Talker can be hooked up to virtually any sonar device and announces the latter's findings every few seconds. I may—my chain saw is reaching the end of its days—go for it and another fisher.

Worth the Work

From now until fall, those who relish the flesh of the Atlantic blue crab will be prowling bays and sounds, tidal rivers and salt ponds in quest of their prey.

I am not a dedicated crabber because the tedium of picking them—removing flesh from shell and claw—usually overwhelms me, particularly when I reflect on the speed with which professionals accomplish this task.

In his delightful book, *Beautiful Swimmers* (Penguin Books), which is devoted to the blue crab and its commercial harvesters in Chesapeake Bay, William Warner notes that in the annual Crisfield, Maryland, National Hard Crab Derby, the top contestants, always women, pick as much as three or four pounds of meat in fifteen minutes. This means, he adds, "that the winners swiftly and surely dissect as many as twenty to thirty crabs within the allotted time."

One golden summer long ago, I did a lot of crabbing because a young woman of whom I was fond enjoyed crab picking. At least twice a week she sat cross-legged on the lawn in the shade of an old horse chestnut tree and worked her way through a bushel of them.

Lacking such a partner in recent decades,

I now—when offering crabs to dinner guests—serve them in the shell. This not only results in a sedately paced meal, but also gives those unfamiliar with the labor-intensive process of crab picking firsthand knowledge of one of the reasons that a pound of crab meat is more costly than a bottle of good domestic wine.

Soft-shelled crabs—those that have just molted—do not require picking, of course. Commercial crabbers look for a narrow black line along the outer and back margin of the crab's carapace that signals the start of a molt and place those crabs in so-called live traps until the event takes place. The black line turns red three or four days after it appears, signaling that shedding is only a day or two away.

Some crabbers use nothing more than a long-handled dip net. This approach requires fast reflexes and a shallow, gradually shelving sandy shore. Another technique, often used in deeper water, is to toss a bait—it might be a fish head, a chicken neck or an eel—tied to a fishline overboard, allowing it to sink to the bottom. After a short wait, one gently retrieves the line, bringing the bait with the crab clinging to it within reach. Crabs usually let go of the bait when they reach the surface of the water, so a net should be slipped under them at that moment.

From boat or pier, crab traps, crab pots or trot lines may be used. The traps—commonly in the shape of a square or a pyramid—have folding sides that the crabber closes by yanking on a line. They can be fished blind, but it helps to be able to see the crabs entering. The various crab pots catch and hold the creatures until the pot is pulled. A crab trot line is a series of baited lines hanging from a buoyed main line, and, again, one must be quick with a long-handled net when the bait and the crabs break water.

If one is crabbing along a shallow, sandy beach, a minnow seine 20 or 30 feet long also works well, but this technique requires a partner. On such a beach, the solitary crabber can also use a cast net. I have found this particularly effective if using a bait to attract the crabs.

Crabbing laws vary from state to state. Sometimes there is a size limit, or a restriction on the gear that may be used. A few states require licenses for family crabbing. In most states, egg-bearing female crabs, sometimes called "sponge" crabs, are protected, and protected or not, they shouldn't be harvested.

Several years ago, I encountered two boys in a Manhattan subway in summer who had several dead blue crabs in a bucket of water. I told them they were running the risk of food poisoning, but they countered that they always transported their catch that way, and had never had any such problem.

They had been lucky.

Crabs will stay alive longer if kept in a container with no water, unless, of course, one has a live well. If possible, keep the container out of the sun and cover the crabs with wet seaweed, burlap or cloth.

Although the blue crab—which ranges from Nova Scotia to Texas along the East Coast—is the most highly prized of the crabs that inhabit shallow water, Atlantic rock crabs are much more numerous and equally tasty. Their one drawback—the picking problem again—is that they're smaller than the blue claw, reaching a maximum of about four inches across the carapace, which is yellowish with reddish purple spots. For the skin diver at least, the rock crab is absurdly easy to catch. It lives in the open, colder, more saline waters of bays, sounds and the ocean itself, and ranges from the shoreline to depths of 2,500 feet and more.

If you spot these crabs while snorkling, all you need do is don a pair of heavy rubber or plastic gloves and dive down and pick them up. Unlike the blue crab, which usually scuttles away when so approached, the rock crab commonly chooses to stand its ground with claws upraised.

Two good books on family crabbing are *How to Catch Crabs by the Bushel* by Jim Capossela (Northeast Sportsman's Press, Box 188, Tarrytown, New York 10591, now in its fifth printing), and William Poppke's *How to Catch a Crab* (Stein and Day, Scarborough House, Briarcliff Manor, New York 10510.

Beachcombing Joys Run Deep

Beachcombing's charm is its infinite variety, and its rewards are not confined to objects acquired. One may comb, instead, coherent thoughts from the wreck left in one's mind by emotional storms.

It is almost impossible to think small thoughts when walking an empty beach alone or with a cherished companion. The sea's insistent, eternal cadence dulls the cutting edges of fear and doubt until they are as smooth as wet, shining stones on a rocky shore. With this also often comes a sense of one's ephemeral sojourn on this planet, not enough to extinguish desire or ambition, only—which makes their present flames more precious—a sweet-sad awareness that all fires must die.

And if such sustenance is not needed, one may look for more obvious rewards. In my salad days on the small New England island where I was raised, there was an old man whose farmhouse was on the edge of a meadow not far from a salt marsh and within sight and sound of the sea. I often saw him moving along the strand in a horse-drawn cart collecting both lumber and logs. It was said that he had built a barn from the sea's largesse. I cannot verify this, but it is certain that a substantial amount of the fuel for his wood stove came from that source.

One rarely sees a wood-gatherer on the beaches anymore, although some owners of four-wheel-drive vehicles cannot resist a particularly good dunnage plank or an oaken pallet lost or tossed overboard from a freighter. But, for the most part, seacoast dwellers now forage inland for wood, having discovered, as have the herring gulls, that town dumps offer better pickings.

The silver-gray patina that cedar shingles quickly acquire on seacoast homes is caused by the weathering action of salt air, and lumber that has wallowed in waves for hundreds, or even thousands, of miles is heavily impregnated with salt. Structures, such as corn cribs or tool sheds, with exposed siding of such material will last three quarters of a century or more, being virtually impregnable to rot or the assault of termites.

He who works with beachcombing lumber will soon find that his saw rapidly loses its edge, because fine grains of sand are driven into the wood's outer surface.

If, when gathering firewood from the shore, you find a ship's timber or plank with copper fastenings in it, save it for a festive occasion, for the copper will burn with a bright blue flame, nearly as blue as the blossoms of beach peas or the electric coloration of a white marlin making his final approach to a trolled bait.

Among the first items that the casual summer beachcomber will find walking the sand from Cape Cod to Florida are the horny yellow-white egg cases of the knobbed and channeled whelks. Each of these disk-shaped cases was home to hundreds of tiny but perfectly-formed baby whelks. Most of the time there will be a single hole on the outer edge of each capsule through which the young whelks departed, but occasionally the string of cases (sometimes called a Venus necklace) will have been washed ashore before hatching took place.

Indians made wampum from twisted spires of these whelks, shaping them into elongated beads. Whelks, as are their southern cousins, the conchs, are good to eat, the major problem in preparing them for the table being to soften their tough, muscular foot. This is often accomplished by beating it with a wooden mallet. Whelks are the main ingredient in the Italian dish scungili.

The channeled whelk is apparently more mobile than the knobbed whelk and may be taken in traps that resemble lobster pots but that have the entrance hole on top. The knobbed whelk cannot be captured in this manner.

The egg cases of the waved whelk, the common edible whelk of Europe and Britain, often wash ashore in the form of sponge-like balls that are often as large as two fists. These empty egg cases are sometimes called sea wash balls and yield a soapy lather if scrubbed in water. South of Cape Cod, this whelk lives in deep water.

Gathering sea shells—any sea shell—interests many northern beachcombers, although the shells of tropical and subtropical waters are much more colorful and varied.

The mollusks are the second-largest group (after the insects) of homogenous creatures, with more than 127,000 species, mostly marine, so the serious shell collector will never complete his quest.

A pleasing find is the circular skeleton of the sand dollar, which can be up to 3 inches in diameter. Its underside has a five-petaled pattern of tiny holes. In life the sand dollar is brownish with red and purple tintings, but when tossed up on the beach it is soon bleached white.

All true skates lay large eggs encased in sea-green or nearly black leathery containers. These empty, roughly oblong egg cases, with a slender point at each corner, are sometimes called mermaid's or devil's purses and are a common find in the flotsam along the high tide mark.

Also on beaches from the Gulf of St. Lawrence to North Carolina are the sand collars of the northern moon snail. These collars—which form a closed circle—are formed of agglutinated sand grains in which the snail's eggs are deposited. They are extremely fragile after being dried by the sun.

Some beachcombers gather bits of glass ground smooth by the waves and sand, and others look for attractive stones. The latter endeavor is harmless enough if confined to a handful of such stones once or twice a year, but many seacoast communities have laws against this because beaches were being ravaged by those who wished to make sidewalks or face fireplaces with such stones. A bit of esoterica: beach sand is unsuitable for making concrete, because the sharp angles of each grain have been worn smooth.

A few beachcombers ignore what the sea offers and concentrate—with the aid of metal detectors—on heavily-populated strands in quest of coins, knives, watches and jewelry. These people are usually abroad at dawn before the sun-hungry hordes arrive.

The acquisitiveness of some beachcombers is muted and involves no more than the shell of a surf clam or a small piece of bleached wood. This same person, who might bring back a single red-gold leaf from an October visit to the North Country, forages for the spirit, seeks only a symbol that will conjure up, as can a cherished line of poetry, an interlude when there was meaning in the marathon in which all are entered.

Skin Diving as a Route to Discovery

There was a time when my idea of the ultimate in swimming pleasure was to cavort in the surf with friends at the end of a long day of pitching hay or to visit Jerry's Pond after dark with a bar of soap, a towel and a bottle of wine, but that ended when skin-diving equipment became generally available after World War II.

Curiosity was the motivation. I had learned to read the surface of the water, to recognize the various kinds of rises made by trout coming up to feed on aquatic insects, to spot the sloughs along the ocean beach where striped bass might lie, to tell a surface-swimming swordfish from a shark, but that was all on top. A world I scarcely knew lay underneath, and when I first looked at it through a mask I was hooked.

Today I rarely go to fresh- or saltwater without mask, snorkel and flippers unless it is at night, too early in the spring or too late in fall, or on a dark, stormy day.

And often if the time and place is right, I can harvest several meals of fish, mussels, crabs or clams.

There is also a psychological benefit that accrues to some when skin diving. When we enter water we enter an alien milieu. As a child and a teen-ager, I always had a vague sense of foreboding when swimming in bay, sound or ocean. Dark shapes—some still, some moving—were below me and tendrils of seaweed or the soft, undulating forms of jellyfish touching me often brought a spurt of fear. The mask changed all that. The unknown became the familiar, so familiar, indeed, that there are long underwater stretches of rocky beach on the north shore of the island where I live that are as well known to me as the streets of my hometown.

Virtually any good swimmer can learn to use skin-diving gear competently in less than an hour. A few people experience a sense of claustrophobia when they wear a diving mask, but sometimes this can be overcome. Scuba diving (involving a tank of compressed air) requires more training and involves certain dangers not present when one is diving with one's own air.

The floating compressors that allow one to go down to a depth of 20 or 25 feet for long periods of time have their place, but one has to tote the compressor and its float to the water, has to tow the rig along behind and has to violate what otherwise might be a preciously silent setting with a noisy gas engine.

The truth is that, for informal observing and much food gathering, skin diving more than suffices.

I once went spearfishing for tautog (blackfish) off the New England coast with a friend who was a good scuba diver. He used his tank. I chose to skin-dive. We were working along a half mile of rock-strewn shoreline in water from six to twenty feet deep. I had more experience with tautog than he, but he had done quite a bit of spearfishing in the tropics. He got the first and the second, and I began to wonder if his approach was best, but by the end of an hour we were even with three tautog each. Then his air ran out, and he had to get rid of his tank and move in to the more shallow water where I was. (At the beginning of a spearfishing expedition, I can handle 20-foot dives for ten or fifteen minutes, but eventually the periods of resting on the surface grow longer and I move inshore.)

At the end of another hour, each of us had five tautog and we declared the informal contest a draw. I considered myself the winner, however, as I watched him sweating under the burden of his tank as we slogged our way a mile or more back to the car. I also reminded him that he would have to drive another seven miles to get his tank filled.

Divers of the Northeast coastal waters of this country who visit tropical or subtropical areas for the first time will be astonished by the water's clarity. It sometimes seems as if one is looking through air. The same is true of certain inland lakes and of water-filled quarries.

Under ideal conditions—bright sun at midday, a flat calm and a minimum of sediment and plankton—Northeast waters only approach the clarity of such places as the Florida Keys, and there are times, during a dark and rough day, when one can only see four feet or less. I have speared tautog, fluke and flounder under such conditions, but it is hard work, particularly when the fish are on or near the bottom, as tautog often do, lurking under the overhang of boulders.

It's one thing to cruise lazily along on top, propelled by the tide or an occasional kick of one's flippers, diving only when a fish is spotted, and quite another to dive continuously. Even at my age, close to sixty, I can do the former for hours at a time in 70-degree water, but a half-hour of the latter endeavor is all I can muster before going ashore for a rest.

Even if one is not interested in gathering food, the pleasures of watching aquatic life are manifold and there is always something to learn. It took me thirty years of skin diving to discover that sand eels, the slim, silvery fish that provide much of the sustenance for bluefish and striped bass, often half-bury themselves in the sand, their heads pointed uptide. In this manner they feed on bits of plankton carried to them even as they gain some protection from predators.

Clear rivers and clear lake are also fun to explore with mask and snorkel, although I must confess that I find the lakes rather dull. The life in them, or at least the life I see, isn't as plentiful or varied as it is in saltwater.

Successful foraging for bivalves in salt or brackish water requires a little training. It was quite by accident, for example, that I discovered how to locate Atlantic surf clams. They rest just below the surface of a sandy bottom, sometimes less than 30 yards from shore, and the only things that show are the black-rimmed holes made by their siphons. Many years ago, I poked at such a hole with a spear and was astonished to find a huge clam below. If your shadow, or that of a fish or boat, passes over a siphon hole, the clam promptly withdraws his feeding tube and the sand closes over, leaving the creature's lair unmarked. It should be noted that spearfishermen and bivalve, lobster and crab hunters should check state and local laws regarding such endeavors.

There are various kinds of flippers available. Stick to those of black rubber, and I personally favor the ones with a closed heel. The simplest mask is oval-shaped, and, again, choose one of black rubber. It isn't necessary to have a mask that allows you to squeeze your nose in order to equalize the pressure on your ears. The same thing can be accomplished by holding the mask hard against your face and blowing through your nose.

People's faces vary greatly in size and shape, so you should test a mask for tightness before purchasing it. Place the mask against your face—without the head strap being in place—and inhale sharply through your nose. If the fit is good, the mask will stick to your face without your holding it there and no air will leak in.

Virtually any open-ended snorkel will suffice. Avoid those with a float or cork or closing device on their ends. The pressure of the air in your chest can keep the water from entering your mouth when you dive and the closing devices can cause difficulties. Probably the best way to make sure that you are getting good equipment is to purchase it at a diving shop.

An easy way to minimize mask fogging is to rub saliva around the inside of the face plate, then rinse before putting it on. Begin your skin-diving efforts by swimming along the surface until you get the feel of the flippers and discover the proper angle for the snorkel and learn to clear water from it. In choppy water, waves will sometimes enter the snorkel. Don't panic, just blow the water out. If it gets in while you are inhaling, tread water and blow the snorkel clean.

Learn to make a clean dive from a swimming position. Tuck your head and torso down, throw your feet up and descend. Avoid kicking until your flippers are below the surface.

When you reach the stage where you are perfectly comfortable with your skin-diving gear, make sure you don't get carried away by the ease with which you move along. Many swimmers who haven't mastered the mechanics of breath control while doing the crawl find they can swim ten times the distance with mask and snorkel and they sometimes venture too far offshore.

It is always a good idea to swim with a companion and, failing that, one should wear a wet-suit jacket or vest, or, if not then some sort of flotation device that can be instantly inflated. With a jacket or vest, it is sometimes necessary to carry a lead weight or two on a belt to assist in getting under.

The simplest spearfishing device is probably the pole with rubber sling attached. Its advantage is instant reloading. Its disadvantage is less range and less maneuverability than the vigorous guns that fling a short spear with line attached. Whatever rig you use, make sure it has a toggled spear point. The trident or two-pronged spear heads won't hold a good-sized fish.

In my salad days, I used to fasten my speared fish to a line at my waist and keep on swimming. Now I go ashore with each fish. I decided to do this when I noticed a large shark following the blood trail of dying fish attached to my waist. It was only a sand shark, but there seemed no point in continuing to entice even that unaggressive species. If one dives from a boat, the sometimes long swim to the beach with one's catch isn't necessary.

A final word of caution. When introducing a youngster to skin diving, keep a close watch on him for signs of chilling. A child is quite apt to become so enthralled with what he is seeing that his body is ignored.

The Edible
Pickerel

For years, this writer has regarded the eastern chain pickerel as little more than passing entertainment, something to be caught and released when other more sporty and edible fish were unavailable.

This attitude prompted the remark in a column recently that several pickerel caught in a Saco River watershed pond were returned to the water for lack of anything better to do with them.

But there dwells in the canyons of Manhattan a man who believes differently. A champion of the toothy, bony pickerel, R. Crawford Livingston writes, in part, "I turned to your column with my usual frenzy and when I read one paragraph [relating to the pickerel] I had a seizure. Everything went black. At first I suspected it might have been ghost-written. I called my doctor but he doesn't make house calls, so I turned to alcoholic sedation and then dragged myself to the typewriter hoping to clarify one point before my condition becomes chronic."

Stating that he is a member of the Lower East Thirty-Fourth Street Gourmet Society and Chowder Claque, Livingston observes that Isaac Walton held the pickerel in high esteem and suggested that one should clean it, stuff its body cavity with salt and hang it overnight in a pillowcase. By morning, says Livingston, the fish's fine, free-floating Y-shaped bones will be gone.

"If you hang one," he goes on, "brush out the residue in the morning and stuff it."

Following is Livingston's pickerel-stuffing recipe:

Chop one medium-sized onion and six mushrooms, a little fresh celery, and fry in butter until tender. Add fresh bread crumbs, chopped parsley, one quarter of a teaspoon of thyme, a little thick brown gravy to moisten, and salt and pepper to taste. Take from the fire and bind this stuffing with two egg yolks.

Put additional sliced onions and carrots on oiled roasting pan. Place stuffed pickerel on top with one tablespoon of whole pickling spices, sprinkle with butter and bake in a slow oven for one hour. When it is half-cooked, cover it.

When the pickerel is cooked, take it out and pour off excess fat. Put two ladles of thin brown gravy in the pan and let it simmer for a few minutes. (Presumably, the thick and thin gravies come from the frying and baking.) Then strain it. Add a little fresh butter and the juice of one quarter of a lemon.

Garnish the pickerel with cucumbers cut to finger length, parboiled and fried in butter, and plain boiled potatoes cut the same shape.

Now that the deplorable subject of pickerel-eating has been brought into the open, it is only fair to add that some anglers say that fillets of pickerel scored from the flesh to the skin every quarter of an inch and fried in very hot fat are also good. This procedure, it is claimed, dissolves the small bones also.

One winter in New Hampshire I brought home a dozen pickerel I had caught through the ice. I removed the heads and tails from their frozen carcasses with an ax and flung the carcasses into a large crock that contained a brine, water, vinegar and spice mixture. These pickled pickerel, cut into small pieces, were a hit of a cocktail party three days later, but I never attempted to repeat the performance having thought, at the time, that my guests' judgment had been befuddled by strong drink.

Nature Has a Way of Forecasting Weather, Too

Watching a television meteorologist wave his little wand across a map of the nation and satellite pictures of cloud formations, many of us forget the time when we relied on natural signs to predict what weather was coming.

Today's television forecasting, at least in the Northeast, is largely geared to the weather's effect on play, such as boating and skiing, and on driving. But when this land was settled, the planting and harvesting of crops were the key concerns. Colonists looked to birds, plants, insects, animals, cloud formations, shifts of wind, and the stars and the moon for indications of what lay ahead.

The immigrants brought a wealth of weather lore to America with them—lore that goes back 4,000 years and more—and they were also given some help from the native Indians who told them for example, that when the dome-like houses of muskrats or beavers were unusually large a hard winter was forthcoming.

Much of this prognostication is obviously ludicrous, but some continues to be as accurate as the television forecasters' efforts.

There is no doubt, and I can vouch for it, that old wounds ache more before a storm, and those suffering from arthritis and rheumatism experience the same phenomenon. Hence the ancient rhyme:

> *A coming storm your shooting corns presage,*
> *And aches will throb, your hollow tooth will rage.*

Rhymes, being easier to remember than prose, were often used to encapsulate weather lore, including this quite dependable one apparently originated by European sailors:

> *Red sky in morning, sailors take warning.*
> *Red sky at night, sailors delight.*

And here is one from my childhood that works quite well:

> *When the wind is in the east,*
> *'Tis good for neither man nor beast;*
> *When the wind is in the south,*
> *It blows the bait in the fish's mouth;*
> *But when the wind is in the west,*
> *There it is the very best.*

I learned those lines when I was in grammar school and for years clung assiduously to the southwind-fish prediction, because on such a day I caught four huge brook trout in a pond where I had taken only small fish previously.

Spiders have long been regarded as good weather forecasters. When spiders are working on their webs, fair weather may be expected to lie ahead, as in:

> *When spiders' webs in air do fly*
> *The spell will soon be very dry.*

Of dubious value is:

> *When the barnyard goose walks south to north,*
> *Rain will surely break forth.*

And I like to think, being fond of squirrels, that the following couplet has some merit:

> When a squirrel eats nuts in a tree
> Weather as warm as warm can be.

All experienced hunters know that wild animals become particularly restless before the onset of a storm, sometimes losing most of their caution. Wolves are said to howl more at such a time and moles to increase their burrowing activity.

Nor do wild creatures carry the forecasting burden alone:

> When pigs carry sticks,
> The birds will play tricks;
> When they lie in the mud,
> No fear of a flood.

And flowers:

> There gay chrysanthemums repose,
> And when stern tempests lower,
> Their silken fingers softly close against the shower.

On the other hand, a wild plant, the pitcher plant, tends to open wider before a rain.

In his utterly charming and highly informative *Weather Wisdom* (Doubleday, 180 pages, illustrated), Albert Lee offers the opinion that insects are the most reliable weather indicators. He writes: "When ants move en masse their patterns are scattered, but when rain is approaching, all mass movements are made in a single-file line, like a long string of soldiers marching."

One has grave doubts, however, about the following:

> When eager bites the thirsty flea
> Clouds and rain you sure shall see.

Although presaging good or bad weather isn't involved, one insect, the cricket, is an astonishingly accurate thermometer. Add thirty-seven to the number of times a cricket chirps in fifteen seconds and you'll have the exact Fahrenheit temperature at his location. Perhaps this is why in centuries past crickets were kept in little cages and regarded as good to have about.

After Man first harnessed fire, it could not have been long before he noted that, although fires were harder to kindle before a storm, once underway they burned better. And those of us whose lives reach back to kerosene lamps and candles may recall that they tend to flare as a storm is approaching.

Frogs are known to croak more than usual before bad weather, and the green tree frog is still used in some countries as a substitute for a barometer.

The green tree frog is kept in a capped jar partially filled with water, and a little ladder is provided him. He is said to remain in the water when foul days are approaching and to ascend as it is clearing.

The condition of harvested crops was once used to predict the severity of the coming winter. Thick, or extra, onion skins were supposed to indicate a tough time ahead, thin skins an easy one.

The first of Eliot Wigginton's *Foxfire* books notes some Georgia hillfolk sayings involving trees and weather prediction. Indicating a hard winter are: thicker bark than usual on trees; bark heavier on the north side; hickory nuts with an unusually heavy shell; heavy moss on trees, and leaves shedding before they turn brown.

And an extensive body of predictions was based on what weather existed on certain days:

> *If ice will bear a man at Christmas,*
> *It will not bear a man afterward.*

And on Candlemas Day (Feb. 2), also called Groundhog Day:

> *If Candlemas Day be mild and gay,*
> *Go saddle your horses and buy them hay,*
> *If Candlemas Day be stormy and black,*
> *It carries the winter away on its back.*

The clouds, the sun, the moon, and the stars all offer some clues to forthcoming weather.

High-flying, fast-moving cirrus clouds, known as mares' tails, have long been known to indicate bad weather drawing nigh:

> *Mares' tails, mares' tails,*
> *Make lofty ships carry low sails.*

If the points of a crescent moon appear unusually sharp, you can expect high winds; if they appear blunt you can expect rain. A halo around the moon is also a good indication of approaching rain. One nearly certain sign of rain to come, and soon, is when the temperature rises sharply between 9 P.M and midnight. Bright, twinkling stars are a result of strong, scouring high-altitude winds that will presumably reach the earth's surface in short order.

The hunger of the mariner, the traveler, the hunter and the farmer of previous centuries to try to gauge future weather undoubtedly accounted for the popularity of the various almanacs, going back to the Middle Ages. There is much chaff in all almanacs, whether past or present, and Lee's book recounts the story of an Irish almanac maker who became famous when he correctly predicted—obviously without any significant justification—that January 20 would be the coldest day in England in 1838.

If the natural world is yours to visit from time to time, or even if you can only sometimes get a smog-free glimpse of the heavens, you might gain enjoyment from making your own weather predictions and comparing them with those of your favorite meteorologist.

Foraging on the Seashore

A few days ago when a hundred surf fishermen were crowded along a quarter-mile of
beach flailing the water for hungry bluefish
that were slashing through schools of squid
and young alewives, a pretty, dark-haired
young woman with a green plastic bucket
walked along the shore seemingly oblivious to
the breaking fish, bent rods, crossed lines and
screaming gulls.

Wearing a soft smile, she wove her way
through the ranks of excited anglers and past
their vehicles that were nosed against the
ocean like cows in a barn, occasionally bending down to pick up something that she deposited in her pail.

I thought of asking her what she was gathering but that proved unnecessary. She paused
and stooped six feet from me and I saw she
was after two species of seaweed, dulse and
Irish moss.

Perhaps she had come to the beach with
her husband and wasn't interested in fishing,
but no matter—she was one of those fortunate people who have discovered the delights
of gathering the wild foods that so many pass
by without a glance.

Learning to identify and harvest wild

edibles is not, for nearly all of us, a way to reduce the food budget or a passport to survival. It is, if it appeals, another passageway to a deeper rapport with the natural world and with the dwellers of a less sophisticated time. And, not incidentally, such a skill provides a welcome departure from our generally mundane diets.

The dulse the young woman was gathering is more prized along the coasts of Scotland and Ireland than it is in this country. You don't make a meal out of dulse. You use it to flavor chowders, stews, salads or simply to chew. In his book *Stalking the Blue-Eyed Scallop* (David McKay Company), Euell Gibbons remarks that dulse-chewing was so popular among the Irish that, in dried form, it was sold at railroad stations and street corners in Boston when Irish immigrants were arriving there in great numbers.

Dulse is rubbery when fresh from the sea, but after a week or two of drying it improves in flavor and texture. It is a red, flat seaweed, somewhat hand-shaped, that grows from the intertidal zone to deep water.

Irish moss is a seaweed of the low-tide area and is deep purple or purple-green in its natural state. Those who gather it on the beach itself are used to its being nearly white, which is caused by the bleaching action of the sun. When I was a lad, my mother used to send me on periodic forays for sun-dried Irish moss, which she used as a gelatinous base—after being boiled—for variously flavored puddings. This nourishing seaweed is not, like dulse, eaten raw, being tough and unpalatable in that state. One might add that live dulse taken from the water is also good for the purpose mentioned.

Another edible seacoast dweller is glasswort, or samphire. It is most commonly found along the edges of salt ponds. It first appears as small, green, vertical spikes no more than three inches high and less than a quarter of an inch thick at the base. Later these spikes "branch" at the various joints. The upper parts of the spikes are tasty and tender and go well in a tossed salad. Samphire may be cooked, although it is not as palatable when used in this manner. In his book, Gibbons has a recipe for samphire pickles, which I have found to be excellent.

Samphire is best in spring and summer. In fall it turns red or reddish-orange, and from August to November in the Northeast tiny flowers appear in the hollows of the upper joints.

Two seacoast plants that are encountered by everyone are the salt spray rose (Rosa rugosa) and the beach pea. The hips of Rosa rugosa can be transformed into a lovely, gentle jelly that is literally bursting with vitamin C. (Do not, by the way, pay heed to the canard that using an aluminum pot for this purpose will destroy the vitamin C content. It just isn't so.) The beach pea is virtually ubiquitous on the seashore, growing in sand where even beach grass has trouble gaining a foothold. Picked when young (they will be bright green), these peas are sweet and succulent. The beach pea's only drawback is that it takes about two hours to gather and shuck enough for two people.

The inland gatherer has an incredible variety of wild foods from which to choose, including such obvious things as blueberries, blackberries, gooseberries, cherries, strawberries and many varieties of nuts and herbs.

There have been times when my urge to eat wild foods on the spot has overwhelmed the original intent of my excursion. I remember a day in late October when I was hunting ruffed grouse in New Hampshire. Halfway up a mountain and alongside a brook I shot a grouse and decided to skin it and clean it immediately. Its crop was jammed with beechnuts which I ate, and as I ate them I noticed that the forest floor around me was covered with more nuts. I forgot my hunt and spent the next two hours eating beechnuts, which I cracked on a boulder beside a tiny waterfall.

Something similar occurred during a fishing trip to Prince Edward Island's lovely and virtually unworked streams and rivers. I had taken a nice brook trout from a stream that flowed along the edge of a broad meadow, had arranged him on a layer of ferns in my creel, had gathered some watercress, which I placed in a plastic bag in the creel when I realized that there were wild strawberries all about me. I lay among the strawberries, eating until the long shadows of early evening stretched out from the trees along the stream.

Wild mushrooms are a gift from heaven, but even though the truly poisonous ones are in the minority and generally easy to identify, one hesitates to recommend mushroom hunting. Those who wish to do this should go out with an experienced mushroom gatherer for a season and should be satisfied with learning to identify only half a dozen species the first year. Indeed, I have friends who have picked mushrooms for years and who are perfectly satisfied with only three varieties.

The various species of mushrooms often appear at different times of year or only when the weather is suitable for their growth. In the Northeast, familiarity with at least a dozen edible species is usually needed to provide one with mushrooms throughout the spring, summer and fall, and if this much of a variety is sought, a good textbook as well as a mycologist friend is essential. There is no general rule for identifying edible fungi. One must be able to recognize each species.

In freshwater marshes (there is also a salt marsh variety), the first green shoots of cattails may be gathered for boiled greens and the roots of the plant when dug in the fall can be dried and pulverized and used, as the Iroquois did, as flour for bread for pudding. The inner portions of the roots and the main stem can also be cut up in small pieces and used in soups and stews.

The wild cherry, or chokecherry, is slightly bitter to the taste but can be combined with citrus fruits and apple to make jelly.

Virtually everyone is familiar with store-bought fiddlehead ferns, and they often grow in abundance in moist places. The young fronds are picked in the spring before they begin to uncurl. The brown, scaly covering must be removed from these fiddlehead fronds with a damp cloth, and they should be chilled before cooking.

The jack-in-the-pulpit—another denizen of wet places—has an edible root, but the root, or corm, must be dried. In its undried state, it has an incredibly acrid taste but when dried, then boiled, it tastes something like a turnip.

One of the best woodland teas is made from the bark, or rind, of the sassafras root. Dig up the roots, wash them, and when they are dried, peel off the bark and store it in a tight container. This root bark is also pleasant to chew. When I was in grammar school, I fancied that I cut a bold figure for the girl who sat at the desk beside me when I pulled a Prince Albert tobacco can from my pocket in class and took out a chaw of sassafras.

(A few days after this column appeared, an alert reader informed the *Times* that sassafras contains a carcinogen and a warning to that effect was appended to a subsequent column. Having made it this far, I rather suspect that I shall continue to enjoy an occasional belt of sassafras tea.)

Those of us who began our foraging before or shortly after World War II had almost no popular references. That's all changed now, and what follows is only a fraction of what is available.

Euell Gibbons's books include *Stalking the Wild Asparagus* and *Stalking the Healthful Herbs* (David McKay Company), and in connection with the latter, Richard Le Strange's *A History of Herbal Plants* (Arco Publishing), provides much fascinating data on the use of such plants by man through the ages. Alexander H. Smith's *The Mushroom Hunter's Field Guide* (University of Michigan Press) is first rate. A good companion volume would be *Toxic and Hallucinogenic Mushroom Poisoning* (Van Nostrand Reinhold Company), by Gary Lincoff and D. II. Mitchel.

A Beachcomber's Botany, published by the Chatham Conservation Foundation, in Massachusetts, is nicely illustrated and covers the seacoast from Long Island to Cape Breton.

Three good paperbacks dealing with identifying, gathering and preparing wild plants for the table are *Edible Wild Plants* (Charles Scribner's Sons) by Erndt Berglund and Clare E. Bolsby; *Eat the Weeds* (Barre Publishers), by Ben Charles Harris, and *Feasting Free on Wild Edibles* (Stackpole Books), by Bradford Angier.

Edible Wild Plants of Eastern North America (Harper and Row), by Merrit L. Fernald and Alfred C. Kinsey, first appeared in 1943 and has been revised. It is accurate, thorough and packed with fascinating historical tidbits. A newer, heavily illustrated—including color photographs—text dealing with gathering and cooking of wild plants is *A Field Guide to Edible Wild Plants of Eastern and Central North America* (Houghton-Mifflin), by Lee Peterson. This book, sponsored by the National Audubon Society and the National Wildlife Federation, includes two appendixes that help in locating a plant by habitat and in preserving or preparing it for food.

In Pursuit of Atlantic Salmon

He who pursues the Atlantic salmon will most enjoy the chase if he is an unlikely blend of gambler, plodder and philosopher.

When, a few months ago, Joseph Cullman 3d of Manhattan invited me to angle the stretches of the Restigouche and Upsalquitch rivers on which he and his brother Edgar lease the fishing rights, I accepted with delight.

Both are first-rate salmon streams. The Restigouche, famous for its big fish (many in excess of 30 pounds) is broad and deep with long stretches of flat water sometimes bounded by drowsy meadows. The Upsalquitch, small and intimate, twists down through a steep-sided valley.

As my visit drew near, I assembled my salmon fly-fishing gear. This included tying new leaders with 8- or 10-pound test tippets. I also gathered my motley assortment of salmon flies even though the guides at the two Cullman camps—Runnymede on the Restigouche and Two Brook on the Upsalquitch—almost always gently suggest that their flies work better.

It is one thing to plan a fishing trip and quite another to arrive on the water at the right time. This is particularly true with salmon. You fish diligently and the rest is up to the gods. About a week before I went to Canada, I learned from Joe Cullman that the rivers were unusually low because of a long drought. In low water, salmon tend either to halt their upstream spawning runs at the mouths of rivers or to sulk—refusing all offerings—in whatever pools they reached before the flow diminished. At Runnymede, I learned that recent heavy rains had produced what is called an "alder stain" in the river. Until that amber tint left the water, there would be little action.

I went out early that evening with Lorne Irvine, a guide to an upriver location called Dee Side. Although we occasionally saw a salmon roll or jump, the sun had almost set before I raised my first and only fish. You angle from an anchored canoe on big rivers, making ever-lengthening casts at a 45-degree angle downstream on one or both sides until you can throw no farther, at which time the anchor is lifted and the craft allowed to drop to a new location. Clearly, the faster you fish each drop the more water you will cover and the better your chances.

When the one fish I raised did respond, I saw the water boil, got a fleeting glimpse of a broad tail and felt a solid jolt before salmon and fly separated. Because the fish had been pricked by my fly, there was no point in importuning it further. As we gathered in front of the lodge's fireplace that evening, I learned that Mr. and Mrs. Joseph Cullman and the Runnymede guests—Robert Marschalk and his son Peter, both of New Canaan, Connecticut, and Mr. and Mrs. Frank Ewing of Washington—hadn't done any better.

Although the alder stain was still in the water the following morning, I was sure I would be successful because my guide, Leonard Moran, and I, fishing a pool called Island Run, saw at least two dozen salmon or grilse rolling or jumping. A grilse is a small salmon, usually from 3 to 5 pounds and almost always a male, that returns to the river of its birth after a year at sea. None responded, however, and Cullman was the only member of our group to raise a fish that morning.

Back at Dee Side that evening with Irvine, I fished hard in a stiff breeze that sometimes gusted to twenty miles an hour. Flogging away with little hope, I was startled when my deep-running fly fetched up solidly. For an instant I thought that I had hooked a boulder, then felt a surge of life on the other end of the line.

The salmon didn't move 10 feet for nearly a minute.

"What is it?" Irvine asked.

"It's a heavy fish," I replied, "but I don't think it has yet realized that it is hooked."

"It will, soon enough," my companion responded, and it did, making a short, ponderous run from the slow current where it was hooked to the fast water between us and the middle of the river. Busy with raising the anchor, Irvine missed the instant when the fish's gleaming form vaulted out of the dark water and crashed back down.

If the salmon had chosen to run downstream, I couldn't have stopped it within 70 yards, but it remained about 35 yards away broadside to me and pointed upstream, an angle that gives the fisherman an enormous advantage. I put a great deal of pressure on it, Irvine poled the canoe to the nearby shore and ten minutes later the fish was netted. Irvine said it weighed about 25 pounds.

The fly was deep in the salmon's throat, too deep to remove, so we cut the leader. Irvine held the fish, a hen, upright in the water for a minute or two until it swam away slowly.

I had tried to make the struggle as short as possible, because the longer it lasts the less chance the fish has of surviving. I relish eating the Atlantic salmon, but Canada and its provinces have severely restricted both sport and commercial harvesting, and in New Brunswick only grilse no more than 25 inches long (two a day, ten for the season) may be killed by sport fishermen. My first catch—on its second jump—in two and a half days of fishing occurred at Two Brook that evening with Denis Moran, a guide.

At the Two Brook camp that night, the Marschalks and I mussed over the mysterious ways of salmon. We had learned, via radio telephone, that the fish had begun taking on the Restigouche that afternoon with everyone—including Mr. and Mrs. George Weissman of Rye, New York, who had shifted to Runnymede from Two Brook—getting some action. The elder Marschalk had another reason for musing. Earlier on that final day on the Restigouche he had put his rod down, leaving the fly trailing in the water beside the canoe's motor. A big salmon, which eventually escaped, seized that fly and headed for the Quebec shore at top speed.

Twilight Awakening

The newly revised edition of Jim Bashline's *Night Fishing for Trout* (Willow Creek Press) has reminded me that one of the graying angler's traits is to slide away from various fishing techniques that delighted him in earlier years.

Long before Bashline's book first appeared in 1973, I was going after big brown trout on various Eastern streams after dark with excellent results. But for a decade—save for post-sunset fly fishing on trout lakes—I've been wading ashore just before twilight.

Why this happened, I have no idea, because I enjoy being on or beside the water at night. And I still do most of my angling for striped bass—mostly surf casting, but some fly fishing—between sunset and dawn.

Whatever the reason for the shift, Bashline's book has me back on track, and I have just finished talking to a New Hampshire fishing buddy about how we should hit a certain brown trout stream in his state in late May or early June.

I have also ordered some materials, including calf's tail, muskrat fur and a hare's mask, with which to tie some large dry flies of the Wulff genre. One tends to use larger flies, whether dry or wet, and shorter heavier leaders when fishing at night.

He who fly fishes at night will avoid much frustration if he has advanced to the stage wherein casting is automatic. All nights are not pitch black—and they can be avoided, of course—but when it is so dark a rising fish, or even the water itself, cannot be seen, one operates by feel.

On such occasions when fly fishing for trout, my approach is to get into position on a pool by sunset and to familiarize myself with the spot—including trees and bushes that might snag the back cast—and to determine the maximum cast that would be needed to cover all the likely water. Sometimes I even cement a few turns of thread around the line to let me know—by feel—when I have stripped enough of it from the reel.

The newcomer to night fishing would be wise to choose nights on which there is at least enough light for him to see the water. I once thought that the dark of the moon was a more productive time, but now I am not so sure, because several times in early summer I have some superb dry fly fishing for rainbow trout on lakes when the moon was full or nearly so.

On one such night, the trout were rising everywhere and a cast in any direction would produce a strike. Because of that—I was fishing from a canoe—I cast into the moon's shining path on the water so I could have the pleasure of watching the fish hit.

Fly fishing for trout after dark is not an early season endeavor because few hatches of aquatic insects are taking place at that time. But from early summer to fall it can be most rewarding.

Big browns that are not visible during the day will be on the prowl in darkness, and rainbows and brook trout may also be taken at such a time whether from stream or still water. For many years, I had the impression that brook trout had little interest in dining much more than an hour after sunset, but now I am not so sure.

Ten years ago I was fishing a trophy brook trout stream that enters the Moosehead Lake in Maine when it was so dark I could barely make out the spires of spruces against the sky. I could hear those big fish feeding and I caught and released several of them.

On that occasion I was using a streamer with a body of red fluorescent floss topped by a healthy hatch of hair from the tail of a gray squirrel and was fishing downstream. Had I known those big trout were going to appear—it was during the fall spawning season—I would have tied on a large dry and worked the pool from its side or its tail. But full darkness had arrived—I had no flashlight—before the fun began, and it had taken me fifteen minutes to get to my precarious waist-deep position in the brawling stream.

On rivers whose daytime temperatures in midsummer become almost too warm for trout, the hours after sunset may be the only ones in which the fish, whether large or small, feel sufficiently energetic—as the water cools—to begin feeding. During the day such fish will often concentrate about springs upwelling in deep pools or where the cold water of forest-shaded feeder brooks enter the main stream. In the latter instance, they may be easily spotted and such locations should be fished from twilight on.

Fly fishermen who fish after dark have to pay special attention to their leaders and flies. Time and again whether casting for trout in some north country stream or for striped bass from a boulder-strewn beach, I have—after several casts among feeding fish have yielded no hits—quelled by my excitement, inspected my fly and discovered that it had been made useless by either a snarl in the leader or a bit of forest debris or seaweed. Another unwanted object you may hook when fly fishing at night is a bat. This happened to me only once, more than fifty years ago, but I remember the distraught and squeaking creature vividly.

If you are fly casting with a rocky bank or shore behind you and feel even the slightest nudge on the back cast, stop and inspect your fly because you may have bent or broken the hook's point.

There is one further caution for those seeking trout after dark. Some states restrict the hours during which this may be done. In New Hampshire, one may only fish for two hours after sunset on streams managed for trout. On the other hand, New York state does not restrict trout fishing after dark on most streams. There are exceptions to this and one should consult the regulations guide issued with every fishing license.

What flashlight you carry with you when night fishing is a matter of preference, of course, but it should be designed to leave both hands free.

The various little penlights with a flexible neck that clip to one's clothing are good, but my choice is the self-contained, lightweight (6.6 ounces, including batteries) headlamp made by Chouinard Equipment of Ventura, Calif. You don't even notice its weight, and the supreme advantage of a headlamp is that its beam goes where you are looking.

While fly fishing for trout at night, one often has the water to himself. When to that sweet solitude I add the common made mysterious by darkness, the solid take of a heavy fish and its first long run across the half-seen pool, I cannot understand how I forsook this happy pastime for so long.

Fly Fishing Draws a Crowd

One of the reasons for fly fishing's burgeoning popularity may be that in no other form of angling is one so lightly encumbered with the necessity of bringing home fodder for one's family.

In fly fishing for trout, the emphasis is on the ritual rather than the kill. In many populous areas of the Northeast, portions of trout streams are set aside for catch-and-release fishing, and on others the limit might be one, two or three trout.

The catch and release, also called fishing for fun, encountered heavy resistance when it was first proposed decades ago as a way to provide quality angling on heavily fished streams of the Northeast.

At that time, there were still a great many of my generation around who enjoyed eating trout and who intended to gratify that taste. I haven't lost my zest for the pink flesh of a wild trout, but I would rather catch several good fish—putting them all back—in a day's outing than flog barren waters from dawn to dusk.

Recent articles in various publications have noted that young, upwardly mobile professionals are joining the ranks of fly fishermen in droves. Fly fishing has always had snob appeal. That didn't motivate me when I became interested in the sport more than fifty years ago. It was simply another way to catch trout. But today when I am fly fishing a trout lake or stream on which spinning gear and lures are also permitted, I do feel somewhat superior to those using the last-named equipment.

During a stint as a commissioner for the New Hampshire Fish and Game Department I advocated, unsuccessfully, that only the cast fly should be used on the few trout ponds set aside for nothing but fly fishing. Trolling a fly behind a boat was an abomination, I pontificated.

I feel less passionately today, but the idea is not without merit. Maine has trout ponds that are so restricted. Maine also has an abundance of trout waters, both moving and still, which makes it politically possible to cater occasionally to fly fishermen, who represent, even with the growing interest in the endeavor, only a small percentage of the angling public.

Part of fly fishing's appeal to newcomers is that one suits up for it. The properly attired fly fisherman has his fly-festooned hat, his short wading vest with its many pockets, his woodframe landing net, his chest-high waders and perhaps an aluminum fly box with its dozens of compartments hanging midway between waist and chin. So caparisoned and carrying a fly rod and reel that could have set him back $500 or more, the neophyte fly fisherman need only appear on the banks of a stream to be regarded by others as a dedicated practitioner of this many-faceted sport.

Indeed, it is possible to achieve this image without wetting a line. One can while away the day capturing aquatic insects in a fine-mesh net, placing them in vials of alcohol or examining them with a hand lens so as to best approximate them with an artificial fly. Add to this an occasional taking of the water temperature and assiduous scribbling in a stream diary, and the image is complete.

Water-watching, always with Polaroid glasses, also marks one as a meticulous fellow to whom fly fishing is an art, and if kept up for two or three hours it tends to unnerve fellow anglers. Clearly, they reason, one is seeing something that they are not; perhaps a giant trout behind a midstream boulder that will be wooed and won as dusk descends. Protracted water-watching also creates the impression that one knows the stream so well that one doesn't waste time fishing until conditions are just right.

If one confines his fly-fishing activities to catch-and-release sections of streams, one need not produce trout to prove one's prowess; a little truth-stretching at the local tavern at the end of the day is all that is needed. Another gambit is to let it be known that one regards trout with such reverence that one returns all of them to the water, no matter what the regulations.

The only weak spot in this formula for swift establishment of status involves the actual casting. All else suffers if one cannot throw a decent line, perhaps, as an example, 75 feet with a No. 6, 7 or 8 outfit. Being able to cast a long line isn't really that important on small Eastern trout streams, where, in most instances, a 35-foot effort is all that is needed, but other anglers, including most fly fishermen, are captivated by a tight-looped, far-reaching cast. "The guy has to be good," they say as they watch him.

Sometimes, as when fly fishing for tarpon with a No. 10, 11 or 12 ensemble, accurate casts of 90 feet and more are essential and often they have to be executed in a hurry: a minimum of two false casts. The sometimes exaggerated emphasis on the long cast is undoubtedly one of the reasons why the fly-casting schools run by such firms as Orvis, Fenwick and L. L. Bean or by individuals like Joan and Lee Wulff, are usually booked well ahead of time.

If one has trouble keeping more than 30 or 40 feet of line in the air, one might go to gossamer rods and lines, such as the No. 1-weight outfit offered by Orvis, with which one would not be expected to reach out more than five rod lengths.

There is also an excellent chance that those who may have turned to fly fishing because it is the "in" thing, will become captivated by it. It appeals to those who don't want to mess with bait, alive or dead, or heavy tackle boxes stuffed with lures. Including their aluminum boxes and fly books, 200 trout flies weigh only a few ounces and can be carried in two or three pockets of a wading vest.

Fly fishing's potential for complexity and refinement also charms many. Just when one thinks he is mastering the sport, a new technique or a new series of flies is born. Conversely, one can say to heck with trends and eschew everything but the venerable downstream drift and a few dozen wet flies and streamers and catch as many or more trout than he who is possessed by a desire to keep abreast of the times.

The Barbless Hook

Although barbs have been on fishing hooks since the Stone Age, some anglers—fly fishermen in particular—have long debated the merits of getting along without them.

The deliberate reduction of a hook's efficiency by doing away with its barb occurs in countries where pleasure rather than food is the fisherman's prime goal.

If one does not plan to release any or all of the fish he catches, there is, of course, no reason to consider suing such hooks. In most states, the regulations applying to so-called "fishing for fun" waters do not call for hooks of the barbless variety, but obedience to the law isn't all that motivates the barbless-hook fraternity.

Long before stretches of various trout streams were set aside for fishing for fun— such stretches are also called "catch and release" areas—many fly fishermen were returning most of their catch to the water, keeping only one or two for a meal, or a truly large fish for a trophy.

The fishing-for-fun concept, which is sometimes modified to allow the killing of one large trout a day, took root in areas where the angling pressure on streams was so heavy that, if all the trout caught were kept, there was no possibility of a decent holdover fish being taken. All one angles for in such streams area pale-fleshed, unsophisticated fish that only days before had been dining on pellets of food tossed them by hatchery workers. Wearying of such endeavors, a small group of enlightened fly fishermen began, a few decades ago, to push for the catch-and-release approach. Among their successes are the stretches on New York state's Beaverkill and Willowemoc rivers that are open year round to such angling.

The attracting of such waters is that one knows that many large and wily trout are in the stream. Because those fish have been there for two, three or four years or more, and because many have been caught and released more than once, they present more of a challenge. And on the restricted stretches of the Beaverkill and Willowemoc, the freedom to fish all year enables one to hone one's skills, to learn about the habits of trout in all seasons.

Because there is little point in releasing a fish that is so badly handled it will later die, the amount of time and effort it takes to detach the hook from its mouth is important. Hence the interest in hooks without barbs.

In a recent newsletter of the Croton (New York) Watershed Chapter of Trout Unlimited, a member, Mark Johnson, writes that he believes barbless hooks hold fish just as well as barbed versions, and that a slack line is the major reason for losing fish. He also notes that the barbless hook not only can be more easily removed from a fish, but also from ear lobes of a fly fisherman or his companion.

There are hooks manufactured without barbs, but otherwise identical with their conventional counterparts, and there are some on which a U-shaped kink replaces the barb. One may also squeeze the point of the barb down until it no longer protrudes from the hook.

On a recent Atlantic salmon-fishing trip in New Brunswick, I had an opportunity to test the holding power of barbless hooks, and I agree with Mr. Johnson that, if such a hook is imbedded solidly in a fish's mouth, it will probably remain there unless the angler fails to keep a tight line. I caught and released salmon every day and am certain that the lack of a barb had nothing to do with the fish that weren't brought to the net.

No angler plays every fish perfectly, however, and a barbed

hook compensates for human frailties. A barbed hook is also less likely to be dislodged by a jumping fish. New Brunswick's angling regulations do not call for barbless hooks, but because the Province this year requires that only grilse—small early-returning salmon—may be kept, the other fishermen, Joseph Cullman 3d and his brother Edgar, whose waters I fished, decided that the barbless approach would be best. We used flies with pinched-down barbs. I lost only two good-sized salmon; my guides and I estimated their weights to be slightly under 20 pounds. In both instances, the fly pulled free when a great deal of pressure was being put on the fish, a situation in which the lack of a barb would not be relevant.

As an aside, I believe that playing a fish for an inordinately long time probably does more damage to it than a few additional seconds added to the pre-release, hook-removal procedure. It is better to force the tackle to its limit and get the fish to shore or boat before it is totally exhausted and wallowing on its side.

Shifting from freshwater to salt, I would like to observe that single hooks are in some ways preferable to the trebles when angling for such species as bluefish. With rare exceptions, I use only one single hook on my bluefish popping plugs. I replace the treble hook on a store-bought plug with a single hook about two sizes larger and install single hooks on poppers of my own manufacture.

This results in my missing a few blues that would have been nailed by a three-pronged hook, but the larger single hook, once embedded, holds much better. It also picks up less seaweed and, perhaps most important, it can be swiftly removed when the fish is on the beach. This last is sometimes critical. The time lost in disengaging treble hooks from a blue can result in an angler failing to take full advantage of the frequently short-lived onshore assaults the species is prone to make.

Clamming

If you relish seafood and have had a series of boring days uselessly flogging ocean or bay for striped bass or bluefish, try clamming. Clams stay put. Once you have located them, they are yours, and the same is true of mussels.

In the Northeast in summer, the bivalves most cherished by the amateur digger are the steamer, or soft-shelled, clam and the hard-shelled clam that is known as a quahog in New England. Both may be harvested with the hands alone in shallow water or on flats exposed by the falling tide, but that's hard on the fingers. A shovel or a flat-tined garden fork is helpful with the former and a clam rake with the latter. The clam rake has a wire basket into which the uprooted quahogs tumble. There are also short-handled, flat-tined rakes designed for harvesting steamers.

Unlike the quahog, the body of the steamer clam is always a few inches below the surface of the mud or sand in which it dwells. It reaches up through that bottom with its long neck, or siphon, to feed on minute organisms brought its way by wave or tidal action. When underwater, steamer clams can be located by the small round holes those siphons create, but when their habitat is exposed to the air by low tide, the holes often disappear because the siphon has been withdrawn.

Most of the time, however, small depressions can be spotted. One can also locate the hiding places of steamer clams on flats exposed to the air by judicious foot-stamping. This will produce a squirt of water from the startled bivalve. Steamers tend to favor a mud-sand habitat, and they will sometimes be found along a beach that contains many small rocks and pebbles. It's worth walking along such a beach at low tide, striking the rocks with a shovel and looking for the telltale jets of water.

The steamer needs less salinity than the quahog in order to survive, which is why it is often found in or near the mouths of tidal creeks and rivers or in salt ponds. The quahog dwells in bays, sounds, the ocean and in harbors subject to strong tidal action.

The basic technique for gathering steamers involves inserting shovel or fork into the muck several inches away from the clam holes, then prying downward. With luck, some clams will come up in that first effort. At that point, drop on your knees and explore with your hands, enlarging the hole. Work rapidly, because the clams you have disturbed will immediately start digging deeper using a muscular "foot" at the end opposite its neck.

The quahog is only partly buried because its siphon is much shorter than that of the steamer. One can simply "tread" for quahogs, walking barefoot in shallow water, feeling the bottom with one's feet until something smooth and hard is encountered. One then reaches down with one's hand and prizes the quahog from its lair. The drawbacks of this technique are the possibility of cuts from broken shells or manmade rubbish, including bits of glass.

The quahog rake does away with this problem and is more efficient. With it, as with treading, it takes a little practice to distinguish one's quarry from a rounded rock. One clue is that it often takes a surprising amount of pressure to dislodge a quahog from the bottom. When stalking either steamers or quahogs in water that is knee-deep or more, a wire basket floated in an inner tube and tethered to one's waist with a short line is needed. If you enjoy using mask, snorkel and flippers and the water is relatively clear, you can easily spot quahogs from above.

About two decades ago, the common blue mussel—whose

orange-yellow flesh is delicious when steamed—was ignored by most seashore foragers in this country. That is no longer true and rock jetties from which one could readily gather them at low tide now offers slim pickings. The mussels need only be torn from their moorings, scrubbed clean and steamed. The skindiver who enjoys exploring rocky shorelines will have no trouble finding undisturbed mussel beds out of reach of the landbound forager.

The same skindiver may also be able to locate extensive beds of the Atlantic surf clam, the largest bivalve mollusk on our coast, sometimes reaching eight inches end to end. In bay, ocean or sound, the surf clam may sometimes be found in only a few feet of water. Because its siphon is longer than the quahog's but shorter than that of the steamer clam, it lies just-covered by the sand. The skindiver should cruise along the surface looking for what appear to be two joined, dark-rimmed twin holes—each about the size of a quarter for a large specimen—created by the surf clam's siphon. If the sun is directly overhead and the water is clear, they can be spotted at least to a depth of ten feet. The surf clam is remarkably alert to danger from overhead and if the diver's shadow passes over it, the siphon is instantly withdrawn.

The diving surf clammer should carry a nylon mesh bag in which to carry the clams. Because the clams are so large and heavy, the diver must wear the jacket of a wet suit for flotation if he wishes to harvest more than a dozen on one sortie from the beach. With practice, one should be able to gather two clams on each dive. Unlike the quahog, mussel, oyster or bay scallop, the surf clam's shells do not have perfect occlusion, being slightly separated at the location of the siphon. One opens a surf clam by inserting a knife through that separation and severing the adductor muscles.

Although many popular reference books say that only the sweet-fleshed adductor muscles of the surf clam are edible, that is a canard. Run everything—adductor muscles, stomach, stomach contents, mantle, the muscular foot—through a meat grinder set to cut coarse and you'll have the base for a superb clam sauce for pasta. That same base, when mixed with Bisquick, a little cooking oil and an egg or two, will also result in splendid clam fritters. One can, by the way, store such a base—it can be made with large quahogs also— in a home freezer for six months without any loss of quality.

Although, as one might expect, surf clams dwell close to ocean beaches, the water is rarely clear enough for the diver to spot them. Seacoast dwellers have long made a habit of visiting the shore after an onshore gale, in which the clams are often washed up by the thousands. The trick is to get there at dawn before the gulls have had time to reap all of the storm-caused harvest.

When, more than fifty years ago, I began gathering clams, oysters and mussels, no permits were needed, nor was there any need to worry about pollution. This is no longer true in my old haunts and the same could be said of most coastal areas in the Northeast. So, before you begin your foraging, check with the appropriate town officials or the local shellfish warden. In some instances, state regulations govern the size of the clams and the amount that may be harvested for home consumption. For those who would like to do more homework before sallying forth on a shellfish expedition, *The Compleat Clammer* by Christopher Reaske (Nick Lyons Books, 1986) is highly recommended.

About Trout

We crept from our tents after a night of thunderstorms and intermittent rain to be greeted by a brilliant dawn and mist rising from the Delaware River.

We had hoped that the big rainbow trout that were feeding on aquatic insects the evening before would be similarly active at daybreak, but such was not the case, and up and down the long pool before us only a few fish were rising.

The man who had suggested that we fish this section of the river, Ed Van Put of Livingston Manor, who is a fish and wildlife technician for the New York State Department of Environmental Conservation, had told us that during the summer nearly all the good fly fishing for rainbows would be at night, and he was correct.

Turning from the pool, my companions—Paul Updike of Roscoe, New York, and Terry Williams of Elmira, New York—and I soon had a small fire burning briskly. Dead rhododendron branches, of which there were plenty, make a clean, quick, hot fire, we discovered.

Bacon, eggs, toast, hot coffee, and large glasses of Tang made with icy water from a nearby spring soothed our hunger, bedding

was hung out to dry and there was really little to do but fish for
trout with wet flies and nymphs in the fast water at the head and
tail of the pool, or do a little exploring.

There was no wind before 8 A.M., making it easy to see down
through the water, which, by the way, had cooled 2 degrees over
night, being 70 at dawn. With this enhanced visibility in mind, I
took our skiff and drifted down the pool, which is more than 200
yards long.

Common American eels were plentiful and feeding on the bottom, as were large and small fallfish, or chub. But infinitely more
exciting to me were the rainbow trout I saw, a few grubbing for
nymphs, but most simply resting in the gentle current above the
rocks. In that one twenty-minute float, I saw at least a dozen rainbows of better than 2 pounds. On several occasions, I tried to
entice them with nymphs and a sinking line, but they would have
none of it.

Van Put, I realized, had known whereof he spoke, although
Williams did manage to take one 17-incher during the daylight
hours.

In early and mid-June and again in September and October, the
big Delaware rainbows may be caught during the entire day. The
trout season closes September 15, but one may catch and release
trout during the closed season. Van Put, as a matter of fact, releases
all the trout he catches. The Delaware rainbows in the Hancock-
to-Narrowsburg stretch of the river have a muddy flavor, he said.

At sunset, as he had done the day before, Van Put joined us,
and from shortly after nine until it was no longer possible to see
the trout rising, we took more than half a dozen rainbows, ranging
from 16 to nearly 20 inches.

Angling for these fish at night takes a bit of practice, for often
only a tiny dimple marks their presence and the cast must be made
directly to them. Although we were fishing from 20 to 40 yards
apart, the evening was so quiet it was always possible to hear a
trout take and the whine of the reel as the fish headed downstream. Several trout made runs of thirty yards or more, but in the
spring and fall, Van Put says, an 18-inch fish will often clear a reel
of its backing. Van Put favors a No. 14 or 16 Adams dry fly with
a tippet of no more than 4-pound test for these fish.

Catching Dolly Varden Trout in Alaska

Hovering on the edge of a snow-fed stream in water so cold it hurt to drink it, hordes of sea-run Dolly Varden trout smashed our flies recklessly.

Fighting hard, and often using a peculiar rolling motion in an effort to escape, the fish, which ranged from half a pound to 5 pounds, were clearly visible against the gravel bottom of the stream where it emptied into a small lake.

In two hours of angling we caught and released forty or fifty of them keeping only a few for supper, the largest a 3-pounder taken by Bing Crosby, who may have coaxed the trout to its demise with his mellifluous rending of "Oh, What a Beautiful Mornin'!"

We—the party also included Jack Samson of Manhattan and a pilot, Buzz Fiorini—had left Bob and Edith Nelson's Thayer Lake Lodge, which is about 50 miles south of Juneau on Admiralty Island, in Fiorini's Cessna 185 float plane shortly after eight that morning, flying east across Chatham Straight to Baranof Island and the Dolly Varden stream.

The Dolly Vardens took almost any fly readily, although a pink bucktail bonefish fly, intended to resemble a shrimp, that had somehow gotten misplaced among my salmon and trout flies, seemed to be the most effective. The trout were in excellent shape, deep-bellied and silvery, and their cold, muscular bodies surged with strength when one held them.

In sad contrast to the vigorous trout, his red and wasted body scarred with fungus, a dying male sockeye salmon cruised slowly up and down the stream, sometimes dropping back into the lake, and once resting against Crosby's leg. His procreative act complete, this fish, as is the case with all West Coast salmon, was fated to die.

To one used to stalking brown or rainbow trout in heavily fished Eastern streams, the Dolly Vardens were remarkably unsophisticated. Although the water was as clear as air, the fish did not scatter when a poor cast dropped the line or leader over them.

Leaving the Dolly Vardens with some reluctance, we visited the mouth of one of Admiralty Island's many silver (coho) salmon streams, and while waiting for the coho to appear, we amused ourselves by catching sea-run cutthroat trout, some of which were over 2 pounds.

Because we were fishing the brackish, tidal portion of the river where there is usually a 14-foot tide, we had to keep a constant eye on the moored aircraft, and, twice before I realized how rapidly the tide came in, I found my camera bag and other gear nearly awash.

Several bald eagles soared up and down the river, ravens fed on the bodies of salmon that had died after spawning, a flock of twenty Canada geese flew by, and once a ruby-throated humming-bird hovered beside us.

There were cohos rolling in the river before us, but Fiorini said their dark coloration showed that they had been there for several days. "We want fresh fish—silver salmon just in from the sea," he said. "They are better fighters, they are better eating, and they will hit a fly more readily than the black salmon."

Toward the end of the day a few fresh salmon moved in. One could see them coming, leaping and twisting into the air, bright side gleaming.

When they came by us, however, they were nearly 50 yards away and only Fiorini could reach them. He was using a shooting head flyline backed with 15-pound test monofilament line. Tucking the rod under his arm after each cast, he used both hands to strip the line into a fishnet basket of his own design that hung at his waist.

"I think they hit best on a very fast retrieve," Fiorini said, and a moment later he was fast to a 6-pounder, the only salmon we took from the river that afternoon. Fresh from the sea, the fish put on a good show, making two long runs and jumping several times.

Two hours remained until sunset, the cutthroats were still slashing into schools of tiny stickleback minnows and an occasional fresh salmon broke the dark water before us. But we were hungry, several days of uninterrupted angling lay before us, and the prospect of the crackling fire in the stone fireplace at the lodge was more than we could resist.

Cane-Pole Angling for Pan Fish

John Arrington of Raleigh, North Carolina, and I had at first planned to fly-fish his state's lovely mountain streams for trout. But various circumstances intervened, and so we turned away from the hills and drove south to the coastal plain, where we would meet Rudolph and Helen Inman at their hostelry at White Lake. Our new goal: cane-pole angling for pan fish.

"Inman," Arrington said on the trip down, "is a good man with a cane pole, and he and Jim Davis, a fisheries biologist with the state's Wildlife Resources Commission, will take us out."

The next morning we set forth in two pickup trucks—a canoe in one, a johnboat in the other—for the Black River. Arrington and Davis launched the canoe, and Inman and I were in the johnboat with Walter McDuffie of Elizabethtown, North Carolina.

There were four or five cane poles in the johnboat, and as soon as we were on the water McDuffie offered one to me. I was prepared for this, having decided during the forty-five minute drive that if Black River's various pan fish, mostly of the sunfish family, would respond to a cane pole and crickets, they would also hit a fly-rod popping bug. This attitude was borne of decades of fly-fishing or casting artificial lures for both freshwater and saltwater species, and was abetted, I must admit, by a tendency to regard bait-fishing as somewhat pedestrian. Like most other devotees of the cast fly or the artificial lure, I was unaware of the intricacies of cane-pole fishing as it is practiced on certain rivers in the South.

"Try your fly rod if you want to," Inman said as we began to fish, "but I don't think you are going to do much. The tide is rising, and the river is higher than usual because of recent rains. The fish are going to be back among the trees, where you can't reach them with anything but a cane pole."

The Black River runs for about 25 miles southwest through Pender County before joining the Cape Fear River. It is a deep, gentle stream with almost no high banks, meandering through a lowland wilderness. Although the lower third, the area we visited, is affected by the tides, the water is not brackish. The lack of high ground allows the rising stream to spread out among the trees, and the pan fish move back with it into shrubbery-canopied pools against cypress and cottonwood boles. I could hit the edges of some of these pools with my popping bug but in most instances couldn't get back inside far enough. Fish were coming into the boat, but they weren't mine.

Having started with a fly rod, however, I felt obliged to stick with it, and my companions understood.

Until my trip on the Black River I had always assumed that cane-pole fishing was the same everywhere. I had therefore believed that my friends would do no more than dangle their bait from the ends of the pole.

Not so.

Faced with situations in which a likely looking hole lay 15 feet away at the end of a narrow tunnel in the brush, each took the baited hook in one hand and the rod in the other, pulled back on the line until the tip of the pole was deeply bent and fired the bait to the target.

The accuracy achieved in this manner was amazing. Indeed Inman and McDuffie argued whether a cricket should be fished 4 or 5 inches to the left or the right.

Their techniques were essentially identical, although I did note that McDuffie always held the rod and the bait at eye level while drawing and firing, while Inman often shot from the hip.

The cane poles they used were about twelve feet long, with limber tips.

"Twelve- or fifteen-pound-test monofilament is about right for the line, and it should be perhaps a foot and a half shorter than the pole," Inman said.

They tape the line to the tip of the pole but wind it down toward the butt for a few feet and then tie or tape it again. This precaution saves the fish if the tiptop happens to break.

Small, oval-shaped cork bobbers, or floats, are fastened to the line about a foot and a half above the hook. (The tiny bobbers, usually in some bright color, are difficult to find in the Northeast. They are designed so that the line runs through a hole in their center, being kept from sliding by a tiny wooden peg.)

"Use light, soft wire hooks," Inman said, "so that if you hang up on brush you can yank the hook free by bending it. If you don't, you'll break the line or the pole."

The crickets, which McDuffie had bought for the occasion, are fished live. They are kept in small, cylindrical wire-mesh baskets open on the upper end. A protruding metal rim on the inside keeps the crickets from climbing out. Eager to show my hosts that I had some knowledge of such things, I told them that as a lad I had caught crickets by hollowing out the center of a stale loaf of bread and placing it in a meadow. Often, I told them, I found several dozen of the insects inside the loaf the following day.

Although it seemed to me that Inman and McDuffie had mastered cane-pole tactics, they said their skill was not equal to that of a lean, lone angler we met, Albert Woodburn of Elizabethtown. Woodburn, who was fishing alone in a small skiff powered by an electric outboard motor, was probing every shore-side pocket with great diligence. At times most of his boat was out of sight, in the bushes.

Today in the Northeast, cane-pole fishing is largely limited to going for horned pout (catfish) on shallow warmwater ponds in early evening or after dark, though in years past the cane pole was an efficient tool for such cooperative fish as yellow perch, crappies, rock bass and chain pickerel.

But the tradition is still strong in the South, where in some counties the residents need no license to fish with a cane pole.

One delight of such angling, on rivers like the Black, is the solitude one encounters. McDuffie made note of this when he said: "I travel around this area a lot, and there are plenty of places where I can catch twenty largemouths in an afternoon. But the Black River is different. I know I can fish it all day and never see more than three or four other boats, and that is important to me."

Although I had caught only two of the more than forty fish—including redbreast sunfish, spotted sunfish, bluegills, green sunfish, warmouths and pumpkinseeds—brought in by the two boats at the end of the day, I was more than content. For, in addition to having learned a new angling technique, I had reveled in the river's mood, its rafts of waterlilies, its Spanish moss, its many water snakes coiled on streamside bushes hanging over the water, its prothonotary warbles, its white ibises and its spotted sandpipers. A special pleasure, at a bend in the stream, was a burst of white spider-lily blooms. The plants are quite common along the state's coastal-lain streams, but I had never before been here at the right time for their burgeoning.

No fishing trip would be complete without the eating of the catch, and, upon our return to White Lake, McDuffie disappeared and then returned shortly with a scrap-iron pedestal to which two gas burners were attached. Three pounds of Crisco went into a 16-inch cast-iron frying pan, and the fish—scaled, beheaded and gutted—were dredged in white cornmeal and popped into the deep fat. When the fish were done a batch of hush-puppy fritters followed.

Immersed in a good Burgundy, fritters and sunfish as the soft North Carolina night descended, I was taken by the idea—and to hell with worry about cholesterol—that this deep-frying technique should be brought East. I thought of clams and oysters and whitebait (silversides and sand eels), horned pout, sea robins, puffers, yellow and white perch, crappies and rock bass.

Those who wish to try cane-pole angling in the Northeast will do well with pan fish in many warm-water streams, lakes and ponds.

A one-piece cane pole costs from $3 to $4, but apartment

dwellers may wish to purchase either a jointed pole or one that is telescopic. These are more expensive.

The tiny cork floats favored by Southern anglers are often hard to find, but a small plastic bobber, or even the cork from a bottle of wine, will suffice.

Bait can be worms, crickets or grasshoppers.

FALL

Hunting as a Sport: A View from Behind the Gun

If one were planning to portray the glories of love between woman and man in a television documentary, then devoted the entire show to the antics of a drunken clod in a bordello, one would achieve the same level of truth realized in the CBS News 90-minute film, *The Guns of Autumn.*

Purporting to be a fair examination of hunting in America, the show instead focused on the shooting of bears in a city dump; the hurly-burly of opening day on a public waterfowl hunting area; running a bear with hounds, Jeeps and two-way radios, then keeping the animal treed until the women and youngsters could gather about to witness the kill; and the slaughter of exotic big-game animals in a mile-square private shooting preserve on the outskirts of Detroit.

Make no mistake about it, *The Guns of Autumn,* shown last Friday night, was powerful stuff and the fragment of the hunting scene it portrayed is accurate, but because it is only a fragment the final result is propaganda.

I find it necessary to become personal to describe some of my thoughts on hunting.

When, for example, the film showed an army of gun-waving men and boys blasting away before dawn at Canada geese and mallards, I thought of a winter day that I spent alone on a salt marsh. All day long I heard no sound save the wind in brown grass and the surf on the distant beach. All day long I saw ducks and geese, but they were too distant for me to shoot at them. Then, just before sunset, a small flock of black ducks came in low out of the last light; I stood to shoot, but they looked so lovely I hesitated. They talked to each other as they descended and I lowered my shotgun, neither, at that time, wanting to kill nor to shatter the soft, sweet sound of the wind and waves.

And when the film showed a band of out-of-shape hunters puffing along the barbed wire fence of the aforementioned preserve, I thought of a log cabin in the wilderness of northern New Hampshire where, at dawn, the several of us who hunt from that spot go forth, each his separate way, into the snow-covered mountains, and where it is possible for us to go all day without hearing a single shot. We hunt that area not because we are sure of killing a deer but because we find the space and solitude that enables us to hunt as we like to do it, each man alone. Deer are scarce there, but so are people, and that is what we want.

Although I slaughtered chickens by the hundreds on a farm as a boy, have had my comrades and once, even, an enemy soldier, die in my arms, have killed other men and have killed big game and small game, I have never become totally inured to the sight of blood and death.

Nonetheless, the spectacle of a bear being gutted (in color) on the film did not disturb me, nor would it disturb any farmer or rancher or veteran hunter, but it is bound to have troubled many millions of viewers. To include it and similar scenes in the show was poor taste, and it had no effect other than to generate revulsion against hunting.

What did disturb me greatly in the film was the incredible botching of the kill, in the Detroit preserve, of a magnificent fallow buck. While the wounded animal raised its splendid head to gaze at the hunters standing about it, they, in an incredible display of ineptitude, had to shoot it six more times with a handgun before it died.

Preserves that offer easy slaughter of big-game animals, whether exotic or native, are, by the way, an abomination.

Space does not allow an examination of the primal urge to hunt, which, when not corrupted, is an honorable endeavor of honorable men.

It might be fitting to note, however, that Dr. Paul Shepard of Dartmouth College had to say in his introduction to a recent publication of the Spanish philosopher Ortega's *Meditations on Hunting*, ". . . he [Ortega] has perceived, by an almost incredible act of intuition into the thoughts of hunters he has known personally and from literature, that the glory of man is a hunting heritage."

The Guns of Autumn gave no hint of this glory.

Hunting According to Ortega

The day is gray and damp. The wet snow that fell during the night is nearly gone from the ground and the last messes of it have long since slipped from the dark green spruce branches.

I am alone in a hunting cabin, my companions having gone forth into the forest; the cylindrical sheet-iron wood stove sends forth a circle of warmth and the pungent smell of wood smoke pervades the room, an aroma that never fails to fill me with leisure that is nostalgia and anticipation.

Last night we talked of hunting and the reason for it, and today that talk is still with me, not only because of our conversation, but also because I have in my duffle bag a dozen letters from readers who expressed shock, bewilderment, sarcasm and sadness at a recent column which, after describing a day of shooting woodcock, I closed with the observation that there is no sweeter sight or sound in the natural world than the singing, spiraling courtship flight of the male woodcock in spring.

One man wrote that the experience of observing the courtship flight was apparently so sweet that I couldn't bear it and had to, therefore, endeavor to eliminate its source.

One wonders if non-hunters can ever be persuaded to understand, let alone endorse the hunter's raison d'être.

Probably the best explanation of why man hunts is in Jose Ortega y Gasset's *Meditations on Hunting,* recently republished by Charles Scribner & Sons. Ortega, Spain's foremost twentieth-century philosopher, has, according to Dr. Paul Shepard of Dartmouth College, "grasped that essential human nature is inseparable from hunting and killing of animals and that from this comes the most advanced aspects of human behavior."

In *Meditations,* Ortega writes: "Thus the principle which inspires hunting for sport is that of artificially perpetuating, as a possibility for man, a situation which is archaic in the highest degree: that early state in which, already human, he lived within the orbit of animal existence."

And again: ". . . hunting has perpetually occupied the highest rank in the repertory of man's happiness . . . it is not essential to the hunt that it be successful. On the contrary, if the hunter's efforts were always inevitably successful it would not be the effort we call hunting, it would be something else."

Of great importance is Ortega's awareness that success is not an essential ingredient of the hunt. There are men who have, for example, gained a great deal of pleasure for more than a decade of unsuccessful hunting for deer. They would, one should hasten to say, have got the same pleasure from pursuing the animals with an empty rifle. It is important that there is a potential for bringing the confrontation between deer and man to a conclusion. Yet there are men, and there is one hunting out of this cabin today, who, when given an opportunity to kill a deer, have passed it up on several occasions. The animals may have been too small, it may have been a doe rather than a buck, the shot offered may not have been ideal—that is to say that there was a good chance the animal could not be killed cleanly—or it may have been that the beauty of the deer, perhaps standing half in sunlight, half in shade, stayed the hunter's trigger finger.

All this is to suggest that most hunters are not brutish men with a lust to kill. Their relationship with wild creatures is much more complicated and sensitive than the average opponent of the pursuit would suppose.

Twilight is descending early outside the cabin. Under the spruces the gloom is deep; the bare lean trunks of the leafless hardwoods on the near hillside are half obscured by mist, and coming through them, empty-handed, is one of my companions.

Peace Lies Beyond the Old Trails

Where the Little Dead Diamond and the Dead Diamond rivers meet in the Academy Grant, a spot about 16 miles up a logging road that runs north of here, they call it Hellgate. This may have derived from the short, steep gorge in the main river's bed at that point, because hell does not lie beyond. Hell, if there is one, is in the opposite direction.

What lies beyond and to the west and east can be called wilderness, although nearly all of it has been worked over by generations of loggers.

But loggers—and their big trucks were rumbling down the road past Hellgate—don't disturb me anywhere near as much as superhighways choked with shiny automobiles or factory chimneys spewing their filth to the skies. The loggers' assault on the wilderness is swift and violent but they are soon gone and given time, if the cutting was done with intelligence, the forest will mend. Far worse, are man's less visible but infinitely more degrading intrusions on the natural world: the acid rain that makes lakes and ponds untenable for trout; the introduction of long-lived toxic chemicals into river and lake systems; and, perhaps worst of all, the continuing proliferation of Homo sapiens.

I visited Hellgate for various reasons. I wanted to revel in silence and solitude, to govern my activities by the rising and the setting of the sun. I also wanted to pursue two daydreams, which I have coddled for more than a decade. Youth may be the best time for dreaming, but in that part of one's life there are too many fanciful flights. In middle age, one stalks less elusive game with greater care.

To be specific, I wanted to float a portion of the Dead Diamond in my canoe and flyfish for the occasional large brook trout the river yields. I have visited the region a dozen times, the first more than thirty years ago, but the river was always passed up in favor of ruffed grouse or deer hunting.

I have also long wished to acquire proficiency in poling a canoe both upstream and down, and the Dead Diamond, in its rocky, shallow, fast-moving stretches, lends itself to that endeavor. My hunger to master poling was born fifteen years ago when Camille Beaulieu, a hunter and trapper, rural postman and raconteur of extraordinary ability stuck me in the bow of a canoe on a downstream run through a series of whitewater stretches on Maine's Allagash River and told me to sit still and keep my hands off my paddle.

The Dead Diamond was low when I visited it. In some places I had to wade—and on every sandbar there were more moose tracks than deer tracks—but after a mile or so I began to get a feel of the downstream effort. The ambience was somewhat tarnished because I was using an aluminum pole rather than one—such as Mr. Beaulieu had used—of spruce that was shod with the discarded iron of a peavey (a lumbering tool).

I cast to all likely looking runs and pools on my way down the river, but no trout responded. That might have been because the water was too cold, only in the high 40's. My failure was softened by four black ducks that flew within 50 feet of me before they spotted an intruder where none should have been, and by a grouse—in the gray phase one often sees in northern New Hampshire—that burst into flight from his perch high on a hemlock and scaled down behind an alder thicket on the opposite side of the river. Both the duck and grouse seasons were open, but my shotgun was in the bottom of the canoe out of reach. It is overly ambitious to try to blend poling, flyfishing and hunting.

Most of the confidence I gained in my downstream poling was lost during the upstream effort. Before reaching my launching point, I did acquire some knowledge of where to plant the pole in order to keep the bow into the current, and I also learned that energy is saved by, whenever possible, shooting across the fast water from one eddy to another.

That night—and here the image, if it ever existed, of a horny-handed outdoorsman fades—I listened to Pavarotti and Beethoven on my portable tape recorder. One need not leave the best of civilizations behind.

Rousing from my music-induced speculations, I remembered that a forest-surrounded, mountainside trout pond lay a little more than a mile south of me, close enough to bear the name of Hellgate, a 3-acre pond about 1,600 feet above sea level from which, I had been told, some truly large brook trout have been taken.

Late the following morning, I loaded my packbasket with an inflatable raft I had brought with me to use in fishing other ponds in the central part of the state, and set forth, shotgun in hand. There was a little wooden sign with an arrow pointing in the direction of the pond, but after glancing at my map I decided it would be simpler to bushwack to it in a straight line. I hadn't reckoned with an extensive beaver bog in which I wallowed for more than an hour before gaining higher ground, where I spent two more hours crisscrossing slopes at the level at which I thought the pond was located. My map was a bit off, however, and I was traversing an area a quarter of a mile or more below the pond.

I abandoned my search and concentrated on moving through grouse cover on the way back, only to discover that while in my salad days when carrying a much heavier load I could successfully mount and swing a gun on a fast-moving grouse, I could not do so when encumbered by the packbasket. Also, only about half of the leaves had dropped from the trees, restricting visibility considerably. I was certain that I had hit one of the three birds at which I shot but gave up after a 45-minute search. A downed grouse lying on newly fallen leaves is difficult to find. At such times one yearns for a good dog.

The next day I took the trail to the pond, had no trouble locating it and learned that my raft was not needed: An old aluminum boat awaited me, suspended upside down between two spruce trees.

Only a small area in the middle of the pond had water up to 12 feet deep; the remainder was much shallower. The entire bottom was muck, and there was a good deal of submerged aquatic vegetation.

No fish were rising, and a cold northerly wind often mixed with rain came and went with regularity. In two hours, I had covered all the likely looking water with no results. I made a long cast, put my fly rod down, lit my pipe and smoked it halfway through before picking up the rod. A male brook trout of about a pound, gaudy in his fall spawning colors, was on the other end, having hooked himself on one of the flies I was using, a gray squirrel streamer with a red body.

Eviscerating him, I found that his stomach was half-full of backswimmer nymphs. It was then I resolved to try no more. That one trout, caught by accident, would suffice.

Later, eating slices of his orange-red flesh raw with a dash of salt, pepper and a few drops of lemon juice, I was more than content.

A Brief Affair with the Parmachenee

Visiting a remote lake for a few days is something like glimpsing the face of a lovely woman in a crowd: the encounter, albeit ephemeral, quickens the heart with wonder and delight.

So it was with Parmachenee, a trout and landlocked salmon lake tucked away in western Maine just across from the northeastern tip of New Hampshire and just below the Canadian border.

Vic Pomiecko of Claremont, New Hampshire, and I were taken to a log cabin on Parmachenee. We traveled with Mr. Pomiecko's fellow townsman, Art Peabody, who had built a camp with his wife, sons and friends, on land leased from lumber interests.

Already at the cabin when we arrived in late afternoon were Paul Bofinger of Concord, New Hampshire, Paul Ordway of Littleton, New Hampshire—two men who had shared in the camp's creation—and Dick Bartlett of Concord.

Some landlocked salmon—our basic prey —had already been caught by the trio and were being meticulously filleted by Mr. Bofinger to prepare them for insertion into a smoker in the woods at the rear of the camp.

Greetings were warm but swift because there was little daylight left, and by six o'clock we all were on the water.

Mr. Pomiecko and Mr. Ordway chose to fish a section of the Magalloway River just below its outlet from Parmachenee; Mr. Peabody and I took one of the camp's boats to the outlet itself. The others disappeared in directions unknown to me.

The stream waters in which we angled were restricted to fly-casting only, which is, at the risk of sounding like a snob, the only enlightened way to go after landlocked salmon or Atlantic salmon. Anglers working those same areas are also, at this time of year, limited to one salmon a day, but it is permissible to catch and release more salmon after one has been killed.

Mr. Peabody and I fished for half an hour, caught and freed a few small trout and then lounged amidst the wreckage—a portion of a wood deck and crumbling, stone-filled wood abutments—of a logging bridge that had once spanned the lake's outlet.

Time was, I told him, when having come to such a precious spot in quest of a precious fish, I would have cast incessantly, but in recent years the hunger to always be successful at angling has become muted. I seem, I confessed, to be fishing for something without shape or form—perhaps, I added, for the essence of a September evening such as ours in the Maine woods when a nearly full moon is rising behind the cathedral firs and spruces.

The moon appeared, bats plunged about in the dusk, and far out on the lake a loon wailed.

Returning to camp, we heard singing and guitar music as we approached and this was puzzling because no one of our group possessed such a talent.

Two large figures rose from the steps of the camp when we approached and Mr. Peabody recognized one of them as Joe Connolly of Portland, Maine. The other man, the singer and guitar player, was Tim Joy of Scarboro, Maine, and more of him later.

The other members of our party returned a few minutes later, and they had caught several salmon.

Proper libations followed and sometime around ten o'clock, Mr. Pomiecko and I remembered that we had seen a magnificent batch of edible mushrooms on stumps just outside the backdoor of the camp. It was imperative, we said—emboldened by wine and good bourbon—that they be transformed into a sauce for the evening meal.

We assured the others—who expressed some doubt about the enterprise—that we weren't going to poison everyone. Mr. Pomiecko remembered the Polish name for the mushrooms. I had forgotten the Latin and the English, I admitted, but observed that Mr. Pomiecko and I had been amateur mycologists for thirty-five years.

The mushrooms were a brilliant success, one that was repeated the following evening.

Tim Joy eschewed the fungi and all other food, preferring to play his guitar and sing, and some time around midnight, when I tried to engage him in conversation, I triggered a display that— even considering my euphoric condition—seemed to me to border on the remarkable.

Music poured from his guitar, and from his mouth, in song, came the answers to my queries, always in rhymed couplets. I had the feeling, which developed into a certainty as the rhymes flowed on, that he was telling me, a stranger, things more directly than he would have in ordinary speech.

Refusing our repeated offers to have supper with us, Tim Joy and Joe Connolly stepped out into the moon washed woods bound for their fishing camp on another body of water a few miles away.

The next day, the only full day for me and my traveling companions at the spot, Mr. Peabody showed me other portions of the lake and the Magalloway River—including Little Boy Falls and pool where a bronze tablet, placed there on a boulder by the Maine Federation of Republican Women, proclaims that President Dwight D. Eisenhower fished there in 1955. I made a dozen casts in the pool, wondering how it would feel to fish with a dozen or more pairs of watchful eyes of security personnel peering at one from the gloom of the nearby forest.

That evening, by no prearrangement, all hands finished up at the Lake Parmachenee outlet and Mr. Bofinger, as meticulous with a fly rod as he is with a filleting knife, took me in hand and informed me that I was covering too much water and sometimes even standing where salmon might lurk.

"Try my rod," he said. "It's got a little dry fly to it. Work that area right in front of you. There has to be a salmon there."

His rod was a delicate little thing—about a No. 5, as I recall.

Twenty casts later a salmon of about two pounds engulfed my fly and danced upon the dark water. Mr. Bofinger netted it for me, and he and Mr. Peabody—who I think was beginning to worry if I'd ever catch a salmon—offered their congratulations.

The next day, the last for all of us, we had to leave by late afternoon. I rose at 6:30 A.M. and found the Messrs. Ordway, Bartlett and Pomiecko pulling on their boots and getting ready to go fishing.

They had not even taken time to eat breakfast. I told them it was uncivilized to begin the day with an empty gut, but they paid me no heed.

I remained in camp that morning to cut green alder wood for Mr. Bofinger's salmon-smoking operation.

"Choose alders about as big around as your thumb and cut them up in pieces from four to six inches long," he said.

I was engaged in the last-mentioned operation. Mr. Bofinger had brought his salmon fillets—which had been rubbed with salt and brown sugar the day before—up to the smoker when the trio of early departing anglers returned bursting with glad tidings.

Mr. Bartlett and Mr. Pomiecko each had a splendid cock salmon of about three pounds taken on Magalloway waters to which Mr. Ordway had guided them, and Mr. Bartlett, who has been fly fishing only a few years, had also been helped by Mr. Pomiecko.

"I had caught my salmon and was watching Dick fishing," Mr. Pomiecko said, "when, on two casts in a row, a salmon made a pass at his fly, a streamer. The next cast, I told him to strip the fly in much faster. He did, and the fish never hesitated. It was great to watch. As much fun as catching one yourself."

Early that afternoon, Mr. Ordway and I floated a short section of the Magalloway above the lake in a canoe, our main goal being to work a pool called Cleveland Eddy, which is often highly productive. I fished hard because time was running out, and my companion, who throws a beautiful line, did the same, but the fish weren't responding.

Late that afternoon, the pre-departure chores done, I stood on the porch of the camp and looked out across the lake. The hills beyond were already touched with red and gold; the strong westerly wind that was whipping the water to a froth moaned in the birches and conifers above me and I was both sad and content.

The Parmachenee is only one of many excellent landlocked salmon lakes in Maine. As one example of this, Azicohos Lake, also part of the Magalloway flowage, is only a few miles downstream of Parmachenee and has a commercial fishing establishment where one will find food, lodging, boats and guides. This is Boebuck Mountain Camps, Wilsons Mills, Maine 04293.

There is a public access and launching area at the foot of Aziscohos Lake, and there are primitive camping sites on its eastern shore. One could put in a canoe at the launching area and, if stream fishing was the goal, paddle up the lake to where the Magalloway River enters.

Dick Frost of the Rangeley Region Sports Shop in Rangeley, Maine, and those who work with him are always willing to suggest how to go about finding a fishing lodge and a guide, or waters to try on one's own.

The Rangeley Chamber of Commerce, whose address is Box 3117, Rangeley, Maine 04970, is also a good source for such information.

Bayberries Are Always a Good Pick

A short while ago when a cool, dry wind from the northwest ended an enervating series of hot, muggy days, my youngest daughter, Alison, and I tucked her six-month-old son, Morgan, into a packbasket and went bayberry picking.

There were probably few others doing the same thing on our island, Martha's Vineyard, Massachusetts, that day, even though the berries were plentiful.

Prized in other, less hectic and simpler times for its waxy exterior—by boiling or near-boiling, and used to make fragrant candles—the bayberry is largely ignored today, and this is a pity for there is no more pleasant way to spend several hours afield.

We picked in reasonably diligent fashion, stopping occasionally to watch small flocks of Canada geese flying low over the scrub oaks and pitch pines. In three hours we had nearly ten pounds of berries which would, I hoped yield about a pound of gray-green wax.

One can pick bayberries in late fall, but snow and ice storms and strong winds tend to knock them to earth and when the ground is snow-covered and other berries and insects aren't available, birds will dine on them.

The bayberry, of which there are several species, can be included under the generic term wax myrtle. One species, Myrica pensylvanica, is found from Newfoundland to North Carolina and inland near the Great Lakes. It is a stocky shrub usually not much more than three feet high, and its grayish berries are about three sixteenths of an inch in diameter by late summer.

The best-known use of bayberries is candle making, but both the leaves and the berries have been used for food flavoring. In years past, cooks often tossed a few bayberry leaves into a soup or stew in lieu of tropical bay leaves, and the berries were sometimes used for this purpose. Bayberry leaves will also impart a pleasing flavor to a cider or wine vinegar. Seacoast housewives also rubbed their flatirons with little muslin bags containing bayberries to give the clothes they pressed a pleasant aroma.

It takes, as mentioned before, about ten pounds of bayberries to produce one pound of wax, and a pound of wax will make about seven tapered candles ten inches long and an inch thick at the butt. Some bayberry candle makers, and I among them, mix the bayberry fifty-fifty with commercially available white candle wax. Candles so made have a pleasing color and enough of the haunting bayberry aroma to satisfy most.

A bucket or a good-sized basket is best for bayberry picking. One simply strips the clusters of berries from the branches and often the container can be put on the ground while one works with both hands. If the bushes are high enough, the container can be strapped to one's waist. One should not strive to keep leaves and twigs of the berries because they will have to be removed before the candle-making process begins.

One should also, after the leaves and twigs are removed, shake the berries in a colander a handful at a time to remove fine grit and dust.

The berries are then placed in a large, wide-mouth pot with water added until the pot is full. Some old-time candle recipes say that iron pots should not be used for this purpose because the iron will discolor the wax. I have always used either copper or aluminum containers.

Some bayberry-candle literature suggests boiling the berries gently for about three hours; other texts advise keeping the pot on the back of the stove (obviously this reference is to an old black iron kitchen range) overnight so that the water becomes hot but never boils. (This can be achieved with a "warm" or "simmer" setting on a modern gas or electric range.)

The idea of all this is that the wax separates from the berries and rises to the surface, where after the mixture is allowed to cool for several hours, the wax congeals and may be lifted off the liquid beneath.

I followed the low heat suggestion until this year, when, being in a hurry, I tried rapid boiling with five pounds of berries. I also, I must confess, was not particular about removing all the debris, figuring that I could strain it out at the end. The result was disaster. Only a little wax came to the top. The rest was mixed with the junk and cooked berries on the bottom of the pot. I am not sure whether it was the boiling or the debris (or both) that caused the problem, but upon reverting to the first method, and not omitting the cleaning process, I had good results.

Re-melt the wax acquired after simmering your bayberries in clean water and strain it through a couple of thicknesses of cheesecloth to get rid of remaining foreign matter. You can rescue most of the wax that clings to the cloth by pouring boiling water through it.

Once this is done, you can either combine the bayberry wax with a certain proportion of the aforementioned commercial wax, or, if you have enough of it, you can use it alone.

Some enjoy making candles by the dip method which involves repeatedly lowering and lifting the wicks—which are suspended from a horizontally held stick—in the wax. This is an interesting technique, but it takes a lot of time because you must wait for the wax to harden after each dipping.

My own approach is to use an antique candle mold that I borrow from a neighbor. With such a mold—the one I borrow is for the conventional, tapered candles—use a wick that is a couple of inches longer than the mold. Dip the upper end of the wick—the end that is to be lighted—in the melted wax. This will help hold it in place in the mold and aid the first lighting of the candle. If you have the mold sitting firmly in an upright position, you can hold the wick centered with one hand while you do the pouring of the wax with the other. If the candles stick in the molds, they can be loosened with hot water.

Molds can be fashioned from a wide variety of common objects such as paper cups or short sections of mailing tubes. Tape circular cardboard disks to their bottoms to keep the wax in. The wick can be pushed through the center of the bottom, and held in place in a variety of ways including a knot. The wick can be centered on top by tying it to a rod that rests across the top of the mold.

If mailing tubes are used as molds, be sure to coat the interior of them with cooking oil to facilitate the candle's removal.

When pouring large candles save a little wax with which to fill the depression that will soon form around the wick. Allow the wax to cool for several hours before removing from the mold.

I procure candle wax and wicks from the Cape Cod Candle and Gift Shops in Orleans, Massachusetts, but they are really only being good to me and are not in the candle-making supply business. One retail company—offering wicks, wax and scents for sale—is the Williamsburg soap and Candle Company, RFD 3, Box 305, Williamsburg, Virginia.

If you want to try making your own wicks, soak cotton yarn overnight in a mixture of two tablespoons of borax, one tablespoon of salt and one cup of water and allow to dry before using.

Elusive Muskies
Turn Challenge
into Ordeal

Although I have resisted it, the urge to once again go muskellunge fishing is growing within me.

If consistent success is one's goal, muskie fishing cannot be justified, for there is no other freshwater species that is so uncooperative. Some experts say they have to spend an average of seventy-five hours of fishing for each muskie caught.

I am not an accomplished muskie fisherman, nor would I ever have the temerity or the time to seek such status. In my sporadic efforts to catch muskies—they are the largest of the pike family, and the rod-and-reel record muskie, caught in the St. Lawrence River in September 1955, weighed 69 pounds 15 ounces—I estimate that I have cast over 5 miles for every response awarded me by my intended prey.

"Response" is a good word in this context. Unlike certain violent, ever-moving saltwater species such as the bluefish, the muskie will not always delight the angler with a savage strike. He is capable of such an act, but most of the time he will either ignore the angler's offering, make an inaccurate pass at it, or simply follow it to the boat, sometimes coming to a stop, part of his head and eyes protruding above the water, before turning away. There were occasions, in the days when such shenanigans weren't regarded with great alarm and weren't illegal, when an angler frustrated by his sight yanked a .45-caliber pistol from his tackle box and blazed away at his tormenter.

There are various scientific explanations for the muskie's recalcitrant behavior toward anglers, but scientists often clutter their judgments with unemotional data and thereby miss the truth.

The truth is that muskies dislike people and will do all they can to irritate them.

Unlike the bluefish or the slim, athletic trout in a fast-running mountain stream, the muskie lives in large lakes or rivers, and he can, if he wishes, lie motionless for days at a time, neither eating nor swimming, merely finning gently and devising ways to annoy the hordes of anglers that toss immense lures at him year after year.

And sometimes, most rarely, muskies go on a lure-chomping rampage. But they did so in 1955 during a two-week period on Leech Lake in Minnesota when 160 of them were caught.

I am not sure how long a muskie can go without eating, but there is a story about one in a Minnesota aquarium that cared so little about nourishment that over the years his keeper saw his charge eat only three yellow perch, two frogs and one Hershey bar, the last-named tossed in by a well-intentioned tourist. Now that is somewhat apocryphal, but the captive muskie did exist and he did, for weeks at a time, do nothing but refuse food and glare at his captors.

The muskie's sedentary life is logical. He is lord of his domain. Once he is a few years old—and he may live to thirty—there is no predator other than man that poses any real threat.

I began my muskie fishing a decade ago on the broad reaches of the St. Lawrence, the mighty river that separates New York State and Canada.

My guide was Jimmy Brabant, an affable, accomplished angler whose roots reach deep into the area and its history.

He took me out trolling among the Thousand Islands. I detest trolling, but he said that inasmuch as I had only one day to try for muskies, trolling was probably better. We boasted two muskellunge that day, and I returned home persuaded that catching a muskie was a simple affair.

Since that time, more than a dozen muskie trips to the St. Lawrence, Minnesota and Wisconsin have yielded nothing.

Faced with such minimal success, the average angler reacts by resolving never to try for the species again. But as the months go by, the cutting edge of failure is dulled and replaced by a vague yearning to go once more, if only to see one of those huge, toothy creatures following a lure to the boat.

This is why I will go again this fall when an event billed as the World Musky Hunt will be held in Minocqua, Wisconsin, even though the nearly thirty anglers taking part in last year's two-day tournament caught only two legal-sized fish.

Truly dedicated muskie anglers apparently gain sustenance from failure or near failure. Talk to several of them in the evening after they've caught nothing all day and you'll never find one who is depressed. They will be filing or honing even sharper points on the hooks of their lures, and their cheeks will flush with excitement as they describe a "follow" or a strike that missed.

Both casting and trolling are effective when muskie fishing—or as effective as any approach to the species can be. The supreme advantage of casting is that it gives the fisherman something to do. It also allows him to work certain weedy areas where a trolled lure would hang up. Some muskie anglers use bait, including live fish and frogs.

The usual gear for muskies is a heavy casting rod equipped with a conventional (revolving spool) reel and 20- or 30-pound test line, monofilament or braided. Short wire leaders are almost always used. Lures include spoons, bucktail-spinners, so-called "jerk baits" and plugs. The last named embrace surface, sub-surface and deep-running varieties.

Most muskies are caught over weed beds in water from four to fifteen feet deep, but often those areas are close to dropoffs. A few trolling specialists have good luck in deeper water, however. A windy day, or at least one with a slight chip on the water, also improves the chance for success.

There is no complete agreement among veteran muskie anglers as to what time of year is most productive. On the St. Lawrence, for example, muskie fishing starts in June and continues into November. Fall is considered a good period on the St. Lawrence, but one long-time resident of the area, Harold Herick, Jr., points out that one reason the muskie catch is down in midsummer is that few anglers go after the fish then.

In the Clayton-Cape Vincent, New York, region of the St. Lawrence there are good reasons for diminished muskie fishing in fall. That's when large catches of coho salmon are being made in nearby Lake Ontario and on the river itself jigging for walleyed pike—among the most tasty freshwater fish in the world—up to 12 pounds has been amazingly successful.

Ron Schara's *Muskie Mania* (Henry Regnery Company, Chicago) is probably the best modern muskie fishing text available.

States with muskie populations are Alabama, Delaware, Illinois, Indiana, Iowa, Kentucky, Maryland, Michigan, Minnesota, Missouri, Nebraska, New Jersey, New York, North Carolina, North Dakota, Ohio, Pennsylvania, South Dakota, Tennessee, Vermont, Virginia, West Virginia and Wisconsin.

Ouananiche Get Hit with a Mickey Finn

Rain rattled against the windows of our Norsman float plane as we came in for a landing on a small, unnamed body of water that lies a quarter of a mile south of Bohier Lake. As we were taxiing toward shore, where the plane was tethered to two spruce trees, the squall passed overhead, however, and sunlight streamed down between the steep, green hills.

This small lake, which is about a forty-minute Norsman flight north-northeast of the St. Lawrence Fishing and Hunting Club's Musquaro Lake bush camp, has produced ouananiche (land-locked salmon) of more than ten pounds. After landing, Gordon Blair, the club's founder, suggested that we fish the lake's outlet first.

My third cast with a Mickey Finn streamer fly produced a solid strike, and a moment later an ouananiche of about 8 pounds rose majestically skyward and crashed back into the water, ridding himself of the hook. An hour later we taxied to the upper end of the lake, having taken no fish from the lower end, and there, where the fast-flowing, boulder-strewn stream from Bohier Lake enters, we caught five ouananiche, averaging about four pounds, in two hours of fishing.

The aforementioned Mickey Finn took most of the fish. Indeed, if one had to bring a single fly pattern to the trout and ouananiche waters of eastern Quebec, it probably should be the Mickey Finn. And if the trout are rising to a hatch of aquatic insects, the dry-fly selection does not have to be elaborate. A Number 12 dry fly, as far as size is concerned, will meet most situations.

Because the frost comes down to the shore all around the small lake, we shuttled the party, which included Mrs. Blair, Mr. and Mrs. John N. Weiss of Southampton, Pennsylvania, Armand Jenniss, the guide, and Greg Peel, the pilot, to a sandy beach on Bohier Lake. The freshly caught salmon were split, then were brushed with butter, salt and pepper and coated with brown sugar, and grilled over an open fire.

A Bad Move Produces a Harrowing Spill

Having purchased a lovely, new, 18½-foot Kevlar-Airex canoe from Mad River, I then proceeded to tip it over on a remote New Hampshire brook trout pond with Vic Pomiecko, my fly-fishing companion of nearly thirty years, aboard.

We got to Chapin Pond shortly before noon on a gray day of intermittent rain. We chatted with a family that was already there—William (Bud) Raymond of Claremont, New Hampshire, his wife, Fran, and their two children, William 3d, ten years old, and Jeremy, six—and then set forth in a heavy fog that sometimes cut visibility to 150 feet.

Within minutes, using sinking lines and a simple red-bodied gray swirl tail streamer that Vic designed for brook trout twenty-five years ago, we were catching fish. One of the purposes of the expedition was to bring home a nice mess of good-sized trout to my mother, and we began releasing the smaller ones. Even so, we had a half-dozen on our stringer when I made my bad move.

A little background information is needed to bring the ensuing debacle into focus.

In more than forty years of canoeing, I had never turned one over on a lake, pond or ocean, although I had flipped several times while running white water. And in our decades of trout fishing on lakes and ponds, Vic and I had, without mishap, often cast for hours from canoes while standing, although those craft were either his big wood and canvas Old Town rowing canoe or my 20-foot Grumman.

Throughout those years, I had lectured him for occasionally making sharp, sudden movements while casting, and I had nearly cured him of the habit.

On our Chapin Pond trip, we were so anxious to get on the water that we forgot our flotation cushions. When we were 50 feet from shore, I looked at my non-waterproof aluminum camera case resting on the bottom of the canoe and said, "I ought to leave my cameras on shore or put the case in a couple of garbage bags so it will stay dry if we go over."

But even as I spoke, a trout of more than a pound leaped out of the water before us and, caution forgotten, I paddled on.

We had anchored and I was kneeling in the bottom of the canoe and casting when it became obvious that we were going over. Later, it occurred to me that I had lurched violently to one side because I still have a slight loss of balance as a result of a recent illness. My first reaction was incredulity, and after we were floundering in the cold water, I thought of the more than $2,000 worth of cameras and lenses in the case, which was bobbing beside me.

I grabbed it and tried to hold the canoe with one hand and the case above water with the other. That didn't work. My heavy rubber knee boots (they have steel shanks) were pulling me down, so I kicked them off.

Vic, meanwhile, was supporting himself on the overturned canoe, and I could see that he was all right for the present.

I would, I thought, swim to the shore, which was only 40 yards away, holding the camera case over my head.

I had gone about half the distance when it became apparent that, encumbered by the case and by my clothing, which included a heavy wool sweater, I probably wasn't going to make it. I let go of the case and began treading water.

The difficulty I was having in staying afloat astonished me. I am a good swimmer. A few weeks before, for example, I had spent the better part of an afternoon skin diving for Atlantic surf clams 8 to 15 feet down in choppy bay waters.

I began to shiver violently, sank lower, swallowed a little water and reflected that I might be engaged in a rather ludicrous final act. Oddly, I felt no fear, only self-disgust at having gotten in such a situation. This emotion was so strong that I made no attempt to cry out to the people on shore, nor did I look in that direction. Vic, thankfully, did yell, and Mr. Raymond went into action. He paddled to us, tossed me a flotation cushion, rounded up Vic and our canoe and towed us ashore.

While his wife and children got a fire going to warm us, Mr. Raymond picked up various floating items, including my hat and pipe, paddles, Vic's Thermos jug and creel and our Styrofoam cooler.

I took my camera case to my four-wheel-drive vehicle and discovered that it was not completely filled with water. One camera and several lenses were obviously ruined, but one Nikon body appeared to be salvageable. I dried it as best I could with a kerchief and the vehicle's heater and that night placed it in Vic's oven on low heat. It came through unscathed.

After dealing with my photographic equipment at the pond, I went out with Mr. Raymond with a grappling line that we rigged with a sinker and a treble hook. The water where Vic and I had tipped over was only 12 feet deep and exceptionally clear. Within twenty minutes we had retrieved both my rods—Vic already had his because his line had tangled on his foot—my boots and my big, custom-made flybox, which contained several hundred flies.

The following morning, a Sunday, Lou Smith, who owns a photography shop in Claremont, kindly opened his doors for me so I could get a couple of new lenses for the Nikon body. Vic and I returned to Chapin. At that time, the camera case remained on shore, and flotation cushions were in the canoe.

For years I had never brought anything but my waterproof camera, a Nikonos, on such ventures, but because of its lack of versatility I had begun leaving it behind. Three years ago, I purchased a waterproof flotation envelope of heavy plastic intended for cameras, watches and other gear that can be ruined by water, but I never got around to using it. It will be with me henceforth on every endeavor involving small boats or canoes. I will also make sure that gear which can sink, such as flyboxes and extra fly rods, will be lashed to the craft.

Some of my trout-fishing trips involved hiking in to remote ponds, where one might get out on the water in an inflatable raft or "doughnut" or perhaps a small aluminum boat that someone dragged in over the snow. Flotation cushions are too bulky and heavy for backpacking, so I had already ordered a couple of light-weight life vests that I will bring with me on such excursions.

There is another precaution that can be taken when fishing from a canoe with a companion. Unless the craft is a huge, beamy affair, each angler should tell the other when he plans to change position. Vic and I do this, but it is easy to grow lax near the end of a long day of angling.

With the memory of the previous day fresh in our minds, Vic and I were exceptionally alert during our second day on Chapin Pond. The afternoon was bright and the fish weren't quite as responsive as they had been twenty-four hours before, but in three hours we each had a limit of seven trout. Mother will savor them in the weeks ahead.

Fresh Blues Don't Have to Taste Fishy

No one denies that the rapacious, powerful bluefish is fun to catch, but there is sharp disagreement over its merit on the dining table.

Many people who eat saltwater fish with regularity favor white-fleshed species such as the flatfishes or cod. The blue, they say, is simply too fishy. A bluefish (even one consumed minutes after capture) does have a more assertive flavor than, for example, a summer flounder, but a strong fishy taste means that the fish has begun to deteriorate, and bluefish do not keep as well as many other species.

A. J. McClane was thinking of this when he wrote in his *Encyclopedia of Fish Cookery* (Holt, Rinehart and Winston, 1977), that when dining out, he would "never order bluefish except at seaside restaurants where freshness is guaranteed, assuming the proprietor is credible."

Treated properly, the bluefish is excellent eating, with mild, flaky meat, although larger specimens (those over ten pounds) tend to have a stronger flavor than their smaller brethren.

Many who have been put off by the flavor of a poorly cared-for blue would find the species to their liking if certain precautions were observed between the catch and the feast. The current cycle of bluefish abundance makes such postcatch care, if one fishes for food as well as pleasure, of particular relevance.

Bluefish eating within two or three hours of capture are usually first rate, although if they were caught at noon on a searing day and exposed to the sun for forty-five minutes, they would be in sorry shape. At the very least, whether in a boat or on the beach, one should contrive to keep fish protected from the sun. This might involve nothing more than placing them in the shade under one's vehicle or placing a wet burlap bag over them.

The suggestions that follow for the treatment of bluefish after capture represent an ideal, but between the ideal and the reality lies the shadow of circumstance. If you reach a certain spot at the end of a tide and are almost certain that the blues will stop hitting as soon as the water becomes slack, the limited time you have (unless you are extraordinarily disciplined) will be devoted to catching fish. You should realize, however, that the process of spoilage cannot be reversed.

Bluefish should be placed on ice immediately. Ice chips or flakes or a mixture of ice and water will remove body heat from fish more rapidly than a block of ice, or ice frozen in a container, but I tend to use the last-named approach because it is easier. At the end of a day's trip, all you have to do is place the water-filled containers back in your home freezer.

The shelf life of a bluefish can be extended by bleeding it immediately after capture, either by cutting off its tail or by severing its gills. Stun the fish beforehand (you usually have to do that anyway to remove the lure safely from its sharp-toothed mouth) and its heart will pump out much of its blood.

Richard Lord of the Fulton Fish Market, a student of fish and fish quality, favors gill-cutting because it is easier to accomplish, less messy and results in more complete bleeding. Lift up the gill plate and cut, from front to rear, the gills in half with the point of a knife, then repeat this on the other side of the fish's head. Among other things, bleeding allows the fish to cool more rapidly and makes its flesh less dark.

When surf fishing, I nearly always gut, or fillet and skin, blues on the beach, using a length of plywood on the tailgate of my vehicle as a cleaning table. This early separate of the edible flesh from powerful digestive juices retards spoilage. The carcasses and innards are returned to the ocean, where they will be quickly consumed by a variety of creatures. Better there than in a town or city dump.

A bluefish in rigor mortis is eminently fresh, of course, but Lord recently pointed out to me that one should not fillet a fish in that state if one has to force it into a flat position, a maneuver that tears the musculature and creates a ragged-looking fillet that tends to fall apart. If the fish has gone into rigor without a curve, go ahead and fillet; if not, wait until rigor leaves.

The dark strips of meat that one finds under the skin down the sides of a bluefish may have too strong a flavor for some palates. Those strips are easily removed after the fillet is skinned. Without slicing through to the opposite side, make a wide, shallow V cut on either side of the dark meat and lift it out. Filleting and skinning a blue and removing the dark meat is a good procedure for another reason. At certain times of year in certain regions, large bluefish have high levels of PCB's (polychlorinated biphenyls), which tend to concentrate just under the skin and in the dark meat. Dangerous PCB levels have not, to my knowledge, been found in blues of 4 pounds or less.

Bluefish that have received the best of care retain their quality for two or three weeks in a home freezer. Unfrozen in the average refrigerator, three days is the limit. Some fish markets have a sideline in wrapping and flash-freezing fillets at temperatures far below zero for anglers who then put them in their home freezing units. This extends the shelf life of the frozen fish dramatically.

Bluefish recipes abound, but those that call for poaching or a chowder should be avoided. When so treated, the blue's flesh has the texture of straw. Broiling is the best way to cook bluefish fillets. Sprinkle the inside of the fillet with lemon or lime juice half an hour before cooking, and rub cooking oil on the other side before putting it in the pan to prevent sticking. Salt and pepper the side that will be facing the flame or heating element, and dot with butter. The fillet should not be turned. If it becomes brown before the flesh flakes readily under gentle pressure from a fork, turn the oven off. The remaining heat will finish the job in a few minutes. Serve with wedges of lemon and chopped parsley.

Battling a King Mackerel

The pink balloon that served as a float to hold the live pinfish bait near the surface of the water bobbed violently and then disappeared.

Tom Earnhardt of Goldsboro, North Carolina, an attorney, handed me the rod and I watched 300 yards of line spin off the reel in a little more than a minute.

"My God," said the third man in Earnhardt's 20-foot Robalo, Joel Arrington of Raleigh, North Carolina, "you've got a good one."

On the end of the line was a king mackerel of undetermined size, but clearly one of considerable energy. The fish slowed its run, but continued to take line in short bursts.

"We'd better cast off from the anchor," said Earnhardt, "or we'll lose this fish."

Arrington did so—tossing overboard a floating plastic jug attached to the anchor line—and we moved after the fish. Twenty minutes later, I had only half the line back and was becoming rather embarrassed at the duration of the struggle.

"Are you hurting him as much as you can?" Arrington asked. "The drag is as heavy as I dare to set it," I replied.

"Must be a truly large fish," said Earnhardt.

"Either that, or I've hooked him by the tail," I replied.

King mackerel are lean, toothy and incredibly fast. The largest taken off United States shores on rod and line weighed 67 pounds. The all-tackle record, caught in Dominican Republic waters, is 78 pounds 12 ounces. The North Carolina record is 57½ pounds, but the average king in the region we were fishing is about 15 pounds.

We had left Paul Hodges's Calico Jack's Inn and Marina on Harkers Island at about 8 A.M., and after an unsuccessful effort to find a school of small bluefish that we hoped to catch for bait we anchored off the mouth of Lookout Bight and Barden Inlet, which separate Cape Lookout from Shackleford Banks. There, we bottomfished for croakers, spot and pinfish. The latter-named species are most commonly used in the area when floatfishing for kings, but Earnhardt believes the young blues are much better.

"All those little bottom fish do when you float them out there on a hook is try to get to the bottom," he said. "The bluefish swims away from the boat and keep up a constant struggle that excites the kings."

The lean and intense Earnhardt sprays his hooks and leaders black, believing any brightness makes the kings reluctant to hit. His king-mackerel rig is about 6 feet of uncoated, and therefore limp, braided wire leader, at the end of which is usually a 6/o single hook that is run through the live baitfish just ahead of its dorsal fin.

Fastened to the eye of that single hook on about six inches of the same leader material is a 2/o or 3/o treble hook that is allowed to swing free. All hook points are filed and honed to needle sharpness. The free-swinging treble hook usually snags the mackerel under the chin.

King-mackerel fishing off Cape Lookout is best from October until Thanksgiving, and throughout this month and next anglers with their own boats and charter-boat fishermen flock to Hodges's place (the telephone number is [919] 728-3575).

Although many kings had been taken the week before our arrival, very few boats were leading any the day we were out. The fish I was fighting was our first and for this reason, if no other, I probably handled it a bit gingerly.

Forty minutes after he first took the bait, my king was gaffed aboard. He was not truly large, only 27½ pounds, but the reason for the long battle was obvious: The single hook was not in him at all, and the treble had snagged him in the forward part of his belly making it necessary for me to pull him sideways through the water.

That fish, alas, was our first and last, but we felt a little better when we learned on reaching the marina that evening that it was the largest caught that day.

Family Outing

A few days ago, while on a fishing trip with my grandson Morgan, I learned that something of the child lurks within me still. Morgan, who will be four years old in February, suggested such an excursion after learning that my granddaughter Lucy, who is a few months older, and I had gone on a white perch expedition that, when we couldn't locate the fish, had been transformed into a picnic.

Morgan is an outgoing fellow and was delighted when his mother, Alison, asked if she could tag along, even though he knew that meant that his brother Jesse, who was one in July, would be included.

I chose the largest canoe I own, a 20-foot aluminum Grumman, for our excursion on Tisbury Great Pond on the island of Martha's Vineyard, Massachusetts, because there was a sharp, northeasterly wind and an astonishing amount of equipage, which included a cooler, light spinning rods, and minnow seine, extra clothing and diapers, big surf rods and two tackle boxes.

Unbeknown to Morgan, who sat beside me in the stern, his hand under mine on the tiller of the tiny, aircooled outboard, I was yearning for experiences past.

Town Cove, where we launched our canoe, is the place where I caught my first white perch and where, nearly fifty years ago as a lad of twelve on Christmas Day, I wandered alone across the brown marsh and shot my first black duck with a single-barreled shotgun that I found under the Christmas tree. There were, even then, laws against twelve-year-olds hunting alone, but no one paid attention to them.

The entire pond is where I ran a trapline for muskrats, had trysts with a summer girl and on warm May evenings lay on a sandy beach listening to alewives splashing in the shallows in a pre-procreative ritual that would be consummated in Mill Brook.

We put up a flock of more than two dozen Canada geese that had been grazing on a horse-cropped meadow along the shore; a single mute swan labored across our bow, wings hissing. We passed a little knoll on the west shore where, in my salad days, an otter often devoured his just-caught alewives and perch, leaving bones, scales, scat and a smooth trail to the water. A newly built summer home now occupies the spot.

From his vantage point is a carrier slung from his mother's shoulders, Jesse turned to grin at his brother and me, brandishing his bottle, and my mood began to brighten.

Our destination was a narrow cut leading to one of the pond's east shore coves. The pond itself is open periodically to the sea by man and often serves as a nursery area for young bluefish, striped bass and Atlantic mackerel. During World War II, near the end of my parachute infantry regiment's participation in the Netherlands jump, a company runner came panting through the apple orchard where we had dug in for a few days of rest and gave me a V-mail letter from my father that filled me with envy. He had, he wrote, spent every day for a week at that cut with his flyrod, catching stripes from 3 to 6 pounds. I vowed to repeat his performance when I returned home, but never found bass there again.

As Alison and I beached our canoe near the cut, a gleaming shower of silverside minnows burst from the water a few yards away, and she grinned happily, knowing the larger fish, probably the baby or snapper bluefish we were after, were pursuing the silversides.

Alison and I had often been fishing companions, and she has a genuine knack for the sport. The baby had fallen asleep, so we made a bed for him in the bottom of the canoe.

My third cast with a little spoon produced a snapper, but it soon became clear that there was too much weed in the water for this approach. We made two passes through the cut with our seine, gathering several hundred silversides, baby flounder, mummichogs, one pipefish and an occasional shrimp. Using the silversides, suspended under bobbers as bait, the three of us were soon hauling snappers ashore.

Morgan was ecstatic and questions poured from him: "Why did you cover the snappers with eel grass?"

"To keep the sun from drying them out."

"Did it hurt the minnow when a hook was run through him?"

"Not much."

"Am I a good fisherman?"

"The best."

"What will we do with the snappers?"

"Have them for supper."

And then a statement: "I'm having fun. I like to be with you, Grandpa."

The baby's arms flailed above the canoe's gunwales. Alison changed his diaper, put him in his carrier and resumed fishing with him on her back. She and I were, I realized, as excited as Morgan.

Pointing to the southwest, where the pond's opening to the sea lay, Alison said, "Daddy, look at the gulls and terns over the surf. There are big bluefish there. We ought to get a few."

We had brought the surf rods with that in mind, but heavy clouds that had been building up all day obscured the sun, the temperature had fallen 15 degrees and it was late in the afternoon. I declined the gambit. Grandfathers are supposed to be imbued with wisdom.

I cleaned the snappers on the beach. From the stomach of one emerged the head of another of its kind, and I explained to Morgan—an observation that probably should have been more delicately phrased—that bluefish sometimes eat their own brothers and sisters.

We also brought home several dozen silversides and ate them and the snappers that night, popping off their heads between thumb and forefinger, rolling them in flour and frying them in oil.

"Can we go again tomorrow?" Morgan asked, the tail of a silverside protruding from the corner of his mouth.

Feast from Water's Edge

If you have ever driven along the shores of a bay or a salt pond on a late summer or fall night, you may have seen silvery cascades of small fish erupting skyward wherever your headlight beams touched the water.

The leapers were, for the most part, sand eels and silverside minnows, two of the most important forage fish for such species as striped bass, bluefish and mackerel.

Although sand eels range from Labrador to Cape Hatteras and silverside minnows from Nova Scotia to Virginia, very few people think of them as anything but bait. That is a pity, for they are splendid eating and an incredibly prolific and scarcely utilized food resource.

They are, in essence, the whitebait of the European gourmet, the dish on which the British Ministers of the Crown for many years dined before Parliament's close. (The Trafalgar Restaurant in Greenwich was the one setting for this repast.)

I use the phrase, in essence, because in England and elsewhere, other small fish are eaten as whitebait, including sardines, smelts, sticklebacks and pipefish. In America, sardines, silversides, herring, anchovies and Pacific surf smelts are all marketed as whitebait. To my knowledge, the sand eel is not gener-

ally available commercially on the East Coast, and it is often difficult for restaurants to find a source of them or silversides.

New York's 21 Club once offered an occasional whitebait feast,
and when whitebait was on hand, the first person the restaurant
would notify was Governor Rockefeller, who was very fond of the
dish.

The fragility of sand eels and silversides may account for their
scarcity on restaurant menus, for they cannot stand extended
storage.

From experience with whitebait in my own kitchen, I can only
observe that the passage from the water to the table, for both sand
eels (also called sand lances) and silverside minnows, must be un-
commonly swift, for the little creatures deteriorate rapidly. When
netting whitebait, don't put them in water; they die and become
soggy almost immediately. Instead, put them in a bucket between
layers of eelgrass or seaweed.

From late May through October in the Northeast, seiners need
wear nothing more than a bathing suit when they gather these
little fish. Earlier or later than that, hip boots or chest waders are
required. Both species are in shallow water all year round, but it is
my impression that substantial numbers of the sand eels move off
shore when the weather is truly cold.

A good rig for capturing whitebait is a minnow seine 4 feet
deep and 20 feet long, equipped with leads and floats. The seine
will come rolled up without poles, but with two lines dangling from
the top and bottom of each end of the net. Find two poles about 5
feet long and fasten one to each end of the net. Make sure the
ropes on the bottom, or weighted portion, of the net are tied close
to the ends of the poles.

With the bottom ends of the poles slanting slightly forward,
and a person on each pole, make a sweep along the shore, then
turn inshore. If children are about, it helps to have them splashing off the ends of the seine to deter any fish from trying to escape.
Keep the seine in the water all the way to the beach and you
will, with any luck at all, be astonished at your haul, which will
include not only whitebait but often baby herring, mummic hogs,
blue claw crabs, small flounder and a host of other aquatic deni-
zens.

It is impossible to move rapidly with the seine in deeper water, but as you approach the shore with it, walk as fast as possible to keep the fish from end runs to freedom.

Both sand eels and silversides grow to about 6 inches in length, but keep only those 3 inches and under. Whitebait is eaten whole and the bones in the larger specimens do not readily soften during cooking.

When you get your fish home, rinse them in fresh water. If they are not to be cooked immediately, put them on ice.

The usual approach is to fry them in fat. Before cooking, place the chilled whitebait on paper toweling and blot them dry. Dredge them in flour and fry in vegetable oil, bacon fat or shortening until they are a light brown. Drain each batch on more paper toweling and place them in a warming oven as the others are being cooked.

A cucumber, lettuce and watercress salad would be an excellent adjunct to whitebait, but this is not really necessary.

I have always fried them in a skillet, but I suppose that a deep fat fryer would also work well. Care should be taken to keep the fish separated while cooking.

Let each diner use salt and pepper to taste and no forks are necessary. Just pop the little fellows into your mouth, and you'll not notice the bones, only a superlative flavor, unlike any other fish you've ever eaten.

Although I find sand eels very good, it is my impression that the silversides are a bit more tasty, but this may be a personal idiosyncrasy.

Every once in a while, you will encounter a silverside that seems slightly bitter. I am not sure of the reason for this, but eight years ago, Kenneth Godfrey of New York City wrote to me, suggesting that the diet of one species of silversides is different from that of another. There are at least two species of silverside minnows in the Northeast, but it is difficult to tell them apart.

The sand eel, or sand lance, may be readily distinguished from either the silverside minnow or the smelt by a long dorsal fin that extends nearly the entire length of its back. Its forked tail makes it impossible to confuse with a young specimen of the common American eel.

The silverside, which gets its name from a band of bright silver that runs the length of the lateral line on each side, may be told from the smelt by its two dorsal fins and no adipose fin.

Grouse Are Plentiful, and Good

Hurtling on throbbing wings through the bare bones of fall-shorn trees, the ruffed grouse can make a competent wing shot look like a tyro.

Except for his moments of madness in fall when he sometimes rockets through the picture window of a hillside home or dashes himself to death against buildings and automobiles, the grouse is marvelously adept at avoiding humans.

Because of his wariness and the effort involved in pursuing him—a great deal of walking in rugged country or pushing through thickets and brambles—the grouse never significantly augments the hunter's larder.

The grouse is something extraordinary, and if you wish to share the eating of a brace of grouse with someone it is important for your emotional well-being to be certain that your dinner companion knows what a rare gift is being offered.

Although man's works have nibbled away at some of his habitat, the ruffed grouse exists in good numbers in thirty-four states and much of Canada.

In his splendid, recently published *The Gallant Grouse*—to which this writer is in-

debted for some of the information that appears in this piece—
Cecil Heacox notes that hunters in the United States and Canada
kill about six million grouse annually.

That is a great many birds, to be sure, but the beginning grouse
hunter shouldn't be led to believe that going after grouse is easy.

It is awkward to generalize about this because grouse populations vary a great deal in density throughout the bird's natural
range, but the average hunter in good or fair grouse country
will probably bag about one bird for every three or four days
afield.

The grouse hunter is not a meat hunter. He is after something
ephemeral, something gained from being abroad at a glorious
time of year in quest of a magnificent bird that was well established
on this continent—the only place he is found, by the way—some
25,000 years ago.

Grouse populations go through cyclical ups and downs—cold,
wet weather during the nesting and brooding seasons in spring
and early summer is one of the causes of a downturn—and, of
course, population densities vary from state to state.

In the section of New Hampshire where I do quite a bit of
grouse hunting, I have felt fortunate in recent years if I flushed
eight to ten birds on a long day's hunt. Some of these get up heard
but not seen and others, although seen, afford no decent shot. I
would estimate that I shoot at less than 20 percent of the grouse I
flush.

I have talked with hunters from our prime grouse states and
have been told that they've frequently flushed twenty-five or thirty
birds a day, but this is something I've never experienced.

The hunting that I am describing is by a man alone without a
dog. Very few pointers or setters—animals that might be superlative performers with quail and woodcock—are adept with grouse.
Most of them either move too fast or too incautiously, flushing
birds without a point, or range so far one spends a third of each
day trying to locate them in some thicket.

For me, at least, it is simpler to hunt without a dog.

On rare occasions, as when it flushes and flies down the middle
of a logging road, a grouse offers an easy shot, but many times the
bird will, by the time you've swung on him and pulled the trigger,

already have gone behind a tangle of limbs or the boughs of a conifer.

If the bird is within range at such an instant, don't hold fire. This is not careless hunting, for more often than not if you are "on" a grouse at the time of disappearance enough pellets will reach him to bring him down.

If you can't locate a bird immediately after such a shot—and this is a time when a dog would be most helpful—but feel certain that you were on him at the moment of firing, spend plenty of time looking for him. Search carefully for a feather or two the charge may have knocked off him and keep looking even after you are becoming sure that you missed. A grouse lying on a blanket of red-gold leaves is sometimes incredibly difficult to spot. I once shot a grouse that fell into a stream and lay floating in a raft of leaves, and I looked at that place half a dozen times during a twenty-minute search before the form of the bird emerged.

Another thing to remember when hunting grouse is to be prepared for a bird flushing after you have stopped walking and started moving again. Grouse will often sit tight and let you go by a few yards away if you are proceeding steadily. A halt, whether short or long, seems to unnerve them. Perhaps they feel they have been spotted. This can sometimes happen with only a slight pause, as when you are stepping over a fallen tree or a tumbled-down stone wall.

Most grouse are shot at less than 30 yards, so a tightly choked gun is a disadvantage. If your shotgun is a repeater or an automatic, improved cylinder would be a good choke and it could also be wide open. When shooting a side-by-side double or an over-and-under, either improved cylinder and modified, or improved cylinder and wide open is good.

An ounce of 7½ or 8 shot suffices for most grouse hunting, and this load can be had in 28, 20, 16 and 12 gauges. Remember that grouse shooting is snap shooting, so the gun should be light enough and short enough for you to handle it speedily.

You will find grouse in abandoned apple orchards, overgrown fields and along the edges of new fields and in thickets and logged-over forests where there is considerable undergrowth. Never neglect a stand of aspens, for in their succession from youth to age aspens are an important source of food and shelter for the birds. Grouse are essentially vegetarians, and eat a wide variety of buds, seeds and nuts, including the beechnut.

When snow or rain is falling, it is best to forget grouse hunting, for they would usually be holed up in thick stands of fir, pine or hemlock.

Remember that if you flush your grouse and don't get a shot at him you will often find him in the same location or nearby the next time around. Grouse don't move very far, except for some of the young birds during the aforementioned fall crazy flights. Grouse can fly rapidly for short distances, but one researcher reports that they are not capable of even a mile's sustained flight.

Ambling After Grouse

If putting meat on the table is an important part of your reason for hunting, you had best ignore the ruffed grouse, for there is probably no other upland bird pursued so passionately by so many with so few results.

There are grouse hunters who sometimes take their daily limit of birds, but for most of us, the restriction is usually academic, whether it be one bird, as on Long Island or four, as in the rest of New York State. If you meet a grouse hunter trudging home in the twilight and ask him what luck he had, a typical response might be: "I walked ten miles, put up twelve birds, saw seven and shot at four."

If you are a grouse hunter yourself, you won't ask how many he bagged. If he didn't connect at all, he will shift to describing all the deer signs he saw, and if he was successful, he will show you his bird. You will both regard it reverently in the failing light, and perhaps you'll hold it in your hand and heft it and murmur something about its being good-sized, or you might fan out its tail and see if the tail band—a broad, dark stripe that runs around the outer edge of the tail feathers—is continuous. If the two center feathers aren't so marked, you'll pronounce it a female. Both of you know that this isn't an infallible test, but it's a harmless ritual and a way to establish rapport.

Although I have talked with grouse hunters who have had days when they put up, or flushed, twenty-four birds, I feel most fortunate if in northern New England and in New York, I encounter half that number. The average is below that figure. I use the word "encounter" because sometimes I don't. About a third of the time, it's only the thunder of the bird's tumultuous takeoff that tells me I have sent one aloft.

If I wasn't deaf as a post in one ear, some of those flushes would be seen. I can hear the birds get up, but can't pinpoint the source of the sound. When hunting grouse, one usually has about two seconds to mount one's gun and fire. Sometimes I look in the right direction and sometimes I don't. This used to trouble me, but I've come to accept it, as I have the awareness that my reflexes aren't as quick as they were thirty years ago. I don't dodder through the woods, but there are, of late, long periods when—even though I have my gun in hand—I am not really hunting at all, just wandering about in a nostalgic mist while savoring the solitude.

Nonetheless, I am pleased when I bag an occasional bird. With that in mind, I always put a jar of beach plum jelly in my pack basket when I drive north to grouse country because it (whether in a sauce or in its pure form) provides a piquant contrast to the bird's sweet and firm white flesh. Last year's jar was never opened, but I spent only five days in quest of grouse.

One tends to remember with absolute clarity an occasion when a grouse is bagged. Recently, I have been thinking of a late afternoon several years ago when a companion and I decided to use the last of the daylight to go back to a stand of old hemlocks where we had flushed two grouse early in the morning. During the course of the day, we had put up half a dozen birds but had missed on the two occasions we were able to shoot.

We were no more than 50 yards into the grove's pre-sunset gloom when a grouse took off from the ground 30 yards in front of me. It was a scarcely visible brown-gray wraith, but when I fired I was certain, although I didn't see it fall, that I was on target. The bird was dead when I reached it, and when my friend came over, he congratulated me for my successful execution of a difficult shot. His praise so warmed me that I handed the bird to him. He lives in the city and has little chance to hunt, and I had used up two jars of beach-plum jelly that fall.

Although the ruffed-grouse season is underway in all of New York State save Long Island, where it opens November 1, it is best to wait until nearly all of the leaves have fallen. Until that happens, most of the birds will fly away unseen.

Grouse hunters tend to divide into two groups: those who use pointing or flushing dogs to find the birds, and those who simply walk through as much likely cover as their spirit and legs will allow. There are highly successful practitioners of both techniques, but if you can afford a good dog, you will probably locate more grouse, including those you hit but cannot find. A fallen grouse becomes part of the forest floor, and if you haven't been able to mark its descent, you eventually decide, after a half-hour of unsuccessful searching for it, that you didn't connect.

If you are reasonably sure that you were on the bird—even if it went out of sight behind trees or bushes at the moment you fired—persist in your search for the better part of an hour. Many years ago, it took me nearly an hour to find a grouse that was floating in the center of a raft of brown leaves eddying about in a pool in a small trout stream.

Veteran waterfowlers don't shoot sitting ducks, and longtime grouse hunters look askance at those who pot birds that are on the ground or perched on branches. Grouse often venture onto logging roads to dust themselves, and if you see one ahead of you as you are driving along, stop, get out of your vehicle and walk toward it. It may take wing down the road, affording you an easy going-away shot, or it may dart into the forest on foot, but whatever it does, you'll feel better about giving it a chance to fly.

Once in the past decade I violated that rule because the bird and I were in a hellish tangle of young hemlocks that wouldn't have allowed me to swing on a moving target. Even though I took special pains with the beach-plum sauce that night, the meal wasn't what it should have been.

How to Find the Woodcock

A woodcock hunter guards the location of his favorite coverts as zealously as a recluse his privacy, but it is possible for a newcomer to a region to find birds if he is willing to do some exploring.

The hunter's desire to keep secret those places where he discovers woodcock is understandable, for these migratory birds use the same areas year after year.

But even the veteran hunter must keep his eyes open for new spots when he ventures forth in the fall, because most ideal woodcock coverts—usually young stands of alders, birches, poplars or pines—pass into mature woodland in a quarter of a century or so, and at the end of that time birds no longer use them.

The woodcock—the average female weighs a little more than 7 ounces, feathers and all, when fully grown; the male is an ounce or so lighter—lives mainly on earthworms and can eat its own weight in worms each day. The woodcock probes the moist earth with its long bill for these worms, and it prefers a feeding ground that is relatively open, free of tall grasses and small shrubs, which enable it to move about freely under a low canopy of leaves.

Alder swamps or alders along the edges of moist meadows are good places to look for woodcock, as is an abandoned meadow grown to hardhack, a low shrub with pink, and sometimes white, flowers that appear in clusters from June to September.

Prospecting for new woodcock cover presupposes that one is in an essentially rural area. One can do this with road maps alone or no maps at all, but I am addicted to maps of every description, so try to find those of the topographic variety covering the area that I plan to scout. Look for sparsely settled country laced with streams and swamps.

Once on the site, look further for an abandoned farm with an apple orchard and spend some time there because worms are often plentiful under those trees. Such orchards are also favorite feeding places for ruffed grouse. Ponds and swamps created by beaver dams provide good woodcock habitat, as well.

During the middle of a really warm day, one may find woodcock under the shade of pines of hemlocks, and when it is raining hard, one may locate them on hillsides above alder swamps.

Flights of woodcock frequently remain on high ground above a swamp—perhaps a hillside of birch and poplars—until dusk, then drop down to the swamp to feed. Several times I have seen dozens of woodcock fluttering into an alder swamp just as the last color in the west was fading. Clearly, because these birds travel at night, they have not come from any distant spot. This is another way of saying that woodcock may rest in one spot and feed in another. Most feeding takes place in early evening and just before dawn.

The American woodcock's existence was once threatened by commercial hunters and later by excessively long hunting seasons and too large bag limits. But the species is now plentiful, with an estimated two million shot in the United States and Canada each fall and winter. It breeds, in spring, from Ontario and Quebec down through the eastern half of the United States to northern Florida and Texas. Its winter range is primarily in the coastal states from Delaware and Maryland to Texas, with most of the birds finally gathering in Louisiana.

Because the woodcock breeds all along its north-south range, hunters are continually dealing with both flight birds and resident birds. Weather is an important factor in the timing of migrations in either direction, but the southward fall flights begin in the northern limits of the bird's range by early September. Most of Louisiana's migrant birds arrive by mid-December.

There are times when entering a woodcock covert that you will discover your quarry has come and gone. You will find the little holes made by their probing for worms, and their droppings but that is all. Remember, however, if birds were there once, others will arrive.

About all the hunter can do is look at likely spots and keep track of the weather north of him, realizing that cold and snow will speed the hegira south.

Equipped with a large heart and heavy dark breast muscles, the woodcock is ideally suited for sustained flights of up to 100 miles. Its flight speed has been the subject of much speculation, with 25 miles an hour suggested as the average. It can fly much faster than that, however.

As with all migratory birds, there are some species that break the pattern. Good numbers of robins spend the entire winter on islands off the Massachusetts coast, and a few woodcock do the same.

Some time in the distant past, the woodcock left the marshes and seashores for the uplands, and it strongly resembles another migrant, the Wilson's—or common—snipe, which is a shorebird. The woodcock is a chunky fellow, almost reckless, while the snipe has a graceful neck. The woodcock has a barred crown and the snipe a striped crown. The snipe, which prefers open, boggy places and wet meadows, has pointed wings and flies in a zigzag fashion; the woodcock has rounded wings and its flight is direct.

Hunting for the ruffed grouse, an upland bird whose habitat often overlaps with that of the woodcock, can be done successfully without a dog, but the dogless woodcock hunter is at an incredible disadvantage.

The magnificently camouflaged woodcock will often hang tight when the hunter walks by a few feet away, and for every one that is flushed, ten will not move. This is one reason that the casual woods wanderer rarely sees a woodcock.

Any decent pointing or retrieving dog can do a good job on

one woodcock. The pointer or setter is more fun—there is nothing quite like the excitement of moving up behind a dog on point—but labradors and Brittany spaniels and springer spaniels will give you pleasure and help you bag your limit. Although purists will wince, many obedient, intelligent mongrels with good noses that would be useless on quail or grouse can perform well on woodcock.

Wide-ranging pointing dogs that excel in open quail country can be a problem in thick woodcock cover. Any dog used for woodcock should have a bell hanging from its collar. This helps the hunter keep track of his animal.

A 20-gauge is probably the ideal woodcock shotgun. If it is a double or an over and under, an excellent choice of chokes would be open cylinder and improved cylinder. Being parsimonious, this writer gets by with a 20-gauge over and under that is bored improved and modified that he uses for everything from woodcock to ducks. No. 8 or 9 shot in low brass loads is just about right for woodcock.

A Memorable Hunt for Duck

A strong northwest wind was blowing and the temperature was near freezing as we pounded across the St. Lawrence River toward Canada in the predawn darkness. The two flat-bottomed skiffs were laden with six hunters, two retrievers, shotguns and more than fifty duck decoys, and I was pleased that our skippers, Harold Herrick, Jr., of Cape Vincent and his son Harold 3d, knew the waters well.

The elder Mr. Herrick, whose riverfront cottage gives him and his wife, Mary, a magnificent view of the stream they love, told me when I was fishing the St. Lawrence for smallmouth bass early this summer that my waterfowling experience wouldn't be complete without participating in the opening day of the Ontario duck season.

"There's nothing quite like it," he said. "There will be black ducks, mallards, pintails and gadwalls, and they will fly no matter what the weather.

"And you've got to see my setup. I've got two stone blinds, one on a pile of rocks in the river near Wolfe Island and one nearby on the shore of another island."

The Herricks, Malcolm O. MacLean of Lawrence, Long Island, and his son, Malcolm,

Jr.; Craig Koch of Fort Lauderdale, Florida, and I were in those blinds by dawn on the first day of the Ontario season last week.

We had spent most of the previous day getting our gear and decoys together and crossing the Thousand Islands Bridge to Canada, where we purchased our $40 nonresident Ontario hunting licenses and the $3.50 waterfowl stamps.

The international boundary snakes down the approximate middle of the river in the Thousand Islands area, and, whether fishing or hunting, one needs navigational charts to know which country one is in.

Angling for such species as smallmouth and largemouth bass, northern and walleyed pike or muskellunge is open to all with the proper licenses, but hunting is another matter. The islands are privately owned, and one needs to arrange permission for erecting blinds and shooting.

Mr. Herrick who spent much of his youth on the river and who returned to it a few years back, has friends scattered throughout the islands who are sympathetic to his passion for waterfowling.

A few weeks before our hunt, Mr. Herrick had spent a day rebuilding his blinds, which are torn apart by ice each spring.

When we arrived at the blinds, the young men—as is only proper in the duck-hunting tradition—put out the decoys.

Sitting beside me as the sun streamed through rifts in dark clouds above the eastern horizon, Mr. Herrick, who is always seething with enthusiasm, said:

"This river is incredible, a splendid resource scarcely used. I miss the smell of the ocean and the salt marshes of Long Island sometimes, but I don't miss the crowds."

He rummaged in his tattered hunting coat for shells for his venerable and lovely, lightweight 12-gauge Charles Daly (circa 1890) side-by-side double, loaded it and rested it in the corner of the blind. I observed that the gun, which is worth as much as a new automobile, looked infinitely proper against the ancient, water-worn stones from the river.

We had entered into a discussion of the new, nontoxic steel shot (waterfowl can be killed by ingesting spent lead pellets), when a pair of mallards flashed by downwind.

Remarkably agile for a man of his bulk, Mr. Herrick stood,

swung and fired, and the second of the birds fell, cleanly killed.

It had been a nicely executed shot, and I told him so.

He grinned and said: "I've got to admit that I was going for the first one. But I'll get better."

He did, indeed, get better, and by midafternoon the six of us had a mixed bag of the aforementioned species, twenty-two in all. The basic Canadian-Ontario duck limit is six a day, per hunter.

We lost only one cripple, thanks to diligent boat work by the young men and an inspired search and retrieve of a wounded duck by Mr. Herrick's two dogs, a young black Labrador bitch named Samantha, and her eight-year-old mentor, Dusty, a golden retriever.

By four o'clock, the wind was blowing about forty miles an hour, sending waves crashing against our rocky outpost, and, with only a few birds flying, we picked up our decoys and headed for home.

No successful waterfowl hunt should end without eating a few of the birds the same day, so all hands pitched in and picked eight of them for supper that night.

The elder Mr. MacLean, a Wall Street stockbroker, handled the roasting of the birds, and I made a thin gravy from the hearts and livers and pan drippings, one that is particularly good with wild rice.

That night, as the wind buffeted the house and the lights of giant tankers slid by on the dark river, we ate what we had killed, and it was good.

Hunting with Muzzleloading Firearms

As one who hovers on the edge of being totally captivated by hunting with muzzleloading firearms, I am trying to comprehend the fascination.

I know that reading James Fenimore Cooper's *The Deerslayer*—a title that would inhibit book sales today—when I was nine or ten years old has something to do with it. My boyhood was passed during the early 1930's, when a few oldtimers in the New England seacoast community where I lived were still using muzzleloading fowling pieces. Most of the others had moved on to modern shotguns and smokeless powder, or were shooting all-brass shells, which they hand-loaded with shot and black powder.

As a child, I was delighted by the clouds of smoke belching forth from a muzzleloading firearm, and the phenomenon still pleases me, as does the peculiar, acrid odor of exploded black powder, or its more stable modern substitute, Pyrodex.

The post-World War II burst of interest in muzzleloading weapons in this country is not confined to hunters. There is, for example, an annual contest, sometimes referred to as the "Black Powder Olympics," put on by the National Muzzle Loading Rifle Association in Indiana in August. The association's address is Friendship, Indiana 47021. And twice a year, members of the North/South Skirmish Association meet at Fort Shenandoah, Virginia, where teams representing various regiments that fought on both sides in the Civil War compete. Cannon marksmanship is an important part of these encounters.

For those who enjoy hunting, many states have so-called "primitive weapon" seasons for deer. One advantage of hunting during those special seasons is that one has the woods pretty much to oneself. One can also, if one wishes, hunt with a muzzleloader during the regular season. Those contemplating such an endeavor should check out the laws of the state, which often specify a minimum caliber, the type of projectile and whether one's weapon should be flintlock or percussion.

Pennsylvania limits the rifles used during the special season to flintlock. The flintlock, which is more primitive than the percussion-type firearm, poses a greater handicap to the hunter. Its ignition system is less certain, slower and more difficult to protect from rain or snow. The phrase "a flash in the pan"—when the priming powder, but not the main charge, ignites—has special significance for the gunner armed with a flintlock.

Some hunters are fortunate enough to own antique firearms in shooting condition, but the average black powder enthusiasts must content themselves with modern replicas, of which there are a plethora, including many of first class workmanship and design. My own muzzleloading rifle is a .50-caliber Thompson/Center Hawken.

Although I have taken deer with a muzzleloader, my favorite endeavor when so armed is waterfowling. I own one antique muzzleloading shotgun in excellent condition, but because it is small-gauge, about 28, and cylinder bore in both barrels, it is only adequate for quail, woodcock and rabbits.

Some years back, I purchased a modern, European-made reproduction of a 12-gauge percussion side-by-side double from Turner Kirkland's Dixie Gun Works, a firm that specializes in antique firearms or reproductions of them. Whether after Canada geese or ducks, I have done as well with it as my companions who were shooting modern firearms, even though there were many occasions when I couldn't reload fast enough to get a shot at a new flight of birds. It takes a little practice to get used to shooting such a weapon at a moving target. There is a distinct lag—albeit only a fraction of a second—between the time the trigger is pulled and the time the pellets are on their way.

Another difficulty for waterfowlers with reproduction muzzleloading shotguns—whether antique or new—is that they tend to have little or no choke. Choke in a shotgun is in a constriction in the barrel that as it increases sends the shot forth in a denser pattern. The greater the distance the quarry is, the tighter the choke should be. If you buy an antique or modern muzzleloading shotgun, it is absolutely essential that you determine its choke.

The most onerous aspect of black powder shooting is cleaning the weapon afterwards. Black powder residue is highly corrosive, and hot, soapy water pumped through the barrel with cleaning rod and patch is the classic approach, followed by liberal oiling. This procedure must be done the day of shooting, or, at the very least, within twenty-four hours.

On a volume-for-volume basis, Pyrodex matches black powder in ballistic performance, is less corrosive and, because it is more stable, the laws involving shipping it and storing it are less restrictive. It requires so-called "hot" percussion caps, however, and cannot be consistently ignited by a flintlock.

A good way to learn more about muzzleloading and antique firearms is to obtain a copy of the Black Powder Gun Digest, which is published by Digest Books, Inc., 540 Frontage Road, Northfield, Illinois 60093. One of the aforementioned Mr. Kirkland's latest catalogues—the address is Dixie Gun Works, Inc., Gunpowder Lane, Union City, Tennessee 38261—would also be helpful.

Vermont Bird Hunt Ended Successfully

A full moon had risen above the valley through which 20 Mile Stream Road wanders. Two wraiths fluttered past my truck's windshield, appearing and disappearing before I had time to slow. They were woodcock moving south ahead of the cold weather, and seeing them seemed to augur well for the two-day grouse and woodcock hunt that lay ahead.

My destination was the home of Russ and Ann Carpenter, and the directions for reaching it were reassuring to one who feels confined if the nearest neighbor's house is within earshot. "Take Twenty Mile Stream Road out of Proctorsville," Mr. Carpenter had said over the telephone. "Go north on it for several miles until it turns to dirt. Go a few miles more, turn right off it on Newton Road, go up the hill and our house is the last one."

Living at the end of the road on a remote, wooded hillside in Vermont suits Mr. Carpenter, an accomplished outdoorsman and gunsmith and a contributing editor to the *American Rifleman*. A big, friendly man, he came out to meet me as I pulled into his dooryard. A few minutes later I was beside the woodstove in his log home, coffee in hand and a trio of Brittany spaniels soliciting my caresses.

The dogs deserted me upon the arrival of

the two other members of our hunt, Bob Elman of Stewartsville, New Jersey, and John Falk of South Salem, New York.

The temperature went well below freezing that night, and by dawn a near gale was blowing out of the northwest, filling the woods with sound.

We began hunting in excellent grouse cover, a mixture of hardwoods and conifers often interspersed with abandoned apple orchards. Some of those trees were festooned with well-formed fruit, and I marveled that this could happen after a half century or more of neglect.

Apples and fall hunting are intertwined. I never pass such trees without sampling the fruit, which has a bittersweet flavor, one that suits my mood in autumn more than in any other time of year—moving me alternately to pleasure and sadness. One moment I am delighting in the crisp, cool weather, the smell of wet leaves, and the apples, beechnuts and acorns underfoot. The next moment, I am grieving over summer's short stay.

Grouse are also fond of apples, and in less than a half hour, Mr. Carpenter's seven-year-old Brittany bitch, Muffin, was becoming decidedly birdy as she worked her way through an old orchard.

Twice she went on point and twice the grouse she had located took wing before we could move within range, a phenomenon that is called flushing wild. Grouse tend to do this on windy days because, one assumes, they cannot accurately pinpoint the noise made by an approaching hunter. There were other occasions on that day when one or more of us thought we heard a grouse taking off, but we could not be sure. That was particularly true when Mr. Carpenter and I were involved because both of us have lost a great deal of hearing, largely the result of too much target shooting in an era when there was little or no awareness of the need for hearing protection.

Although no shot was fired for the first two hours, Muffin worked superbly the entire time, ranging back and forth in front of us, neither too close nor too far. Most upland bird hunters put a bell on their dog's collar. This serves two purposes: it helps the hunter keep track of his animal when it is in thick cover, and when it stops tinkling, it lets the hunter know that the dog is motionless and on point.

Shortly after midday, our host bagged a woodcock that flushed wild out of an alder swamp as the three of us stood talking on a dirt road. I was the first to see that bird coming but could take no action because I was stuffing my pipe with tobacco. We harvested only one more woodcock that day and found none the next.

A short while later, Mr. Elman was embarrassed when he missed, with both barrels, a grouse that flew across that same road. Any grouse hunter worth his salt has to kick himself under such circumstances, because the birds are rarely seen without trees or thickets intervening.

The temperature was less than 20 degrees the following morning, some of the upper trails of two nearby ski areas were filled with manmade snow and the wind had abated only a trifle. Because woodcock were so scarce, we focused on grouse habitat.

We put up ten grouse that morning—two of them were probably birds flushed a second time—but shot at only two and bagged none.

Early in the afternoon, we came down out of the hills and repaired to a coffee and doughnut shop in Ludlow to plan our strategy for the remaining three hours of daylight. Mr. Elman and I, in my truck, would follow the others in Mr. Carpenter's truck. I failed in that mission and Mr. Elman and I wound up in a gas station wondering what to do. Up to that point, I hadn't fired a shot on either day and had decided, after losing our guide, that I was doomed to a birdless hunt. Because we were unfamiliar with the area, Mr. Elman suggested that the only thing we could do was return to one of the locations we had visited that morning.

"Wouldn't it be great," he said, "if we could pick up a grouse on our own without the dog?"

We reached the spot with perhaps fifteen minutes remaining before the sunset hunting curfew. The valley was deep in shadow; under the white pines where we entered, the woods' darkness was at hand. I had chosen that spot because I had seen two of the grouse we had put to flight earlier in the day head in that direction. We were less than 100 yards from our starting point when a grouse burst forth before me and flew straight away—more phantom than bird—into the gloom. My first shot was high and to the left, but the second was on target and the bird fell, killed instantly. I found it breast up on the dark forest floor and gave it to Mr. Elman, who has less opportunity to hunt than I do.

Borrowed Gun Bags Sage Hens

"Have you ever hunted sage hens?" asked Jack Brodie, a Lander rancher, as we sipped our brandies stand-up style in the dim, noisy, crowded confines of the Pronghorn Lodge Bar.

The occasion was the end of the Lander One-Shot Antelope Hunt, an annual event that draws sportsmen from all over the world, an event in which this writer competed ingloriously a few years back and attended this year as an observer.

"I have no shotgun with me," I replied.

"I'll loan you one," he said.

Thinking of the poor showing I might make with a borrowed gun (why do we strive so hard to avoid tarnishing our reputations in such simple things?), I replied, "I have a thick neck and a fat face. The gun might not fit."

"One of my guns will fit," he countered, ordering us another brandy and I knew there was no way to resist the persuasion of this friendly man who has so often made a visitor from the East feel welcome at the Brodie home in Sinks Canyon.

The following morning was still young when, with Brodie's two sons, Jack and Mike, the rancher and I reached sage-hen country in his four-wheel-drive truck.

The one gun that fit me was a 16-gauge pump, but because I had never shot a pump gun in my life I was a little ill at ease as I wandered across the rocky terrain breathing deeply of the crisp, gin-clear air that was laden with the odor of sagebrush, and lamenting, privately, my indiscretions of the night before.

Mike found a covey of birds and we moved in on them together.

With a clatter of wings, a sage hen lumbered aloft before me—an easy straight-away shot—and I brought him down. Another took the same course, but I had forgotten to pump another shell in the gun and after a suitable pause in deference to the guest, Mike bagged that one.

In less than an hour, the boys and I took eight birds, only one short of our limit of three each. There were only a few misses, for sage hens are slow to accelerate, although they can be deceptively fast when in full flight down the side of a canyon. They are also surprisingly large. We skinned and eviscerated them in the field and I was astonished to find that they were about the size of a mallard duck.

"All but the really large and old birds are good eating," said my host. "We'll wash these off at my place, pack them in ice and put them in a cooler and you can take them with you on your elk hunt."

A few hours later, made more alert by several cups of black coffee and a hearty meal prepared by Brodie's wife, Irene, I left for the high country of the Shoshone National Forest with eight sage hens in my dunnage.

An Antelope Hunter Is Led Astray

High in the snow-covered foothills of Wyoming's Wind River Mountains, a Lander rancher, Jack Brodie, crouched, then waved for me to approach. Peering over a rock, I saw a herd of antelope 150 yards away. "There's a nice buck in the center. He's walking around. Wait until he gets clear of the others, then take him," Brodie whispered.

The buck moved ahead, then turned broadside. Settling the crosshairs of my scope just behind his right front shoulder, I fired. The animals scampered off, their rumps whiter than the snow, and the most agile of them all was my buck.

That clean miss set the precedent for my performance throughout the day. I missed another standing shot, a walking shot and two running shots and, given the chance, would have undoubtedly missed more.

A man should have an excuse for such a day. Mine is that hunting with Beth Williams is distracting. The widow of C. C. Williams, the astronaut who was killed in an air mishap a few years ago, Mrs. Williams was a guest, as I was, of the Lander One-Shot antelope hunt, an annual event in which members of three-man teams go forth with one bullet each.

An astronaut team of Gene Gornan, Ron Evans and Jack Kousma was entered this year, and two other astronauts, Jack Smitt and Rusty Schweickart, were also present, although not shooting as team members. Beth, a slim and lovely North Carolina country girl who had a .22 rifle in her hands before she was twelve, had to climb, with the rest of us, the foothills of the mountains in six inches of snow.

Each time a buck was spotted, I murmured, and with increasing fervor as the morning wore on, "You take him, Beth," or "Ladies first," sometimes adding to Brodie, hopefully, "It's Beth's turn, isn't it?"

Ten minutes after my third miss, a buck appeared on a nearby hillside.

"He's yours, Beth," I whispered. "I'll be damned if I'll shoot."

Breathing lightly although we had been walking rapidly over rough terrain at high altitudes, she dropped to one knee in the snow, sighted and fired in an instant and the animal was hers.

"You can hunt harder now that a woman is out of your hair," said Beth as we dragged the antelope back to Brodie's Jeep truck. But clearly, the damage had been done.

By early afternoon, Dale Wunderlich of Littleton, Colorado, had got his buck, as had Larry Hughes of Tucson, Arizona. Harold Mares of Appleton, Wisconsin, who had invited me to the hunt, made a brilliant shot on a buck that was running at right angles to him more than 100 yards away.

By mid-afternoon, only Schweickart and I were empty-handed. We were walking half a mile apart up a steep hillside when the largest buck of the day went running across in front of him and Schweickart dropped it.

Back at the ranch house, where Irene Brodie had prepared us a splendid breakfast at sunrise, the party ate heartily once again and, happily, no one asked me to account for my shoddy marksmanship.

Battling for Hard-Fighting Amberjacks Offers a Lesson in Proper Technique

A seething wall of rain met us fifteen minutes after we had left Hatteras Harbor in the 43-foot charter boat, the *Early Bird,* and Capt. Emory Dillon tucked her bow into a secluded cove on the Ocracoke Island side of Hatteras Inlet and waited for the squall to abate.

Half an hour later we were trolling the outer inlet for small bluefish, one pound and under, which we planned to use as teasers while flyfighting for amberjacks.

The blues were hard to find but in an hour and a half we had a dozen of them swimming in the live well and then ran several miles offshore to a wreck that lay in 32 feet of water on the southern edge of Diamond Shoals. Using his compass, a Fathometer and ranges from shore, Captain Dillon soon put us above the wreck and we anchored a buoy over it as a reference point.

Amberjacks, which range from the West Indies to New Jersey, are a handsome hardfighting fish, and are frequently found around wrecks.

Lashing a short length of leader wire to a 14-foot surfcasting rod blank, we fastened the other end to a live bluefish which we held struggling on the surface of the water alongside the boat. The object of this was to bring amberjack to the surface and then, by lifting the bluefish from the water as they were about to take it, to goad them into a frenzy in which they would hit a flyrod lure. (Off Key West the year before, Captain Bob Montgomery and I had taken cobia on a flyrod with the same technique.)

Less than five minutes after the bluefish were in the water, the amberjacks appeared and soon were slashing back and forth under the bluefish.

A good amberjack hit a large white popping plug I offered it. That fish broke off (we were using 12-pound test tippets) and Karl Osborne of Vero Beach, Florida, cast to them with a similar plug. He hooked a fish and a little more than twenty minutes later boated a 24-pounder.

At one point it took out all his fly line plus 200 yards of backing. His fish was, by the way, a North Carolina record for the species in the 12-pound-line class.

After Osborne landed his fish, I took one of 22 pounds on a large white streamer fly, and the third member of our party, Joel Arrington, who is outdoor editor for the North Carolina Division of *Travel and Promotion,* had the misfortune to lose three in a row. All his fish sounded, as amberjacks do, and cut him off in the wreck.

By the time Arrington was casting to his last fish, rain was driving down in torrents and we had lost all of our live bluefish to the amberjacks, being unable to lift them from the water in time.

When the last bluefish was gone, we switched to spinning rods, popping plugs and bucktail jigs and took a few more amberjacks, which were released.

Those who would wish to try this form of angling from a charter boat should check with the skipper beforehand. Not all captains are as amenable to such shenanigans as Emory Dillon or his mate Bill Bazemore.

We had broiled amberjack for supper that night, although there is some feeling in this region that it is not safe to eat. This probably stems from the white, wormlike parasitic copepods that tend to mass in the tail section of the fish. The copepods are not toxic, however.

Certain members of the jack family, more commonly the Caranx gnus, have been responsible for ciguatera poisoning in humans.

Dr. Ross Nigrelli, director of the Osborn Marine Laboratory in New York, says that the natives of certain areas of the Bahamas will not eat amberjacks afflicted with parasites. Eschewing the parasitic portions of the fish and chewing the others, we found them to be good eating, being somewhat similar to cobia.

Vermonters Open Hearts to Stanley Moose

One wonders why nearly fifty thousand people journeyed to Shrewsbury, a hamlet in a sparsely settled section of southwestern Vermont, to witness a bull moose's month-long courtship of a Hereford cow named Jessica.

While noting that a moose is a majestic animal always exciting to see, Ted Levin of Hartland, Vermont, a naturalist and freelance writer and photographer who several times went to see the moose at Larry Carrara's farm where Jessica and others of her kind are domiciled, adds that part of the national interest in the affair may reflect the average person's hunger for news that does not deal with murder, drug abuse, war, famine, disease and deception in high places.

There was also—to those romantically inclined—the unquestionable appeal of a quest that could not succeed, the impossible dream acted out in a serene New England pasture in early winter, its hero a besotted 700-pound bull moose. This is not farfetched. Levin and others have been besieged with requests from newspapers and magazines for stories and pictures, and Carrara, not your typical taciturn Vermont farmer, has been selling T-shirts, sweatshirts and baseball caps commemorating the event.

He also works for General Electric's aircraft engine group in North Clarendon, Vermont, and has been given a leave of absence to deal with his bonanza. A country music song is already celebrating the event, and according to Levin, there is at least one book about it in the offing.

One foresees an effort similar to the best-seller sixteen years ago that anthropomorphized and idealized a herring gull, a scavenging species that finds municipal dumps as attractive as a lonely stretch of surf-battered beach and takes over nesting grounds needed by hard-working, self-sustaining terns. It could be dedicated to "the real Stanley Moose who lives within all of us," and the opening chapter might begin something like this:

"October's Hunter's Moon had passed, the last of the once-flaming leaves had been ripped from swaying branches by an early November gale, and the needles of the cathedral tamaracks were yellow.

"At one moment there was no living creature visible on the vast marsh that the forest ringed, and the next, a gigantic black form parted the willows, materializing without a sound and lifting his great antlered head to survey his domain. Stanley Moose was young and strong and he had already spent a week dallying with a girlfriend under the eternal twilight of ancient hemlocks on the nearby mountainside, but he was not content. And worst of all, he somehow knew that he could not find contentment with his own kind.

"Stanley was no ordinary moose. From the time he left his mother and father and set out on his own to browse on shrubs and buds and aquatic plants, he believed that life had to be more than wandering about bogs and hillsides enduring black flies in summer and slogging through belly-deep snow in winter, and even his recent dating spree had been only mildly exciting.

"He had never been able to talk of this with his parents, but a week ago on a moon-washed ridge he had met an old whitetail buck. The deer had been ready to bound away because moose and deer don't fraternize, but in his wisdom, the old animal sensed that the huge young fellow that had stepped out from behind a giant beech meant no harm. They discussed the coming winter and both agreed that because their hair had grown longer than usual and the Canada geese had passed overhead on their way south earlier than usual, that bitter cold and much snow lay ahead.

" 'There has to be more to it than this,' Stanley suddenly blurted, stirring the sodden leaves with his right forefoot. The ancient buck raised his head at this and fixed Stanley with a glittering eye.

" 'There is more, much more,' he said. 'I've seen it all and I've come back to finish out my days on this mountain, but I know how you feel. South of us beyond the mountains there are places called farms that in summer have green fields and tender, succulent trees sometimes no higher than your knees that when full grown will bear sweet nuts without husks that are called apples, and the winters are milder and some of the fields are filled with docile, friendly creatures called cows. The farms are built by men.'

" 'I know about men,' said Stanley. 'My parents moved here from Maine when men began hunting us there. Tell me about cows.'

" 'There's not much to tell. They're bigger than me and smaller than you, and—I'm sure you won't be offended—they smell something like you.

" 'My kind,' the old buck continued, 'have been visiting farms for a long time, but only twice have I seen your people down there. If you do decide to go I must caution you to cross the roads, particularly those called superhighways, with great care. They are much wider and smoother than logging roads and the vehicles travel at great speed. It is worthwhile to look for the signs men have put up telling us where to make a dash for it.'

" 'You have tasted it all, haven't you?' Stanley said admiringly.

"The old buck regarded him with compassion, 'I suppose I have, but if you choose to do this thing, remember that it marks you for life, that you will never be able to rejoin the herd. The herd cannot tolerate—even though some of its members may se cretly admire it—such naked individuality.' "

The book could then describe Stanley's entry into a new world, his awkward and unrequited wooing of Jessica, his grief when he learned she was destined for an abbatoir, and his return to the wilderness, where, rejected by his own, he lived alone on the shore of the great marsh, nourished until death by the knowledge that he had not been afraid to reach for the stars.

Casting Calendar Aside

Having bade summer farewell, I was startled by the three-day warm spell earlier this month that ended the night the moon was full.

By late October, I usually put my surf-fishing gear away, even though I know I may drag it out one or two more times if weather and schedule permit and if bluefish and striped bass have not yet departed the beaches of southern New England and Long Island. Although bass in particular can sometimes be caught throughout November, the conditions under which one fishes for them are frequently horrendous. And, more important, the angler who also hunts experiences a sea change in late fall: just as leaves turn red and gold, so does he begin to think of grouse thundering aloft, of black ducks flying low over a wind-torn marsh or deer slipping as silently as snow through the winter woods.

November's first gentle day came on my return to Martha's Vineyard from upland bird hunting in northern New York State. Because the temperatures had been below freezing on two mornings during that endeavor, I immediately, upon arriving home, busied myself banking my strawberries with hay and putting up storm windows on my mother's house. By late afternoon, shirtless and sweating, I was furiously uprooting the last of my leeks when I realized that I was wasting what might be my final opportunity of the year to catch bluefish or stripers.

I grabbed an assortment of gear, including a light surf rod, a fly rod and a tackle box, and drove to Lobsterville beach in Gay Head. I chose Lobsterville because the 30-mile-an-hour southwest wind that had been blowing for two days would be at my back, facilitating casting. I arrived a half-hour before sunset. Neither birds nor fish were visible, and only two other anglers were present. Heavy clouds moved in and a light rain began to fall. Full darkness was near when bluefish began breaking close to shore. I caught three that averaged about 5 pounds and lost two more, using my big rod and a wooden needlefish plug, before remembering that the conditions were ideal for fly fishing.

I switched to the fly rod and hooked and lost a fish on my first cast when it cut through my leader and departed with the fly. My tackle box was a quarter of a mile down the beach, and by the time I reached it and tied on a new fly, the fish were gone. While cleaning the fish on a dunnage plank at the water's edge, I reminded myself that when fishing from shore in bay, sound or surf, one should carry assorted lures and flies in a shoulder bag. This leaves one's hands free to cast continuously as one walks along the beach. I was, nonetheless, content with what I thought would be the finale of the 1987 season, even though I had caught no bass and had missed a fly-fishing opportunity.

Although the strong southwest wind persisted, the following day was warm and cloudless, and I was once again assailed by a desire to be on the beach. Some of this can be attributed to the moon's phase. When the moon is full, or nearly so, a vast uneasiness possesses me and I yearn to roam. I yielded to this urge when Luciano Rebay, who is the Giuseppe Ungaretti Professor in Italian Literature at Columbia University, gave me a call. More than twenty years ago, I introduced Luciano to surf fishing and he has been devoted to the sport ever since. Luciano's call revealed that he was on the Vineyard for a few days closing up his summer home and that he would be free to fish late that afternoon and evening. We agreed to meet at Lobsterville, with perhaps an after-dark foray to the surf on the south side of the island.

Mindful of my poor preparations the day before, I spent an hour readying my gear, which involved rigging a surf rod with a wire leader and a dropper fly and carefully choosing flies and lures that went into a shoulder bag. The dropper fly, which hangs about 18 inches ahead of the terminal lure, usually a plug, sometimes entices stripers that ignore the main offering. Knowing that the half-gale would be in our faces if we did visit the surf, I also included one heavy plug, a Stan Gibbs darter, that would enable me to cast a reasonable distance under such conditions. That darter is also an excellent after-dark striper lure.

I got to Lobsterville a half-hour before sundown, and when I reached the top of the dunes I could see a snarl of gulls and breaking bluefish extending for half a mile along the beach. I caught three of those fish, one on the dropper fly, and lost four more before Luciano arrived. He had several hits and beached one blue before the action stopped.

The nearly full moon was so bright that even on a long cast one could see a gleaming burst of spray when the lure struck the wind-ruffled water. Luciano and I dallied there, occasionally pausing from our casting to marvel at the glorious evening the gods had given us.

When he suggested that we visit the island's south side, I agreed, although I was not overly enthusiastic because it seemed to me that the wind's velocity had increased. I knew that the surf would be wild, and it was. Long, unrolling scrolls of white water thundered on the rocky shore and the warm half-gale in our faces was laden with the aroma of seaweed and salt. Several times I was staggered by breaking waves as I made three or four casts before there was a pause in the ocean's almost-continuous assault on the beach. When that happened, there was a lull of about five seconds during which I could feel that the plug was working properly, not being tossed about in the tumult. A small fish hit, and a few minutes later, it was on the beach, a striper of about 8 pounds, far below the legal limit of 33 inches, and I quickly released it.

I had two more hits before repeating the performance with a slightly smaller bass and then hooked one that was considerably larger. How much larger I do not know because, after taking out 20 or 30 yards of line, it pulled free. Having no plug heavy enough to cast effectively into the wind, Luciano had hooked no fish and we departed, a sensible decision because it was nearly ten o'clock and neither of us had eaten anything since breakfast.

It had been a marvelous evening, made particularly pleasurable for me because Luciano and I had not fished together for several years and because a former student of mine had nearly attained his professorship in surf fishing.

WINTER

Time for Waterfowling

Although it might seem ludicrous to some nonhunters, this is the time of year when grown men devote considerable time, money and physical energy attempting to outwit ducks and geese.

There are several approaches to this, ranging from jump and flight shooting to fixed or floating blinds with elaborate spreads of decoys, and judicious quacking and honking on a variety of breath-powered calls.

The typical country boy begins his waterfowling career by easing down a brook or creeping up on a marsh or pot hole where he suspects such species as black ducks or mallards may be resting or feeding. This is called jump shooting. Later he learns to flight shoot, to locate himself at various points, particularly on stormy days, over which the birds are wont to fly.

Some hunters never go beyond these two techniques, a decision that has merit because one can set aside pen, hawk or handsaw, don proper clothing, grab one's shotgun and be on one's way in fifteen minutes. He who has succumbed to the lure of decoying must gather up his bogus birds, set them out when he arrives on location and retrieve them—often in bitter cold—at sundown.

The species one is after determines the number of decoys needed. If one is hunting black ducks in a salt marsh, only three or four decoys could suffice. If mallards are about, double or triple the size of this spread. If one is hunting bluebills on Long Island Sound or similar big water, at least fifty bogus birds would be needed and a hundred would be much better. Bluebills, or scaup, tend to remain in huge flocks that usually won't pay attention to a small rig of a few dozen decoys. In Connecticut's Thimble Islands area of the sound, bluebill shooting involves going forth in a beamy skiff laden with a hundred or so decoys, one, two or three hunters, and perhaps a retriever.

The location one chooses is always determined by the wind's direction, but wherever it is, the gunners will have no blind. They will simply huddle on windswept, spray-drenched rocks waiting for the birds to arrive. Scoter shooting on the Sound is equally demanding, although not as many decoys are needed and they may be of the nested-pair silhouette variety which makes putting them out and taking them in much easier. A decent scoter rig would be twenty-eight birds in two strings of seven pairs each.

One often has to venture a mile or more offshore for the Sound's scoters. If one is lucky, one can simply hunker in the skiff, anchored near the decoys, but if the big boat frightens the scoters away one has to resort to a less conspicuous layout boat. It's a tiny, one-man flat-bottomed craft with a few inches of freeboard in which one lies on one's back, creaking upright to shoot when the birds arrive.

Successful gunning from one of these rigs, particularly if there is any significant chop, is beyond the capabilities of most. One really shouldn't use a layout boat if one is alone. The best approach is to have your companions anchored in the main boat a quarter of a mile or so away and take turns. They can also pick up the occasional bird you manage to down.

In general, more decoys are needed for the divers—among them bluebills, scoters, canvasback, redhead and whistler—than for the shoal water, or dabbling, ducks, which include the mallard and black duck, the teals, pintail and widgeon.

The only waterfowl worth bothering to try to call in (and this is a personal opinion) are mallards, black ducks, Canada and snow geese and brant. If you have reason to suspect that your importuning of these species lacks verisimilitude—watch how the birds respond and watch your companion's face—either eschew it or keep it to a minimum.

Live decoys have been illegal for a long time, but when they were allowed, it wasn't uncommon to find several mallards in a pen next to a duck blind. The ultimate refinement of the use of live decoys came in Canada goose hunting, where adult birds were tethered on the water's edge while their offspring of that year were sent winging forth to lure distant flocks back to the waiting gunners.

It is difficult to be specific about how a decoy rig should be arranged, because the location and the wind direction are constant variables, but one should always leave an opening within the spread, and within shotgun range, that the birds will aim for on their final approach. Some of the decoys can be out of range, 50 or 60 yards away, but the shooting should be limited to 35 or 40 yards.

A few fortunate gunners have access to private land where they may build onshore waterfowl blinds, but there are also situations where natural shrubbery can be filled in with brush to make a serviceable hiding place. There are many portable blinds—some for one hunter, some for more—on the market. All that I have seen effectively hide the hunter or hunters, but many are not designed for a half-gale wind. You might wish to invest in a one-man blind that doubles as a decoy. A modern version of the Trojan Horse, this is a giant fiberglass Canada goose for use on land in which the hunter lurks until the moment of truth. These are manufactured by Honkers Supreme, whose address is 433 Gardner Avenue, Department U, Twin Falls, Idaho 83301.

There are still many wooden decoys around, but soon after World War II, decoys fashioned from cork scavenged from surplus life rafts began to appear, and today several firms offer much lighter cork decoys with wooden heads. Although most longtime waterfowlers believe that wood or cork decoys are best for rough water, their plastic counterparts are lighter and cheaper and are effective under most conditions. In general, one does better with oversized, or magnum, decoys.

Although one sometimes sees silhouette plywood decoys used in field-shooting geese, they have largely been replaced by shell or full-bodied plastic decoys. There are also goose decoys fashioned from a lightweight fabric that work like a wind sock, filling out in even a light breeze.

Sources of excellent waterfowl decoys include L. L. Bean in Freeport, Maine 04033; Cabela's, 812-13th Avenue, Sidney, Nebraska 69160; and Herter's Waterfowling Specialists, P. O. Box 518, Beaver Dam, Wisconsin 53916. Carry-Lite, Inc., of Milwaukee specializes in rubber-bodied inflatable decoys. Two first-rate books devoted to the art of decoying waterfowl are Ralph Coykendall's *Duck Decoys and How to Rig Them,* which first appeared in 1955; a second edition as issued by Winchester Press in 1983, and Zack Taylor's *Successful Waterfowling* (Crown Publishers, Inc.)

Hunting from an Unusual Blind

Although the excuses offered by waterfowlers who fail to shoot their limit of birds are as plentiful as pinfeathers on a young duck, I have one that is, I believe, without precedent.

Whit Manter of this town and I bagged only four Canada geese instead of the ten allowed us because our blind was an outhouse.

Those who have never hunted out of an outhouse cannot appreciate what a handicap such a hiding place presents, but before I expand on this I should explain why we were using it.

The structure is smack-dab in the middle of a farmer's field adjoining a salt pond. There is a conventional blind on the pond's shore, but we were not in it because the geese have of late been settling down in the middle of the field no matter how many decoys were spread about the shorefront location. That the pond has been frozen solid for the past couple of weeks probably has something to do with this.

The alert reader might also wonder why an outhouse is situated on a windswept plain. It was put there, held upright against northeast gales by two iron fence posts driven into the earth, to accommodate those who attend the annual picnic of the town's volunteer fire department.

Arriving there forty-five minutes before daylight, Whit and I set out two dozen oversized shell decoys. Bogus birds of this genre weigh very little and their heads and necks are detachable, making it possible to stack as many as a dozen bodies together for transportation and storage.

We missed our first chance of the day when a lone goose came in low over the pond, remaining silent and unseen until it was too late, just as we finished arranging our rig. Our guns were leaning against the outhouse 6 feet away, so all we could do was stand motionless while the bird set its wings and landed about 35 yards away. The instant I made a move toward my gun, it departed.

We regarded that as a good omen, even though the day was far from ideal for goose hunting, with bright sunshine and only a whisper of wind from the west.

Half an hour later, we got a taste of what lay ahead when a flock of fourteen geese appeared in the distance. We entered the outhouse from whose interior Whit began calling them. I have neglected to mention that although the structure was a good-sized two-holer, it was divided in half by a wooden partition, making it impossible for us to see each other unless we stuck our heads out of our respective open doorways. The geese were coming from the blind, or back side, of the building, so all we could do was to listen for their approach.

Their clamoring grew louder and a moment later we saw their shadows as they passed directly overhead, well within range. From the twilight of our cubicles, we watched them circle until they were once again out of sight behind us. A muffled consultation through the partition wall resulted in an agreement to go for them if they came that close the second time around.

When their shadows appeared once more, we jumped out of our hiding places and shot one bird each, and at the sound of our guns, five that had already landed out of sight on the other side of the outhouse took wing and were out of range before we could fire.

Before we could pick up the downed birds, we saw another flock of about twenty birds approaching and darted back into our lairs.

Thinking of what had happened only two minutes before, I tapped on the partition to get Whit's attention and told him that this time around I would await his signal to leap forth.

Being more than three decades younger than I, his hearing is acute, and I thought that he might be able to better estimate the moment of truth.

Once again, the honking of the geese drew near. Whit cried, "Now!" He stepped outside and fired twice, dropping one. I lurched forth too late to do anything, my gunning coat having caught on the edge of the door.

The lack of wind was also adding to our problems. Had there been a stiff breeze, the geese that did respond to our decoys and our calling would not have been so indecisive.

Whit remarked that if we had a brace and bit, we could drill peep holes in the back of the outhouse. We could also have shot peep holes in it, but declined that gambit because the structure wasn't ours. We decided that our best bet was to remain inside until the birds landed. Even though we wouldn't know their exact location, that would we reasoned, give us an extra second or so to spot, flush and shoot them.

Three or four times after that decision, small flocks of geese, always gabbling incessantly, came in to look at our rig, then became indecisive and left. On each occasion, had there not been a roof over us, we would have been able to fill our limits. The five-bird daily limit applies during Massachusetts's experimental coastal region season for Canada geese, which began January 21 and ended at sunset February 5. Canada geese have proliferated in the Northeast during the past decade and in some areas have become a nuisance, raising havoc with crops and golf courses.

Sticking to our game plan, Whit and I lurked within the outhouse as long as birds were visible. Between eight-thirty and nine the flights stopped and we were about to call it quits when a huge flock of about three hundred geese appeared more than a mile away in the west. The flock began to break up into smaller groups, and one of about thirty headed our way. They came to us, talking with great animation, then flew away. As I peered out the doorway, I had the feeling that the departing flock was a little smaller than it should have been.

"I think," I whispered to Whit, whose head emerged from his half of the building, "that a few of them are on the ground behind us."

I eased my head around the corner of the building and four geese were on the ground about 40 yards away. I eased back, reported my finding to my companion, who said, "Go ahead. I'll come around behind you."

The birds were nervous and jumped the instant I stepped around the corner. I shot one and could have shot another if I had remembered to pump a fresh shell into the chamber of my new gun, a slide-action repeater with which I am unfamiliar. Whit had no chance to fire.

As we were picking up the decoys, five Canada geese accompanied by one snow goose came in, and even though we were standing in the open, our guns 30 yards away against the building, they circled us several times, often within range.

The outhouse caper seemed a poor way to end the season, so the next day I went forth with my brother Dan to a field where we quickly put up a blind of camouflage netting against a wire fence, set out twenty decoys, and in two hours had our ten birds.

Handwarmer Search

My 1986–1987 waterfowl hunting ended with a three-hour vigil in the stinging cold, during which several flocks of Canada geese glanced at our decoys, honked derisively and departed with the alacrity of a teen-aged churl asked by his mother to mow the lawn.

The morning wasn't a total loss, however, for it reminded me that I must resume my search for a handwarmer that really works.

The previous day my brother Dan and I had huddled in a hay-bale blind on the edge of a friendly farmer's field from dawn to 9 A.M., waiting for the geese to leave their nighttime resting area on a salt pond a few miles to the south and fly inland to feed. By eight o'clock, the birds began to fly, several hundred in all, but none came near us even though we had set out three dozen decoys. Again and again we would hear them calling and then they would appear in ragged, wavering lines low over the dark woods more than a half-mile away at the meadow's opposite end, but their flight course always carried them far out of range and they paid no attention to our bogus birds.

Dan, who spends more time waterfowling than I, was beside himself with frustration.

"They have done this every day for two weeks," he said. "We need more decoys. We need more wind. This is stupid. Tomorrow is the last day. We ought to move the whole rig to the other end of the meadow close to the woods because they always pass over that spot."

We chewed on that idea for half an hour. Then Dan said: "I quit. I'm going to work."

We both went to work, leaving the decoys in place because we hadn't really made a decision on whether to try the same spot on the morrow.

Three or four inches of heavy wet snow fell that evening. In the early morning hours the temperature dropped into the low twenties. My brother and I met at his house at dawn and decided to set up in the meadow's other end. We wanted to bring the decoys from our hay-bale blind with us, but they were white, frozen mounds and it would have taken too much time to dig them out. He borrowed six more from a neighbor and a half-hour later we were standing behind an improvised blind of camouflage netting strung on a barbed-wire fence.

By eight o'clock, the hour when the first geese had always flown during the last few weeks, the gulls and five crows had been our only visitors.

My fingers began to grow numb and I jogged in place.

"What's the matter, old man, can't you take it?" said my brother, who is twelve years my junior.

I continued to jog without response, remembering the roaring days before I eschewed booze, when butterball fat from food and drink I could gather oysters all day in winter—wet, bar hands red but warm sometimes wading ashore to shed outer clothing and have a slug of port wine when the sun came out. Defeating the demon improved my disposition and fattened my self-esteem, but left my carcass forty pounds lighter and vulnerable to the cold.

During a pause in my hopping, I noticed that Dan occasionally slid his trigger-finger hand into his coat pocket with a smile of pleasure.

"You've got a handwarmer, haven't you?" I asked accusingly.

"I brought it along for you," he said. "I was just making sure it was working."

He handed an uncovered Jon-E handwarmer to me, and after five minutes of clutching it inside my pocket, my fingers had some mobility. Then it began to cool off. I knew that it would because I have never been able—except on my desk—to keep one of them lighted for more than half an hour, particularly if I follow the manufacturer's advice and tuck it in the little flannel bag that comes with it. The bag, one surmises, is to protect one's fingers from the hot metal, but it—as does a tightly closed pocket or a hand cupped about the device—restricts the flow of oxygen to the handwarmer's heart, a burner operating on refined, vaporized gasoline. A few years ago, I experimented with an open-mesh bag made of burlap, and that was a bit more successful.

"It has expired," I said to my brother.

"You choked it to death," he replied, "but never mind. I brought along another. It was made in Japan. I've had it for years. It doesn't throw out much heat but it never fails."

It resembled one of those old-fashioned hard-covered snap-lid cases for eyeglasses and contained a rectangular stick of fuel. Dan lighted the stick, blew on it until it glowed red, closed the lid and handed it to me.

"There you are, old-timer, but remember that it doesn't get as hot as the other one," he said.

It went out in less than five minutes. Dan lighted it again and the same thing happened. "I give up," he said. "You're death on handwarmers."

It was then that I pulled out my ace in the hole, HandiHeat, which the legend on its plastic package said was "the handwarmer that runs on air." Someone sent it to me a year ago. On second thought, it might have been three years. The instructions said to open its sealed covering and remove the four little packets, which contain iron powder, water, salt and activated charcoal and shake them to make them grow warm. From 130 to 150 degrees of heat was promised.

We shook the packets for ten minutes but they remained stone cold.

"How long have you had them?" my brother asked.

"A year or two."

"Or three or four or five," he said. "The years run together for you, and you think that anything you buy should last forever. Remember the ten-year-old peanut butter you tried to get us to eat at deer camp?"

"I was," I replied, "saving the HandiHeat for an emergency and there was nothing—save for a touch of rancidity—wrong with the peanut butter."

Thirty geese streamed over the woods in our direction. We were positioned exactly where they had flown the day before, but they ignored our decoys and our calling and took a different course, as did several more smaller flocks during the next hour.

The flights ended. We waited a half hour and were about to leave when a flock of two dozen appeared. The leader showed some interest in us, then changed his mind and led his entourage to our hay-bale blind half a mile away, where they all settled down among the barely visible snow-covered decoys.

"I don't believe it," my brother said. "I'm going to work."

The Incomparable Oyster

When a companion and I arrived at Tisbury Great Pond small flights of greater scaup flashed by, and six Canada geese beat against the sharp northwest breeze along the shore, well within shotgun range.

The waterfowl season was long over, however, and we were armed with nothing more than potato forks and large plastic garbage cans. As some fortunate winter foragers along the Northeast coast are prone to do, we were going after Crassostrea virginica, the common Eastern oyster.

The oyster's numbers have been sadly diminished in recent decades by industrial pollution, disease, altered environment and over-harvesting. And often, where it does exist in good numbers, it is subject to domestic pollution that makes it unfit for human consumption.

Where you can find this bivalve bountiful and untainted, however, you are in for a feast. Few things are more pleasing to the palate. And, though much is made of the superiority of raw specimens from other regions, in my samplings from New Brunswick to the Gulf of Mexico I have found nothing better than the Tisbury Pond oyster.

The oyster's immobility is another of its charms. Unlike the striped bass, which in winter migrates offshore and south, or huddles in a semidormant state in some estuary or river, the oyster is always available, being unable to move from its original anchoring place.

The season for gathering oysters in this region of the country is generally restricted to the nonsummer months, however, for reasons both palatal and regulatory. (In New England the traditional gathering time is during the months of r's, although it has been my observation that this can usually be extended through May.) In most Northeastern areas oysters begin to spawn in June, and the effort leaves them thin and watery throughout the summer. Further, various state and local regulations protect the species against gathering during its spawning period.

There is another consideration for the oyster gatherer on Tisbury Great Pond, where my friend and I set forth. The pond, separated from the ocean by a narrow barrier beach, is periodically opened to the sea by man. Sometimes these openings last more than a month, but if an onshore storm develops the cut may close in a matter of days. Such a closure poses two problems for oyster hunters. If they are using waders and potato forks, as we were, rather than a boat and dredges, then the pond, fed by rain and brooks, may be too high. Of equal importance, its salinity may be too low, making the oysters less tasty. Most people who eat oysters on the half shell prefer them when they have a tangy, salty flavor.

The pond seemed a little high when we reached it, and the beach was too far away to see whether the opening was closed. But I tasted the water and found it highly saline, and our hunt was on. We waded forth and soon had single oysters, and clusters of them, filling our containers.

The plastic garbage cans we used are not really right for the job, and one of these decades I'm going to invest in a wire fish basket. Such a basket can be inserted into an inflated automobile inner tube and towed beside you with a short lanyard. In addition to being readily accessible at all times, the basket helps to wash the sand and the mud off the oysters.

A single female oyster can release as much as fifty million eggs during one spawning. Most oysters begin life as males and then, in the second, third or fourth year, become females. Later, if they live that long, many revert to their original sex. Off New England the average oyster lives to five or six years. Some may reach ten. A Northeastern oyster is usually big enough to be worth harvesting, at least three inches long, in two and a half to three years.

While an adult female is releasing eggs, the young males are releasing sperm. Water temperature is the key to this spawning time; generally it must be at least 50 degrees Fahrenheit. For a brief period hordes of free-swimming oyster larvae are moving about, many devoured by tiny marine crustacea. Many more perish when they sink to the bottom, being suffocated by silt or eaten by small fish.

Those that survive eventually fasten to other oysters, rocks, brush or, in the case of cultivated oysters, materials put down for them to adhere to. From this point on they are immobilized, resting on the bottom.

In their natural state, oysters tend to build up in clusters on existing oyster beds, a situation that produces crowding and malformed shells. Misshapen oysters, or those with the shells riddled by marine worms, are not valued in the half-shell trade, but the meat itself is generally not affected.

Such crowding occurs in Tisbury Great Pond, and for this reason I always take a short piece of pipe or a wooden hammer handle with which to separate the clusters. One sharp blow near the base, or hinge, of an oyster will usually do the trick.

Having raked the clusters off the bottom, and having found a piece of driftwood to serve as a pounding table, one proceeds in a deliberate manner. If the edge of a shell is broken during the pounding, set the oyster aside, because so injured it will not be able to retain its life-sustaining juices in storage. When half a dozen have been so broken, open them and devour the meat. I find that a glass of good burgundy enhances this ritual.

When the oysters have all been separated into singles, the next step is to wash them—I often take along a scrub brush—and carry them home.

The out-of-water life span of oysters is another of their endearing qualities. Like the hard-shell clam, or quahog, they can be stored for two months or more at temperatures of 40 degrees or so with no ill effects. If you are lucky enough to have a root cellar in your home, that's the ideal place for them. If not, put them in the coolest place you can find.

Those who gather oysters for the first time often lose their zest for the pursuit when faced with the task of opening them. Some, in desperation, pound off the ends of the shells with a hammer, so a knife can be readily inserted; others attack the bivalve at the hinge end with a bottle opener. (The latter technique works sometimes, but often the shell breaks off.)

There is really no easy way around this. One simply has to buy a good oyster knife and practice.

Place the oyster on a table, deep side down and the hinge away from you. Anchor the oyster firmly with the heel of your left hand, and insert the knife on the right between the two shells. After the knife enters, push it in farther, and pivot it so that it cuts the adductor muscle, which will be where the heel of your left hand is. Flip off the top shell, make a pass under the meat with a knife to cut the adductor off the bottom shell, and the act is completed.

If you weary of opening oysters in the traditional manner and plan to use them only in a stew or a casserole, you can steam them open. Scrub the shells carefully before doing this. And steam for only a few minutes, for overcooking spoils the meat. Save the juice, and proceed as you would with an uncooked oyster.

The classic New England oyster stew is simplicity itself. Figure four to six oysters, depending on the size, to a portion. If you're working with raw oysters, shuck them into a pot, saving the juice. Remove the meats from the juice and wash them, making sure to get rid of any bits of shell. Strain the juice, or let the debris in it settle to the bottom and pour off the top carefully. Put the meats and the juice into a pot, and boil for one minute. Add evaporated milk in an amount equal to the quantity of meats and liquids, and reheat, taking care not to let the mixture boil. Add a chunk of butter, and stir. Let people salt (and pepper) to taste, because the oysters may already have all the salt flavor one would want.

In densely populated seacoast areas oyster beds are often polluted, and you should check with a shellfish warden before going off on the hunt. In addition a shellfish permit is usually required.

Long Island's once-important oyster industry is making a comeback, but at present there are not many areas on the Island where you can wade to good oyster beds. Inquiries can be directed to the shellfish permit office of New York State's Department of Environmental Conservation at Stony Brook, Long Island. The telephone number there is (516) 751-7900.

In New Jersey one of the few places where the general public can go oyster hunting is at the mouth of the Mullica River. The water is deep, however, and so, instead of wading, you must dredge and tong from a boat.

Massachusetts offers the best recreational oyster hunting in New England. Nearly all the towns on Cape Cod and in the Buzzards Bay area have pockets of oysters. The towns control the oyster rights, and one must approach the local shellfish wardens.

In Connecticut, according to state aquaculture officials, the pollution line extends too far out into Long Island Sound for any wading for oysters.

Rhode Island has a few places open to the public. That state's once-flourishing Narragansett Bay oyster industry is dead, apparently because heavy metals from industry destroyed oyster larvae.

Where Others Won't

More than thirty-five years ago, when I was a student of limited means at Dartmouth College, I bought a secondhand pair of snowshoes for $10, and they served me well for a decade.

Dartmouth is known for its devotion to skiing, and I suppose if I'd had the money I might have turned to that, but perhaps not, because all I really wanted was something that enabled me to walk through the winter woods.

Since the 1960's, cross-country skiing has become much more popular than snowshoeing in the United States, but I suspect that an increasing number of people will embrace the latter activity in the years ahead.

Snowshoeing appeals to those who do not wish to become part of an organized group. The burst of interest in cross-country skiing triggered the development of a host of lodges designed to cater to that urge. Trails were made and clearly marked, and before long dozens of skiers were following the leader around them.

This is not to say that the cross-country skier cannot strike out on his own, but only to suggest that the American urge for group activity has enveloped the sport. And with that togetherness comes also stylized clothing, from the windproof parka and ski pants to the specially designed boot.

Snowshoers, at least the ones I know, don't care much about their clothing. A heavy shirt or wool sweater and a pair of baggy wool pants takes care of most situations, and foot gear can be anything from moccasins to hiking boots or rubber packs.

The cost of being outfitted for snowshoeing is less than half that involved in skiing, and if one eschews the groomed trails used by most cross-country skiers that expense is also eliminated.

A good pair of conventional (wood and rawhide) snowshoes and bindings can be had for $65 or $70, and a pair of the newest aluminum-frame shoes for about $125.

Other than his ordinary winter clothing, that is all a snowshoer really needs. There are some snowshoers who carry one or two ski poles, but poles are an incumbency most of the time, and one of the advantages of snowshoes is that their users can have their hands free—to carry a rifle or shotgun while hunting, for instance.

In open going on fairly level terrain, the cross-country skier will leave a snowshoer far behind, but when the climbing gets tough or one is working his way through the dense hemlock forest, the snowshoes are far superior.

This high mobility over difficult terrain is what endears snowshoes to me. If I want to make an excursion into the woods alone or with a friend, I don't have to think about trails. I can go virtually anywhere the spirit moves me, which is as far from sights and sounds of civilization as I can travel.

According to William Osgood and Leslie Hurley, whose *The Snowshoe Book* (The Stephen Green Press) gives a splendid account of the sport, present snowshoe design can be traced to the American Indians. The first white men to make wide use of them were probably the French when they began to colonize the St. Lawrence River region in the seventeenth century.

The snowshoe held sway as the primary means of winter woods travel in the North until the 1800's when immigrants introduced the ski.

Downhill skiing became a major winter recreation in this country in the 1930's, but ski touring, or cross-country skiing, did not burgeon until thirty years later.

Skis have never, by the way, replaced snowshoes for the serious hunter or trapper.

Although there are snowshoe clubs and snowshoe races in the United States, the Canadians, especially those in the province of Quebec, have traditionally paid more attention to organized events, both social and competitive.

Vermont Tubbs of Forest Dale, Vermont, is the oldest and one of the largest manufacturers of snowshoes in this country, and a glance at the Tubbs catalogue quickly reveals, as its President Baird Morgan noted the other day, that all modern snowshoes are basically variations of the bear paw or the trail shoe.

The trail shoe is essentially long and narrow with a tail. The bear claw is wider and shorter and has no tail. There are some who feel that the bear claw is much easier to handle, but others feel there isn't that much difference.

The classic snowshoe is white ash and the webbing is rawhide. In years past, the usual material for the latter was cowhide. Today, according to Mr. Morgan, it is water-buffalo hide, which has a high resistance to abrasion. This ash-frame, rawhide-laced shoe—the only kind this writer has ever owned—requires some maintenance. In years past, one used to give them a coat or two of spar varnish. Today, polyurethane varnish is more commonly used. The varnish protects the wood and the rawhide and helps the latter resist moisture.

Many snowshoe bindings—the part that holds the boot of the snowshoe to the snowshoe—have evolved over the centuries. The ideal binding holds the foot firmly in place, does not allow it to slip forward or backward when descending or climbing, and has a minimum of lateral play. Leather is the traditional binding, when it becomes wet it stretches. Synthetic materials have removed this problem.

Snowshoes have a crossbar on which the foot rests and a hole in front of that to allow for the toe of the boot to descend as the heel rises. In the old days, climbing a slope was difficult, the only traction being provided by the webbing of the shoe and the down-dipping toe of the boot.

Tubbs's aluminum-frame shoe, of I-beam construction, has a stainless steel crampon riveted to the underside of the shoe to inhibit sliding when climbing, descending and traversing. The I beam also digs into the snow under the last-named condition.

This same aluminum shoe also has a binding mounted on a nylon-bearing aluminum crossbar, which eliminates side play. The lacing in the midsection of the shoe is a tough, waterproof synthetic as are the solid toe and heel flotation pads. This shoe was, by the way, used in a successful assault of Mount Everest last year.

The Tubbs aluminum shoe is probably the best one for rough terrain, but it lacks classic beauty of the traditional rawhide-wood design. There is really no snowshoe that equals the beauty of the traditional trail shoe, and those sensitive to such considerations have a difficult choice to make.

Mr. Morgan acknowledges that cross-country skiing is much more popular than snowshoeing, but, he adds, "I think we're going to see more and more people who want to get off on their own turning to snowshoeing. Cross-country skiing has become frightfully expensive, and there are some of us who don't enjoy marching around a marked trail with fifty thousand fannies in front of us."

Greater interest in snowshoeing may not, however, result in a major increase in sales for American manufacturers.

"Whether," Mr. Morgan says, "we see any great sales increase in the next few years is problematical. Our sales have been very flat for the last six years, really. We face strong competition from Canadian firms, which are government subsidized. They make good shoes and they can dump them down here for less than our direct cost. They're clobbering us."

One of the problems faced by reputable snowshoe manufacturers is that their products are extremely well-made and last a long time. My own two pairs of trail shoes, twenty and twenty-five years old, are in excellent shape, and with proper care they will give good service to my grandchildren.

In Anticipation, and Remembrance of the Hunt

I am preparing for a deer-hunting trip in northern New Hampshire without the excitement of previous years.

Time was when the ritual of zeroing in my rifle, of looking at the topographic maps of the area, of assembling proper heavy wool clothing and making sure that my duffel bag also includes compass, knife and the backpacking stove with which I heat a cup of soup high on a hardwood ridge at noon after leaving the cabin at dawn, would have set me quivering with delight. Is it merely that a half-century of hunting has dulled my appreciation of it?

An avoid waterfowler—he never hunted big game—as a young man, my father had given it up by middle age, even though he fished to the very end. Does hunting tug hardest at those who have not passed their prime? Does the heightened awareness—sometimes only a vague anxiety, sometimes a shudder as great wings pass over head at dusk—of life's fragility that age brings vitiate the longtime hunter's quest? And why is it that some still-active duck and upland bird hunters—albeit grizzled and stiff of joint—have long since ended their pursuit of large animals? What has the size of the quarry got to do with whether one wishes to bring it down?

In some instances, one stops big game hunting because one can no longer range the hills with the young men. A decade ago I saw this happen at a hunting camp where for years a man—he was in his sixties when I first went afield with him—was the center of the endeavor. It was he who decided who should go where. It was he who after the supper dishes were washed and we were all seated at the rude pine table with coffee, rum or bourbon in hand, announced that it was time for each to tell his story of the day's hunt. These stories were saved for that hour because there were sometimes eight of us scattered about the mountains during the day—we didn't all return to the cabin at the same time. Once one of us shot a deer in a distant ravine in late afternoon, dragged it three miles to the river and then had to use a canoe to fetch it the last half mile, arriving three hours after sundown.

The story-telling ceremony gave form and substance to our wanderings and observations. When it was over, we would slip away one by one to our bunks and our leader was always the last to go, remaining beside the huge cast-iron cookstove that had once served a logging camp, his face reddened by its warmth, eager to talk with anyone who had the stamina to remain awake.

Long before sunup, he was inevitably the first to arise, noisily stuffing chunks of birch and beech into the stove where embers still glowed, and looking at us with pity as we stumbled forth groaning and sleepy eyed.

One year he was going as deep into the hills as any of us, and the next—because of legs that no longer carried him as far or as swiftly as they had twelve months before—he spent most of his time walking on logging roads, hoping to see a deer that we had pushed from the woods.

This caused him great distress and we hoped it would not dissuade him from returning. Back at the cabin the following season, I learned from two of his nephews who had got there before me that he was coming and I rejoiced. The dark November day wore on and late in the afternoon he pulled up beside the cabin, having driven nonstop, some 300 miles.

He flung the cabin's heavy door open and commanded one of his kin to fetch his rifle and his bag from the vehicle.

Ensconced in his traditional spot at the table's end near the stove, he began to talk of deer tracks he had seen in the snow on the way in and of how, on the morrow, we might locate the animals that made them. The day grew darker. His animation slackened, he started to pour himself a drink, then stopped, gazed out the window and announced:

"I'm leaving. Put my gear back in the car."

We made no attempt to dissuade him—his decision was obviously irrevocable—and moments later we could see the headlights of his car as it turned onto the logging road, went across the brook and down the bleak valley of the Dead Diamond.

I can still climb the mountains with my sons who often accompany me to the Dead Diamond cabin, and what time has subtracted from the thrill of the actual hunt has been replaced by the joy of being with them alone in the woods and within log walls darkened by age and woodsmoke. If a father is fortunate, the sons who were his companions before their own lives and wives properly took precedence, will walk with him again in ever greater intimacy.

And, I learned a few minutes ago when I made a call to New Hampshire, all anticipation of the hunt itself is not lost. An inch of snow has fallen in the valley of the Dead Diamond and on the surrounding mountains. More is expected, and tracking conditions may be ideal when we arrive. Tonight as we are loading my truck for the trip, I'll suggest to the boys that we might first concentrate on the area halfway up the mountain behind the camp where we located a large herd of deer last year after the region's first snow. They may have other ideas and if they do there will be ample time to chew on them on our long drive north to the cabin that sits in the shadow of the mountain until the day is half done.

Caymanian-Style Night Fishing

Gentle swells greeted us as we left George
Town at sunset in Sam Ebanks's 16-footer,
outboard-powered skiff, and gentler yet was
the warm night breeze coming off the tropical
shore.

Ebanks, who like many Caymanians, has
spent much of his life at sea, anchored his
boat in 120 feet of water over a reef.

"I understand you want to fish Caymanian
style," he said as he rigged two handlines and
baited them with good-sized pieces of fish he
called sprat.

Sam's weathered skiff contained a variety
of gear, including a medium-weight spinning
rod, two heavy-duty trawling rods, a seat with
a rod gimbal for fighting bit fish, and a lantern atop a five-foot pole.

Not long after our lines were in the water
he lighted the gasoline lantern, which not only
gave us light to see by, but also, he said, served
to attract certain species of fish.

Within ten minutes we were hauling a variety of fish aboard, including mangrove snappers, grunts, yellowtail snappers, groupers
and one 4-foot lemon shark.

Fishing for large groupers with a light
monofilament handline is rather difficult, be-

cause the fish, after being hooked, tend to surge toward the rocks or coral on the bottom, where the line can become tangled. I lost one heavy fish, which I assumed was a grouper, because it could not stop his downward rush.

Ebanks, who fishes commercially from his small boat, did better than I, but that was expected. One rarely keeps up with a good angler on his home waters.

As the last light left the sky, ominous, rolling masses of black clouds covered most of the western horizon and the small, wavering circle of illumination thrown by our lantern became suddenly intimate. Within that circle of light on the dark, heaving water dozens of silvery blue fish appeared, some breaking on the surface, others knifing back and forth 2 to 10 feet down.

"Jacks," said Sam, "and there is but one way to catch them."

Rigging a small hook and sinker on another handline, my companion cut a small piece of fabric from his white undershirt and wrapped it around the hook.

Holding his baited handline with the big toe of one foot, Sam cast his undershirt lure to the jacks, retrieved it rapidly, and before long he had several of them in the boat. (He called the fish amberjacks, but they did not look quite like the amberjacks I had caught in United States waters.)

Not to be outdone, I, having no undershirt, fashioned a small white lure from a plastic Clorox bottle.

"It will not work, brother," Sam said. He was, alas, correct in his prediction.

"We used to catch them with such lures or with feathers, but no longer. Only the undershirt now."

Snook Fishing in the Everglades Is Not for Everyone

Snook were all about us—some 8 pounds or more—streaking away as we paddled our canoe through a maze of mangrove channels.

Each time a snook moved, it left a billowing cloud of mud in the shallow water. These "muds," as they are called, are the snook fisherman's equivalent of rising trout, a sure sign that the fish are about.

My companions were Ed Stephanic of Rockaway, New Jersey, and his springer spaniel, Jay. Stephanic has, over many years, familiarized himself with the remote water regions of the Everglades National Park north of Flamingo.

The first several miles of our trip from Flamingo was made in Stephanic's outboard powered skiff. With it we entered the rarely visited Hell's Bay region of the Everglades, and then, when the water trails through the mangroves became too narrow, we shifted our gear to a canoe that Stephanic caches under a canopy of jungle growth at the entrance of a little creek.

At times we were unable to use the small outboard Stephanic had on his canoe; at others we paddled and pulled our way through innumerable, narrow, mangrove-entangled waterways.

The area we fished is slightly affected by the tides from the Bay of Florida, and the water, even at the northernmost point we reached, had a faintly salty taste.

This region of the Everglades is not for the casual visitor. One cannot, for example travel by compass, for the maze of waterways is intricate beyond description and it is impossible to set a course and maintain direction. One must memorize the many twists and turns, and this is difficult because, to the untrained eye at least, there are few distinguishing landmarks, only mile after mile of mangrove islands with an occasional palm or other hardwood tree rising above the low growth.

Within an hour, Stephanic and I had caught a few snook, none over 3 pounds. We kept two for supper and released the rest. The fish were difficult to locate in any number, and we pushed northeast into a region he had visited only once before. It was in a very shallow lagoon, about a foot deep, that we found a large school of snook, but they were extremely spooky, sometimes racing away when we were more than 30 yards from them, even though we paddled quietly.

These fish, we discovered, could be induced to hit if one made a very long cast. The plugs Stephanic favors for snook in these waters is the floating Mirro-Lure.

Much of this snook water can be fished with a flyrod also— almost any pink, yellow or white streamer fly will do. The flyrod, when there is room to use it for the snook, has certain advantages over spinning or bait-casting rods, for the fly may be dropped quietly on the water, and it may also be presented with greater accuracy. Accuracy is often critical because snook tend to hang under the mangroves or snags along the shore, and will not take when the fly or lure is dropped more than a foot or two from them. This is not always true, however, Stephanic noted, recalling a time when he and Dr. Joseph Ferrara of Franklin, Indiana, had hooked and released several large snook in the center of a good-sized lagoon in Hell's Bay.

Twelve-pound test line is about the minimum weight one should use when fishing for snook, because the fish will, if not stopped, immediately rush toward the mangrove roots where it will snag the line and break free.

Snook, which are an excellent table fish, commonly run from two to ten pounds in this area of the Everglades, although they do reach a weight of 30 pounds or more.

The snook fights hard, hits a fly or lure with all the savagery of a smallmouth bass and may be taken on bait, such as pinfish or shrimp, also. Flies or lures fished on or near the surface provide the most excitement, however.

The Art of
Spearing Eels

I have begun, albeit inauspiciously, an effort
to become a successful spearer of eels through
the ice. No unusual adroitness is needed for
this, because the creatures are lying numbed
and drowsy in the mud. The trick is to know
where to engage in one's blind thrustings into
pond or bay bottom.

Late last summer, I told a friend, Hein
Kirchmeier of Midvale, New Jersey, that I
would have no trouble providing him with a
batch of smoked eels. When I made my promise and prediction, there was still time to set
eel pots in a salt pond near my home, which is
the course I should have followed because that
was something with which I was familiar. But
fall surf and trout fishing, grouse hunting and
waterfowling intervened; cold weather arrived; the ripe adult eels had departed for
their spawning grounds in the Sargasso sea,
and those that remained had ceased foraging
for food.

That was no real problem, I assured Mr.
Kirchmeier, because it was a simple matter to
spear them.

One winter's day more than forty years
ago, I had gone eel-spearing with the late
Daniel Manter, a waterman and a builder who

had always found work for me in the summers of my college years. We had got all the eels we wanted, and my recollection of the endeavor was that it had been singularly uncomplicated.

Two weeks ago, I borrowed an eel spear from Mr. Manter's son, George. Eel spears aren't common items and the only ones I have ever seen were hand-forged by a blacksmith—eight-tined affairs with a central piece of flat metal that reaches about an inch beyond the tines and protects them when the spear is inadvertently jabbed against hard objects, such as rocks, sunken timbers and oysters.

Most of the spears I have seen are fitted with limber handles 18 to 20 feet long, and all the handles are tapered to a long point opposite the spear end, a feature I have not been able to understand, unless it is for esthetic purposes.

Armed with the spear, an ax and a pry bar that over the years I have used for cutting holes when ice-fishing, I visited Tisbury Great Pond on the island of Martha's Vineyard with Sam North, a young friend from Croton, New York.

I had asked a few people about the finer points of eel-spearing, but had received little information beyond the advice that eels were usually found in conjunction with aquatic vegetation and that the "edge" areas—the line between sand and mud bottom—were usually the best. For some reason, the sport of winter eeling has waned in popularity in this region. I blame television for that.

My friend and I began our hole-cutting near the head of Town Cove, and four hours and no eels later, were a mile down the pond toward the ocean. It was snowing hard most of the time and a northwest wind was gusting to 35 miles an hour. Although we found no eels, we did learn something about the pond's bottom, which varied from hard sand and oyster shells to black muck three feet deep. When we were probing the deep muck, I realized that I had no idea how deep in it the eels might be resting.

We persevered into late afternoon, although by the time we had cut our seventeenth hole in the ice that was 5 to 8 inches thick, there was no pleasure in the endeavor. Because I am only an occasional ice fisherman, I have never owned an ice auger, whether hand- or motor-driven, or even an ice chisel, and an ax is not the best tool for such an endeavor.

With an ax, one first cuts a narrow V-shaped groove in the ice defining the perimeter of the hole, then continues around that circle widening and deepening the V. The cut should vary as little as possible in depth, for when the ax breaks through, the water beneath rushes up and one must finish the work while chopping in water, an effort that soon has one's trousers soaked.

We used the pry bar as much as possible for the final cutting, and discovered that it was easier to shove the floating plug of ice under the surrounding ice than remove it from the hole. A decade ago, I saw ice fishermen, wearing foul-weather gear to protect themselves from spray, use a chain saw for cutting holes, but I have always hesitated to do that, particularly in rust-producing brackish or saltwater.

Sam North and I were saved from reaching our arbitrary goal of twenty holes, when the spear shaft broke about 6 feet from the upper end.

The following week, I repaired the shaft, joining the broken pieces with a long splice, clamps and waterproof glue, finishing it off with a wrapping of heavy nylon cord. The joint is strong, but the handle is about a foot shorter.

Piqued by my failure, I consulted a neighbor, Frank Drake, who occasionally does a bit of winter eeling. "You want the grass on the bottom, all right," he said, "but look for a foot, or a little more, of mud. The eels don't go deeper than that."

He also noted, and it had occurred to me about halfway through my day with Sam North, that one should move the spear handle a quarter-turn on each thrust in a specific spot, because the eels might have been lying parallel with the tines on the first jab.

"And don't forget to make a sharp upward stroke after the downward jab," he said. "If you don't do that, you'll probably never catch anything."

The points of an eel spear are rounded and blunt, rather than sharp. The object is to force an eel between the tines on the downthrust, then catch it on a point's needle-sharp, upward-reaching bar on the upward tug.

Certain that a failure to yank as well as jab had accounted for my dismal first effort, a week later I went forth again with Kenneth Child, one of my sons-in-law. I was so sure that we would succeed that I purchased two bags of apple wood chips for my electric smoker and also looked up a recipe for eel stifle.

After two hours of prospecting—the ice had increased to a thickness of more than ten inches in some places—we found the type of bottom we wanted and began jabbing and thrusting with commendable fervor, but no eels lay below.

We had a cup of coffee in the shelter of our truck, which occasionally rocked in the gusts of wind coming out of the north; watched a flight of two hundred Canada geese settle down on the lee shore of the pond three-quarters of a mile away; sallied forth, and called it quits after two more holes had yielded an old oyster shell and a waterlogged branch.

Mr. Kirchmeier may have to wait until early summer for his smoked eels, but there is another possibility. Mr. Drake has told me that in recent years he has enjoyed some good eel-spearing at Anthier's, a salt pond that, unlike Tisbury Great Pond, is always open to the sea. It hasn't been cold or calm enough for Anthier's to freeze, but if it does, I know just where to go.

Hunting for Quail on Georgia Plantations

Less than fifteen minutes after our two English setters had been turned loose to hunt in an open stand of stately, longleaf pines on a sunny hillside, they were locked on point.

The owner of the dogs—Charley Dickey of Tallahassee, Florida—and I moved in, guns at ready. I was pleased when the lone quail the setters had located took off on Mr. Dickey's side.

I was pleased because I felt strangely awkward, not yet ready for the swift movements needed in successful quail shooting.

My companion downed his bird with one shot and twice more within a few minutes repeated his performance.

The third bird had flown straight away from us and I knew that both Mr. Dickey and our guide, John Norman, were wondering about my failure to shoot at it.

"Nelson," said Mr. Dickey, "you can be too much of a gentleman in quail shooting. Don't hold off on a shot that is just as much yours as mine."

I replied that my restraint was born of something else, that I needed a little time to recapture the essence of the endeavor. It had been several years since I had visited one of

Georgia's many magnificent quail plantations (and here, the 4,000-acre Quailridge is one of them). That, plus the odd sensation created by traveling from the cold of the Northeast to a place where the temperature was in the low 80's by noon and redbud trees were putting out their lavender blooms, was a bit overwhelming.

There soon came a time when a covey of birds that erupted from the wire grass at my feet were indisputably mine to shoot. I shot and they continued on unscathed. It had been an easy opportunity, but I knew, as I fired, that I hadn't mounted the gun properly.

My next opportunity was a difficult one on a bird rocketing off to my right and it fell.

My companions, who had remained silent on my previous miss, complimented me, and I entertained a vague notion that my form had returned.

By the end of the next two hours—we quit at eleven because it would have been both cruel and stupid to run the dogs any longer in the blazing sunshine—we had taken nineteen quail, five short of our basic two-man limit of 24. Most of them had fallen to Mr. Dickey's gun, but that didn't trouble me because quail hunting is a passion to which he frequently succumbs. (For a delightful exposition of that passion, which also involves a fascination with the birds themselves and the dogs that find them, read Mr. Dickey's *Bobwhite Quail Hunting*, published by Oxmoor House.)

We returned to the field in the middle of the afternoon after the day's heat had eased off—this time Edwin Norman, John's father, also accompanied us—and quickly shot the five more birds to which we were entitled.

The Normans are a father-son team. Edwin Norman, who is also a field trial judge, comes from a long line of Georgia farmers, and his son is a graduate zoologist.

"We raise corn, peanuts, tobacco, soybeans, milo, hogs, beef cattle, quail, bird dogs and children," Edwin Norman said to me as we drove to one of our shooting areas in a Jeep that is equipped with a raised seat in back from which hunters may more easily watch the dogs work. "We're not making much money but we have a good time and a first-class plantation."

As on all shooting preserves, most of the quail on the Normans' spread are pen raised, because it would be impossible for native populations of the bird to provide hunting throughout the season. Some hunters feel that wild, or native, quail hunting is much more difficult, that the birds are both more wary and better flyers. There is truth in this, but if the released birds are properly raised from good stock there is often very little difference, if any. There is also some mating between the released and wild birds, which further blurs the distinction.

The preserve season for quail is October 31 through March in Georgia. Quailridge is in southwestern Georgia, about 17 miles northeast of the Moultrie Airport. Hunters flying in to Moultrie or to Albany, forty miles northwest of Quailridge, may make arrangements to be picked up.

The hunting lodge at Quailridge is a converted farmhouse that has a 5-acre pond out front stocked with largemouth bass, bream and shellcrackers. During the noon break or in the early morning or evening hunters are free to fish that pond or any of the others, more than a dozen, situated on the plantation.

The Normans do not handle large hunting parties and do most of the guiding themselves. This, says Edwin, enables them to give personal service to their clients. Most bookings are made well in advance. The address is Quailridge, Box 155, Norman Park, Georgia 31771.

Most of Quailridge's dogs are pointers, which, at some risk of offending champions of other breeds, are generally considered to be the classic bird dog of the South.

Hunters who wish to do so may bring their own dogs and the Normans will board and train a limited number of dogs each year for $125 a month.

Among the pleasures of visiting quail plantations are the evening chats with other hunters who are almost always a warm and friendly lot and who—perhaps inspired by a toddy or two—often reveal more of themselves at such gatherings than they would on home territory. Gestures of friendship to a just-made acquaintance are not uncommon.

I, for example, confess that while I would never know what it was like to own and farm a thousand acres, I got great pleasure from maintaining a vegetable garden 100 feet by 100 feet.

This prompted William Brodbeck of Hilton Head, South Carolina, to ask if I was acquainted with the glories of the Vidalia onion.

I said no, and he, ardently supported by Edwin Norman, said it was a magnificent thing, tasty and so mild it could be eaten like an apple.

Where, I asked, could I find seeds or sets for this marvel?

Mr. Brodbeck rose from the table, went outside and returned in a few moments with a handful of onion sets.

"These are Vidalias," he said. "I bought these on the way down. You take them and plant them as soon as you can."

He then went on to describe in detail the depth at which they should be planted and the care that should be given them when the tops begin to fall over.

"Begin eating them when they reach a suitable size," he added, "for they are not good keepers."

They are before me now, wrapped in paper towels, and a gentle, elusive scent comes from them, reminding me of Quailridge and good dogs on point and good friends I hope to meet again.

Finding Your Way in the Woods

Although being lost in the woods is, at best, an unpleasant experience, thousands of deer hunters contrive to do it every year.

Death by exposure sometimes results, but the usual outcome is spending a cold, miserable night in the forest. There is also the embarrassment of possibly being the object of an organized search, a thing that would bother some men more than the physical discomfort.

All this could be avoided by carrying a map of the area and a compass, or, if the topography of the region to be hunted is committed to memory, the compass alone.

Anyone who spends a lot of time in a big forest sooner or later will become confused as to his whereabouts.

The first thing to do when you suddenly are aware that you don't know which direction to take to return to your car or camp is: sit down, think and compose yourself. You should realize that if you've been hunting properly—not moving too fast—you cannot be more than a few miles from your starting places; you haven't entered some strange never-never land.

If you have a map, or if you study the map of the region you are hunting, you should have a good idea, within a mile or so, of where you are. All other clues lacking, you can simply use your compass to backtrack to your start. Implicit in this is that you know, on the map, the point from which you began and the general direction of your travels.

If the sun is out, or if there are mountains or hills you can see and use as reference points, there is really no need for a compass. The same is true when the night is clear and the stars are visible. Every woodsman should, at the very least, be able to locate the North Star.

Sometimes, however, a bright, clear day becomes dark, snow begins to fall, or mist fills the woods, and you have nothing, except your compass, to go by.

Each of us has a sense of direction, and with most people it is thoroughly unreliable.

When you first realize that you don't know where you are and sit down to think it over, you will, after a while, often have a strong feeling about which way you should go to get out of the woods.

Checking that feeling against your compass, you will usually find that you are way off the mark.

This has happened to me several times, and I always marvel at the distinct act of will that is required for me to believe the instrument, not myself. I have even, in extreme cases, felt that there were magnetic rocks nearby pulling the compass needle awry. Always, however, the compass was correct.

Your compass should be of good quality, waterproof and liquid-dampened.

The only maps worth using are the topographic variety, available from both private and government sources.

If you study such maps carefully, you will eventually reach a point where you can actually envision the contours of the land.

If you are completely turned around, following a brook downstream will often lead you to civilization. This doesn't work all the time. To put it another way, the stream on one side of a mountain may lead you to a community in short order while one on the other side may take you deeper into the wilderness. You should, from your topographic map, know the direction in which streams drain if you are using them as a guide.

Following a brook can be a tough job. I once lost my way in the mist on a New Hampshire mountain and elected to use a stream. I was encumbered by a heavy pack, and the brook's boulder-strewn, twisting and often precipitous course down the mountain was a considerable challenge.

There may come a time when you are still deep in the woods at dark. If the walking is good and you are sure of where you are going, you might as well keep moving. If, however, you are on some rugged mountainside or deep in a blowdown where night travel is dangerous, the best thing to do is gather plenty of wood and light a fire.

If you are with other men in a deer camp, they won't start worrying about you—if you fail to appear—until after sundown.

Three shots, closely spaced, are regarded as a universal signal of distress, but don't touch them off until well after dark or they'll be mistaken for those fired at a deer.

Usually, and this should be arranged beforehand with the others, it is expected—if one of the party is missing—that the men at camp will fire three shots when it is truly dark.

If you hear those shots, respond with three of your own.

Thereafter, as the searchers start moving toward you, they will occasionally fire a single shot. Respond with one of your own.

Failing to hear their original three shots—or if you don't have a hunting party—the only thing you can do is fire groups of three at one-hour intervals after dark and hope for a response. (All this shooting presupposes that you have a full box of twenty cartridges with you.)

Some deer hunters, and I am one of them, bring along a small pack which contains a few packets of dried soup and tea or coffee, chocolate bars, a little bag of nuts and dried fruit, rope, a small hatchet and a canteen cup in which to heat water. It usually isn't necessary to carry water because streams, lakes and ponds are common in deer country, and if there is snow it can be melted for this purpose.

This little kit, which weighs only a few pounds, will help making a night in the woods more comfortable, and there will also be times when a cup of hot soup at midday is most welcome.

The pack should be draped with fluorescent orange so that

some other hunter won't mistake it for a portion of a deer. An extra hunting vest of this color is ideal for this purpose.

The average hunter really doesn't need to achieve pinpoint accuracy in his woods navigation, but there are orienteering groups one may join, if they appeal to you. (Orienteering involves traveling as rapidly as possible from checkpoint to checkpoint through the woods.)

To return directly—assuming no impassable terrain is in the way—to one's point of entry into the woods requires keeping track of the distance traveled and the various changes of direction that were made. It is nearly impossible to do this and simultaneously hunt deer successfully. The best one can do is make an accurate guess.

Rather than striving to arrive at one's precise starting point, it is sometimes better to make a planned error. If, for example, one leaves his car on a road that runs east and west for several miles and then hunts to the south, one might simply head north near the end of the day. The difficulty with this is that when the road is reached one usually doesn't know whether the car is to the left or right. It is much better, on the return trip, to consciously veer 10 or 15 degrees east or west of north. Then, upon reaching the road, there is no doubt about which way to go.

Although precise navigation isn't needed by most woodsmen, it can offer both a challenge and a reward. A trout fisherman who wants to visit a little pond 5 miles deep in the woods will, unless there is a trail to it, have to become truly proficient with map and compass. If the pond is, for example, only a quarter of a mile long, he hasn't much room for error.

For this, a specially designed compass—the orienteering models by Silva are excellent—is needed. The ordinary wrist, or watch-pocket-size instrument won't do.

There are government topographic maps available for most of the United States, and they may be obtained in many sporting goods stores and bookstores.

If you can't find what you want from such places, you can write Map Information Service, U.S. Geological Survey, Washington, D.C. 20242, asking for a map index of your state. From that, you can choose the maps of the area you plan to visit. Your orders for maps should be mailed to Distribution Center, Geological Survey, Washington, D.C. 20242 (for maps east of the Mississippi), or to Distribution Section, Geological Survey, Denver Federal Center, Denver, Colorado 80205 (for west of the Mississippi).

The same maps may also be purchased from the United States-Canadian Map Service Ltd., Midwest Distribution Center, Box 249, Neenah, Wisconsin 54956. This concern sells two map catalogues, one for the eastern half of the United States, the other for the west, from which the maps you want may be identified.

Another valuable publication for the hunter, camper or hiker is the huge paperback *The Bantam Great Outdoors Guide* (Bantam Books), which is an excellent reference for planning wilderness trips in the United States or Canada. Topographic map designations for thousands of the areas described are included.

One of the best books on using map and compass, with special emphasis on orienteering, is Bjorn Kjellstrom's *Be Expert with Map and Compass* (Charles Scribner's Sons). It is available in paperback and hardback.

For information on the rapidly growing sport of orienteering, write American Orienteering Services, Department FS, 308 West Fillmore, Colorado Springs, Colorado 80907.

Hunting Scoters Offshore

Trying to ambush scoters from a one-man lay-out boat anchored in choppy seas does not enhance one's wing-shooting reputation.

The scoter—whether white-winged, surf or American—is a so-called sea duck, as are elders and old squaw. All are species for which there are long seasons and liberal bag limits along the Eastern seaboard. Shooting scoters —often called coot by seacoast gunners—can sometimes be done from shore, as from a peninsula jutting out into ocean, bay or sound. But most are taken by gunners willing to go offshore to set up their decoys.

A few days ago, Dixon MacD. Merkt of Guilford and I left Sachem Head harbor and headed out into Long Island Sound on a gray dawn in a beamy 16-foot skiff towing his lay-out boat, a little, low-profile craft in which one lies on his back near the decoys, rising to shoot when birds approach.

Another waterborne hunter was already set up in the area my companion had in mind, so we ran a half-mile more offshore and put out our own rig, two seven-pair strings of silhouette decoys and four cork-bodied bogus birds that were about three times natural size. Even as we were doing this, small flocks of scoters were flying close by, and the other hunter was enjoying some shooting.

A gracious host, Mr. Merkt insisted that I be the first to occupy the layout boat. An easterly wind was blowing about ten miles an hour and the waves were about a foot high. I climbed aboard the little boat, which we anchored near the up-tide end of the decoys, and my companion took the larger one about 300 yards away. Then he shut off its outboard engine and drifted with the wind and tide.

Lying on the straw in the boat's bottom and gazing skyward at distant flocks of birds and scudding clouds, I could have dozed off in my floating cradle. That relaxed mood evaporated when two scoters came within easy range. Lurching to a sitting position, I touched off both barrels of my 20-gauge side-by-side double and the birds flew on. Even as I fired I knew that the bobbing of the boat and the awkward position from which I shot had put me far off the mark. Shooting these birds from a land-based blind is fairly simple. Although strong, fast fliers, scoters are not given to quick, evasive movements.

I did not panic at my inauspicious beginning. Five more scoters visited the decoys, coming so close I could clearly discern their eyes. I will, I told myself as I lifted up to shoot, atone for my previous misses by dropping two of them. I swung on the birds, the boat lurched and again two shots produced nothing.

Having hunted waterfowl for more than half a century, I was aware that there are days when one's timing is off, but I sensed that something more was involved, that I was engaged in an endeavor in which I could not shine.

I had a moment of optimism when I cleanly killed a bird about 45 yards distant.

From time to time in the next hour I bagged an occasional scoter, but was appalled at the number of empty shells that lay about me. This was particularly distressing to one who is prone to boast that he averages one duck for every two shells fired.

I did take some consolation from the ever-increasing wind, which by midmorning had created 2-foot seas on the Sound. I also learned that it was useless to try for birds that passed by on my left, or gun-shouldering side. In the cramped confines of a layout boat, one's swing is too abbreviated in that quadrant.

We changed roles, and Mr. Merkt did much better than I.

I would have been content to pick up his birds, but the skiff's outboard had developed starting and idling problems and much of my time was spent yanking on the starting rope as I was driven to the westward by the wind and tide.

When I finally got underway, Mr. Merkt signaled for me to come to him and we decided to see if the birds would decoy to us if we both shot from the skiff. They did, and given more room in which to maneuver, my performance improved.

By 10 A.M., most of the flights of scoters were trading back and forth far beyond us out in the Sound and we decided to call it quits. We had taken close to our two-man limit of fourteen birds and had enjoyed some excellent decoying.

When boats are involved—and they almost always are—scoter shooting is a rather elaborate procedure, and when winter arrives it is often a bitter test of endurance. Some hunters ignore scoters because they believe that the birds are inedible. Part of this erroneous notion may derive from the infamous New England coot (scoter) stew, which defies all but the most robust palates and digestive systems.

Properly prepared, however, breast of scoter is excellent. The thick, dark-red chunks of meat should be marinated for an hour or so in a mild—about five to one—water-vinegar solution, then seared in a smoking-hot frying pan and removed while still red in the center. Sliced thin and across the grain and served on buttered toast with a piquant sweet-sour sauce—beach plum jelly is a superb base for such a sauce—breast of scoter is superior table fare.

One might add that using only the breasts—which account for more than 90 percent of the edible meat on a wild duck—greatly speeds up getting them ready for the table. One simply peels the skin from the bird's chest, then removes the breasts with a little careful knife work. The entire process should take no more than three or four minutes per bird.

There are some who use this approach with so-called puddle ducks, such as mallards or black ducks, but that is a sin because in order for those birds to be properly roasted, the skin—which seals in the juices—must be left on. The skins of sea ducks contain much of the fishy flavor that most people find unpleasant.

Hunting Deer Indirectly

Although I enjoy a venison steak singed on the outside and red in the middle more than any other fare save rare wild duck, most of the deer meat I eat has been given to me.

Now and then as the seasons roll past, I manage to shoot a deer, but in recent years, this has happened less frequently. Those who frown upon deer hunting might view this admission as pleasing evidence that in my advancing years I am assailed by doubts about the morality of the endeavor, but that is not the case. I want to bag my buck, but between that wish and its fulfillment, various personal quirks obtrude.

I know, for example, that an organized deer drive is a highly successful maneuver, but I haven't taken part in more than half a dozen such endeavors in nearly fifty years of hunting. They involve close cooperation with other hunters—those doing the driving and those placed on stand—and much of the reason I enter the woods is to escape people and schedules.

For the past half-decade, my brother, my two sons and I have had an annual three-day hunt in the wild and rugged northeastern corner of New Hampshire. While in the woods, we rarely see another human. Deer do not abound in that region—one often sees moose instead—but it consistently produces bucks of more than 200 pounds. If seeing many deer was important to me, I would go to the Catskills, where nearly as many deer are shot on opening day as are taken during the modern firearms season in New Hampshire, which runs through most of November.

Part of my desire to escape contact with all but a choice few of my own species comes from a rural childhood in which I devoured such tomes as James Fenimore Cooper's *The Deerslayer* or Gene Stratton-Porter's *The Harvester*.

Early on, I went forth berry-picking, hunting, trapping and fishing, imagining myself a colonial settler or a frontiersman. If there happened to be someone at one of my favorite trout pools or waiting in the salt marsh for black ducks at dusk, I would back away and go elsewhere. If, walking down a pitch-black country road at night, I saw the headlights of a vehicle approaching, I would dart into the shrubbery. That same country road is beside me as I write; if I still took such after-dark strolls and was still so moved, I would spend most of my time in the bushes.

Accomplished hunters and fishermen pursue their sports with an intensity that blocks out all else. When deer hunting, I tend to daydream, to think of work undone or to potter about, neglecting my quest. I prefer still hunting, which, done properly, involves—once one is in a prime deer habitat—easing one's way through the woods, stopping every few yards to examine meticulously all that lies before. One concentrates on details. Often, one sees not the entire deer, but one of its twitching ears, its nose or sunlight glinting on an antler. I always start out in this fashion, but more than half the time, I begin moving faster and faster, sending whatever deer may be nearby into precipitous flight.

My brother, a skilled hunter who says he thinks of nothing but deer from the moment he enters the woods, enjoys describing my coming out on a rocky outcropping over a little snow-filled valley through which I had been wending. He watched me examine a clump of oyster mushrooms on a dying maple. (I was thinking of how they would enhance the spaghetti sauce I planned to make that night.)

I then sat on a log and, my brother says, devoted more than

half an hour to trying to induce a chickadee to share my sandwich with me, after which I had a pipe.

"I thought of whistling to you, but you're so damned deaf I dropped that idea," he said. "I would have spooked every deer in the neighborhood before I got your attention."

(Being nearly deaf in one ear and nearly blind in one eye might also have something to do with my failure to shoot a deer each season.)

Having a pipe is not a good idea when deer hunting, and the same goes for a cigarette; the animals have a superb sense of smell. But I don't fret about that indulgence because the woolen shirt and sweater and the trousers, cap and mittens that I wear when hunting deer spend the remainder of the year stuffed into a plastic trash bag with a handful of camphor balls. I am sure that the reek of camphor is much more potent than the smoke from a pipe.

There are some dedicated deer hunters who store their clothing in an air-tight box half-filled with spruce or hemlock boughs and who would never use a scented shaving cream or a deodorant while in pursuit of the white-tail.

I have also had trouble deciding what gun I am going to use. Less than a decade ago, I became interested in shooting muzzle-loading rifles (I have hunted waterfowl with muzzle-loading shotguns for years with commendable success). After acquiring one, I made my own powder horn and cast my own bullets. For three years—imagining myself to be Hawkeye slipping as silently as smoke through the forest—I used nothing else for hunting deer, getting a nice buck on the first of those seasons. The third year, I had to pass up a standing shot at a big animal because it was about 140 yards away, too far for my black-powder weapon.

This sent me to the other extreme, to a scope-mounted antelope rifle, a flat-shooting .243. The first day hunting deer with it, I took one shot at an animal that was only 50 yards away but behind a light screen of alders. The lightweight, fast-moving projectile either disintegrated or went far off course when it struck one of those alders. The deer didn't even speed up his slow walk, and I didn't bother to shoot again.

The following year, I went back to a rifle better suited for dealing with brush, a scope-mounted, .30/.30. Rain, or rain mixed with snow, fell every day, and the final afternoon the moisture worked its way into the scope, rendering it useless.

Three years ago, I traded a rimfire .22 automatic rifle that I hadn't fired since I zeroed it in a decade before for a Model 94 Winchester lever-action in .375 caliber. Wanting nothing more to do with scopes, I installed a peep sight on it. It is a short-range deer rifle, but it is handsome and evocative of this country's past: the first Winchester Model 94 was produced in 1894, and most of the cowboys in the movies I watched as an adolescent carried one in a saddle scabbard.

The rifle fits me and weighs only a little more than six pounds. Each fall before the deer season, I take it to Harold Rogers's sand pit and fire three rounds. It prints on the button at 100 yards and about an inch high at 50. I have yet to fire it at a deer, but this may be the year, and if it isn't, there will still be the smell of woodsmoke, the gleam of gaslights in the log cabin's windows, the warmth of the logging stove and my sons' smiles to greet me as I stomp in after a day of communing with chickadees.

Man's Best Friend Adds a Touch to Retrieving

When waterfowlers daydream of their sport, they see birds wheeling through dark November skies or pitching down into decoys before a cattail-covered blind in a salt marsh. And a keen-eyed, ever-eager retriever, whether a Chesapeake or Labrador or some less-specialized breed, is always with them.

The relationship between a duck hunter and his dog has provided fodder for generations of outdoor writers. Even when nothing is bagged, some sweet juices can be injected into the story of the day's endeavor with mention of how old Tober retrieved a decoy that had broken loose from its mooring. Or perhaps of the post-hunt rapport in front of a blazing hearth, the man with his tot of bourbon, the dozing dog with a full belly, twitching and whimpering in an ecstatic dream of the chase.

The seriousness of Robo-Duck's challenge to that cozy tradition is difficult to assess. Robo-Duck, priced at $1,250, is a battery-powered, propeller-driven, electronically controlled 15-pound decoy nearly 3 feet long that can lure and retrieve waterfowl.

The waterfowling equipment catalogue put out by the decoy's distributor, Outdoorsmen's Herter's, shows no temerity in describing its capabilities: "Robo-Duck is the most efficient retriever available. No training or handling fees, medication, shots, or cleaning the kennel . . . performs like a champion. You will never again flare incoming ducks. Robo-Duck will retrieve downed ducks and move decoys in bluebird weather or when ice is on the water."

The catalogue goes on to say that Robo-Duck's spring steel fingers can easily grasp two big mallards or a single large goose, adding that it is powered by two batteries that will suffice for a full day's work without recharging. Robo-Duck's top speed—10 miles an hour—far exceeds that of any surface-paddling duck, let alone one that has been wounded.

Wishing to learn more about Robo-Duck, I called Herter's Dennis Faber, who ran Robo-Duck through its paces before advertising it. (Many readers will feel a twinge of nostalgia at seeing the Herter name. For many years, Herter's of Waseca, Minnesota, produced a huge catalogue filled with reasonably priced and often first-rate gear for the outdoorsman. The firm folded in 1980 and Outdoorsmen's Herter's—whose address is P. O. Box 518, Beaver Dam, Wisconsin, and telephone number is 1-800-654-3825—later acquired, among other things, the Herter name, waterfowl decoy molds and manufacturing equipment.)

Faber tested Robo-Duck this spring in a mile-long lake in front of his home, using plastic milk containers half-filled with water as substitutes for downed birds.

"After a couple of passes, I was able to handle and retrieve from any direction . . . going straight away or coming straight in was obviously the easiest, and I was soon able to handle the side approaches as well, although depth perception is involved."

Robo-Duck's steel fingers, about 20 inches long, are opened, then closed, as contact with the object to be retrieved is made.

"It's great," Faber said. "I would bring the container to shore, open the fingers to release it, then throw Robo-Duck in reverse to go back out after another one."

He added that the "basket" created by the closed steel fingers gripped the container tightly.

Robo-Duck's speed and range lead one to speculate that if its use became widespread, regulations—they already exist for waterfowlers in boats—might be needed to prohibit hunters from breaking up dozing rafts of birds on bluebird days. One suspects that waterfowl confronted with a monster duck rushing toward them at 10 miles an hour would either take wing or allow themselves to be herded toward the guns.

Robo-Duck—which has a stainless steel prop encased in a wire basket—can handle rough water, Faber said, adding that its inner case is completely waterproof. "You could, if you wish, easily remove the duck part and replace it with whatever you wanted . . . and one gentleman is interested in mounting the model of a tugboat on one."

Faber said he had been worried that someone might—as when shooting at wounded ducks on the water—put a charge of shot into a Robo-Duck and sink it, but no damage was done when Robo-Duck's inventor—Jack Adelman of Madison, Nebraska—fired a heavy duck load at the device from a distance of 40 yards.

The effectiveness of a few magnum of oversized birds in a decoy rig has long been recognized, and Robo-Duck is placed among the decoys and held in position by closing its wire fingers around a small, anchored float. When a bird is downed, the hunter—using the remote control panel from his blind, opens those fingers and sends Robo-Duck on its quest, returning it to the float when the mission is completed.

The use of live decoys for waterfowling was once commonplace, the most sophisticated example of this being the young, or "flyer" Canada geese that were raised in captivity with their parents and sent winging out over bay, ocean or sound to lure wild birds back to the waiting guns. Live decoys have long been outlawed. Since then, decoys that dip up and down—as if feeding—or flap their wings, have been devised, but Robo-Duck is a new concept.

Robo-Duck cannot, of course, retrieve a bird on land, sniff out one that has crept into the tules on the water's edge, spot distant flying birds that are beyond human eyesight, or regard you with disfavor when nothing falls after your shot. Nor can it, as my son's black Labrador bitch did a few seasons ago, bring back a wounded Canada goose that sailed far out over a mist-shrouded salt pond covered with rotten ice. Long after the bird was invisible to my son and me, the dog watched it descend, then lunged into the murk returning in triumph ten minutes later.

Robo-Duck will not quiver with excitement when you pick up your shotgun, nor will it press against you on the front seat of your pickup on the drive home, but when its motor fails you will not once again lament that you have outlived yet another companion.

No Deer Were Bagged, Just Leftover Groceries

Had there been snow for tracking, had the deer that walked past my son, Steve, been a buck instead of a doe, had the season on black bear not been closed, had moose been legal game, the six of us who recently journeyed to the northeastern tip of New Hampshire for two-and-a-half days of hunting could have come back with more than a box of leftover groceries.

On second thought, bears should not be included in such speculation even though my brother Dan encountered two of them. Neither he nor any other member of our party had any desire to shoot one.

Dan met the bears on the eastern slope of Round Mountain, on a warm, sunny afternoon. He had been standing on an old logging road looking for deer on the hardwood slopes above him, his back to a little ravine through which the north branch of Loomis Brook tumbles on its way to the Dead Diamond River. He heard a noise behind him and turned to see a bear loping uphill beside the stream, less than 60 feet away. A twig snapped under my brother's foot and the bear, alerted to Dan's presence, fled.

"It was a big, beautiful animal that must

have weighed well over three hundred pounds," Dan said. An hour later and a bit higher on the mountain, he came upon another bear somewhat smaller than the first. That one showed more curiosity than fear, allowing him to walk within 25 yards of it.

"It stood up on its hind legs and peered at me and didn't run until I grabbed a sapling and shook it," he said. "Just for the fun of it, I snorted. It stopped short and turned to stand and stare at me again. It really didn't know what to make of me."

On that same day, my son and I, and the others of our group—David Taylor of Littleton, New Hampshire, Henry Sanders of Peterborough, New Hampshire, and Peter Huntington of West Tisbury, Massachusetts—were either on Round Mountain or a little east of it toward the Dead Diamond. Moose and deer tracks and scat were plentiful, as were rubs made by both species, and scrapes made by the latter.

The whitetail buck speeds the removal of the velvet from his newly-developing antlers in the early fall each year by rubbing them against brush, saplings and small trees. During the rutting season (in the Northeast, the peak period is usually between mid-November and mid-December), he resumes these maneuvers, but this time they are more violent and part of the mating ritual, as is the scrape. Evidence of the latter is a patch, often about two feet by three feet, of the forest floor pawed down to bare earth. According to the literature on whitetail deer behavior, bucks sometimes urinate on such scrapes, but in years of dropping to my knees and sniffing such areas I never smelled anything but earth and rotting leaves.

Finding two scrapes that seemed quite fresh, I eased up to a ridge overlooking the area and pulled my secret weapon out of my shirt pocket. The literature that came with it described it as a big buck snort call. It sounded more like a bleating fawn than a snorting buck and after more than an hour of intermittent blowing on it I put it away, fearful that some member of my group would come upon me and think that I had gone over the edge.

Although the only creature that showed any interest in the sounds I was making was a female hairy woodpecker, some hunters swear by such devices. I lack confidence in it and I am equally wary of trying to "rattle up" a buck. Fifteen years ago, I watched a Texas rancher lure a good-sized whitetail buck out of a dense thicket with this technique. It involves banging a pair of antlers together, the idea being to pique the curiosity of the area's dominant male by simulating the sounds of two other bucks engaged in rutting combat. Some deer hunting experts say that the same thing can be accomplished by beating a standing tree with a dead limb, but having spent much of my life trying to learn how to sneak through the woods without a sound, I can't bring myself to raise such a ruckus.

Huntington, who had never before hunted in the region, had told us on the 14-mile drive along a logging road to our cabin that he was just as interested in seeing a moose as he was in bagging a deer. That wish was fulfilled on our first full day in the woods when he came upon five of them bedded down on Round Mountain. Sanders and Taylor each jumped one deer during our trip, seeing only their tails, and I did the same. I also came upon a yearling moose along the Dead Diamond. Taylor's most unusual sighting came at eight o'clock at night. He was ensconced in the outhouse and had left the door open. A shooting star blazed down the sky and while he was still marveling at its fleeting brilliance, a huge, black form, a moose, walked past the open door.

Early evenings in a deer camp usually follow a certain ritual. As the occupants arrive, some after dark, they—with either toddy or coffee in hand—recount their day's adventures. One person lugs in logs for the wood stove, another fetches water from stream, spring or lake, and someone else begins to prepare supper. In our case, Steve performs the last-named duty. He enjoys cooking and is good at it. His major effort on this trip included roast Cornish game hens with a mushroom stuffing, stir-fried vegetables, wild rice, cranberry sauce, just-made applesauce and a tossed salad. It is when the meal and the dishes are done that the format arises. There is comradely gaming, but it is never, at least in my experience, as sharp as the edge of the knife that hangs from each man's belt. The hunting camp is a place where most men make believe that food, shelter, fire, water and the quest for meat are all that counts. Poker is a common evening recreation in such a setting, as is poring over topographic maps of the region and making plans, elaborate or haphazard, for the following day.

Huntington set the stage for one evening's activities, having toted in a blowgun and a large supply of darts for it. Most of us took a turn or two at shooting at a target pinned to the cabin wall, but Dan, who is fascinated by primitive weapons, persisted in practicing until he became so skilled that we devised a moving target for him, a potato swinging from a length of dental floss tied to a rafter. When that became too easy, we fastened the cork from a champagne bottle to the potato, and soon he was hitting the cork with regularity. He was so pleased with his performance that he said he was going to acquire a blowgun when he got back to civilization, and I rather suspect that he will.

How to Perpetuate Your Myth

If, plagued by the various ills that aging flesh is heir to, you wonder how to sustain your reputation as a rock-hard, immensely clever hunter or fisherman, do not despair, for there are some only slightly dishonest ways of perpetuating the myth.

Let us consider the deer camp. The deer camp is not a place where the animals gather, but some log cabin, shack or lodge in the woods that serves as a base of operations for a group of hunters.

If you are the oldest fellow in the camp and have been there several times before, you know more about where the deer are than do your companions, and you also often have a chance to suggest what territory each man should hunt.

It's usually a relatively simple matter to assign yourself the best hunting area and the younger men the worst. You can get around the mild moral discomfort you may feel by telling yourself that deer often change their habits, that a ten-year pattern may be broken this time around.

If it is a well-run camp, the breakfast dishes will be cleaned up just as the tops of the spruces become visible against the eastern sky, and if the thought of lurching up the mountain before your joints have become properly loosened appalls you, there is a way out.

Inform the others that you have a special stew or casserole you wish to delight them with when they return from the hills that evening. Use a little arrogance. Tell them that—just because no women are about—there is no reason to live on canned swill.

With a little foot-dragging, much of the morning can be consumed in that project, and by that time you probably will have reached the stage where you can walk without stumbling. If you happen to be a writer, you needn't bother with cooking—simply make a show of getting out your notebooks, remarking that some people have to work for a living, even when hunting.

Eventually, of course, you'll have to go into the hills. If all has gone well, you'll set for about 10:30 A.M. Perhaps the hot spot you have set aside for yourself will produce a deer immediately; in which case you will drag it triumphantly back, ahead of everyone else, remarking when they arrive empty-handed that you can't understand their problem, that the woods are full of deer.

In youth, taking a deer early in the game is a disappointment, because your hunt is over. Later, you'll welcome this event. It not only relieves you of any more hiking, but frees you to read the book of poems you tucked away in your duffle bag, to toss scraps of food to the camp's Canada jays and chipmunks and to take long naps.

If you fail to get your deer on opening day, there is still an almost effortless way to enhance your reputation. Plan your hunt so that you are, by early afternoon, propped against a sun-warmed boulder on the southwestern slope of the mountain. Settle yourself comfortably, and before long, sleep will come. Remain there the rest of the day, perhaps kindling a tiny fire to heat a cup of tea and to ward off late afternoon's chill.

Near sunset, move slowly downhill toward the camp, but stop a quarter of a mile short of it. Tarry there as darkness fills the woods.

Wait until you hear the others return, until lamplight gleams from the cabin windows, until you know that your friends are becoming concerned about you. This is particularly effective if it has begun to snow, conjuring thoughts of the old-timer being lost in a blizzard.

Deer Season

Dawn was cold and gray. A light snow sifted through the bare black branches of hardwoods, or clung to feather hemlocks.

It was the opening day of the Pennsylvania deer-hunting season, and we were on our respective stands around the periphery of a small ravine.

We—my brother Dan, and Paul Updike, of Roscoe, New York—had elected to remain immobile that morning because we knew as of other hunters would be moving through the woods, pushing the animals before them. Among the hunters would be school students—all the schools in Tioga County were closed for opening day—and youngsters are too jumpy to remain sitting standing for long.

For the most part, however, I was alone in the woods that was silent except for the sound of what was nearly sleet, striking the plastic vest one must wear for self-protection.

I leaned my muzzle-loading rifle against a tree, after cutting a little groove in catch the front site and to keep the weather ping, and placed a leaf over its p moisture from reaching the

You may if you wish remain there until someone goes outside and fires a signal shot into the night sky, but that is carrying it a bit too far.

Arise, tousle your hair, slap your face to make it red, as with exertion, sprinkle pine needles on your garments—or snow if it's possible—and stride to the cabin, kicking the door open and demanding a tot of bourbon.

Stomp your feet on the cabin floor and hang your rifle on the wall, and, glass in hand, immediately launch into a saga that might go something like this:

"I walked clear to hell and gone over Terrible Mountain. On the backside of it I picked up the trail of a big animal that led me down into Black's Swamp. Damndest mess of blowdowns you ever saw. I poked around in there all afternoon. Twice I saw a deer ahead of me, but I couldn't be sure it was the big one. I hung around until near sundown, hoping he'd show. That's a good buck. I'm going back in there tomorrow."

Then, lest you be queried too closely, advance to your stew, give it a stir and say: "Probably shouldn't have wasted my time with this after breakfast, but it sure smells first-rate."

The waterfowl hunter is more restricted in his image-creating maneuvers, particularly if he shares a blind with someone. About all you can do when you have a duck-hunting companion is to avoid all distant shots. Hold off until you can see the bird's eyes—30 yards or less away—and if you still manage to miss, rub the shoulder where you took a bullet in the Normandy invasion and softly curse the sniper who spoiled the uncanny coordination of eye and hand you once possessed.

If you are angling, trout fishing offers the best chance for self-inflation. You can't, for example, fool someone who is standing beside you in the pounding surf, flinging lures at the same school of fish. Fly-fishing a trout stream, however, you and your companion will separate, and as soon as you are screened from each other there need be no limit to your imagination. It is a good idea to enjoy several pipes on the bank of the stream, while you fashion the tale you will tell at the day's end.

If you wish to remove all doubt—or most of it—from your friend's mind, insist on fishing waters in which all trout must be

released. Catch-and-release trout fishing has helped spawn a new breed of anglers who have found total contentment in equip[ment] and approach, in mastering the entomology of stream insect[s], tieing the flies designed to represent those insects and in cre[ating] new fly pattern and angling techniques about which a see[mingly] unending spate of books have been written. Some of the[m] that come to mind are *Nymphs I Have Known, Caddis Ma[ys] Fly Dry*, not forgetting of course, the privately publish[ed] signed copies—*Reeling About*, a singular probing of th[e] tencies of trout, women and wine.

But even if you are flogging a stream where the fi[sh] be kept, there is no reason you have to trouble yo[urself with] them.

Steal along the stream, making sure you don't [cast a shadow] on the water, thereby startling the fish. Indeed, [the best way] is to cast nothing on the water for if you do [you risk an] overhanging branch and lose one of the flies [you always] ever carry—given you by Lord Purslane [as you fished the] stretch of the Itchen as war clouds were g[athering].

And when the cattle are lowing and wi[nd] and the setting sun flames in the west, s[ome angler] who, insensitive to the new tradition, ha[s] rainbows in his creel, and tell of how, f[or many] years, you managed to fool Old Ca[esar, the six-] pound brown trout that has spent [its days in] maid Pool.

Tell how the big fellow's deep, [as the] light from the dying sun as you [ ] slide your silver flask from you[r] trout and old friends, and, di[s] panion will soon cease to dou[bt]

Given time, so will you.

and if the thought of lurching up the mountain before your joints have become properly loosened appalls you, there is a way out.

Inform the others that you have a special stew or casserole you wish to delight them with when they return from the hills that evening. Use a little arrogance. Tell them that—just because no women are about—there is no reason to live on canned swill.

With a little foot-dragging, much of the morning can be consumed in that project, and by that time you probably will have reached the stage where you can walk without stumbling. If you happen to be a writer, you needn't bother with cooking—simply make a show of getting out your notebooks, remarking that some people have to work for a living, even when hunting.

Eventually, of course, you'll have to go into the hills. If all has gone well, you'll set for about 10:30 A.M. Perhaps the hot spot you have set aside for yourself will produce a deer immediately; in which case you will drag it triumphantly back, ahead of everyone else, remarking when they arrive empty-handed that you can't understand their problem, that the woods are full of deer.

In youth, taking a deer early in the game is a disappointment, because your hunt is over. Later, you'll welcome this event. It not only relieves you of any more hiking, but frees you to read the book of poems you tucked away in your duffle bag, to toss scraps of food to the camp's Canada jays and chipmunks and to take long naps.

If you fail to get your deer on opening day, there is still an almost effortless way to enhance your reputation. Plan your hunt so that you are, by early afternoon, propped against a sun-warmed boulder on the southwestern slope of the mountain. Settle yourself comfortably, and before long, sleep will come. Remain there the rest of the day, perhaps kindling a tiny fire to heat a cup of tea and to ward off late afternoon's chill.

Near sunset, move slowly downhill toward the camp, but stop a quarter of a mile short of it. Tarry there as darkness fills the woods.

Wait until you hear the others return, until lamplight gleams from the cabin windows, until you know that your friends are becoming concerned about you. This is particularly effective if it has begun to snow, conjuring thoughts of the old-timer being lost in a blizzard.

You may if you wish remain there until someone goes outside and fires a signal shot into the night sky, but that is carrying it a bit too far.

Arise, tousle your hair, slap your face to make it red, as with exertion, sprinkle pine needles on your garments—or snow if it's possible—and stride to the cabin, kicking the door open and demanding a tot of bourbon.

Stomp your feet on the cabin floor and hang your rifle on the wall, and, glass in hand, immediately launch into a saga that might go something like this:

"I walked clear to hell and gone over Terrible Mountain. On the backside of it I picked up the trail of a big animal that led me down into Black's Swamp. Damndest mess of blowdowns you ever saw. I poked around in there all afternoon. Twice I saw a deer ahead of me, but I couldn't be sure it was the big one. I hung around until near sundown, hoping he'd show. That's a good buck. I'm going back in there tomorrow."

Then, lest you be queried too closely, advance to your stew, give it a stir and say: "Probably shouldn't have wasted my time with this after breakfast, but it sure smells first-rate."

The waterfowl hunter is more restricted in his image-creating maneuvers, particularly if he shares a blind with someone. About all you can do when you have a duck-hunting companion is to avoid all distant shots. Hold off until you can see the bird's eyes—30 yards or less away—and if you still manage to miss, rub the shoulder where you took a bullet in the Normandy invasion and softly curse the sniper who spoiled the uncanny coordination of eye and hand you once possessed.

If you are angling, trout fishing offers the best chance for self-inflation. You can't, for example, fool someone who is standing beside you in the pounding surf, flinging lures at the same school of fish. Fly-fishing a trout stream, however, you and your companion will separate, and as soon as you are screened from each other there need be no limit to your imagination. It is a good idea to enjoy several pipes on the bank of the stream, while you fashion the tale you will tell at the day's end.

If you wish to remove all doubt—or most of it—from your friend's mind, insist on fishing waters in which all trout must be released. Catch-and-release trout fishing has helped spawn a new breed of anglers who have found total contentment in equipage and approach, in mastering the entomology of stream insects, in tieing the flies designed to represent those insects and in creating new fly pattern and angling techniques about which a seemingly unending spate of books have been written. Some of these titles that come to mind are *Nymphs I Have Known, Caddis Madness and Fly Dry,* not forgetting of course, the privately published—1,000 signed copies—*Reeling About,* a singular probing of the inconsistencies of trout, women and wine.

But even if you are flogging a stream where the fish may legally be kept, there is no reason you have to trouble yourself catching them.

Steal along the stream, making sure you don't cast your shadow on the water, thereby startling the fish. Indeed, the best approach is to cast nothing on the water for if you do you may hook an overhanging branch and lose one of the flies—the only ones you ever carry—given you by Lord Purslane when you angled his stretch of the Itchen as war clouds were gathering over Europe.

And when the cattle are lowing and winding slowly over the lea and the setting sun flames in the west, seek out your companion, who, insensitive to the new tradition, has a lovely brace of 16-inch rainbows in his creel, and tell of how, for the third time in as many years, you managed to fool Old Cannibal, the monster seven-pound brown trout that has spent more than a decade in Dairy-maid Pool.

Tell how the big fellow's deep, bronze sides gleamed in the last light from the dying sun as you slipped him back into the water, slide your silver flask from your hip and propose a toast to old trout and old friends, and, disarmed by good brandy, your companion will soon cease to doubt your tale.

Given time, so will you.

Deer Season

Dawn was cold and gray. A light snow sifted through the bare black branches of hardwoods, or clung to feather hemlocks.

It was the opening day of the Pennsylvania deer-hunting season, and we were on our respective stands around the periphery of a small ravine.

We—my brother Dan, and Paul Updike, Jr., of Roscoe, New York—had elected to remain immobile that morning because we knew dozens of other hunters would be moving through the woods, pushing the animals before them. Among the hunters would be high school students—all the schools in Tioga County were closed for opening day—and most youngsters are too jumpy to remain sitting or standing for long.

For the most part, however, I was alone in a world that was silent except for the sound of snow, which was nearly sleet, striking the plastic orange vest one must wear for self-protection.

I leaned my muzzle-loading rifle against a tree beside me, after cutting a little groove in the tree to catch the front site and to keep the rifle from slipping, and placed a leaf over its muzzle to keep moisture from reaching the powder charge. Each of our trio was using a muzzle-loading rifle, or so-called primitive weapon, because such a rifle, with its single shot and limited range, offers more of a challenge.

Early in my vigil a pair of small deer walked by about fifty yards away, but I didn't even reach for my rifle because the light was too poor for me to discern if either had the 3-inch-long horns that make them legal game in Pennsylvania.

From then until nine-thirty, eight more antlerless deer went past at varying distances and then a fair-sized animal came sneaking through the hemlocks below me about forty yards away, and when it lowered its head to feed I saw a set of horns about 8 inches long silhouetted against the snow.

At my shot, the animal ran a few yards then fell, killed cleanly with a bullet that later proved to have gone through the lower portion of its heart.

After dressing it out—I saved the heart and liver and placed them in plastic bags in my pack—there was nothing left for me to do but put my rifle aside and wait until darkness or until the others of my trio were similarly successful.

By ten-thirty, guns were sounding with startling regularity from the surrounding hills, not the occasional shot one hears, for example, in New Hampshire, where fewer deer are taken.

Pennsylvania is one of the nation's top whitetail deer states, second to Texas. Last year, more than 64,000 bucks were killed in the regular season, which lasts about two weeks, and nearly 58,000 more were killed during the special two-day antlerless deer season, for residents only, that follows.

In the Northeast, only New York State comes close to this total, with nearly 100,000 deer taken annually in recent years.

About 1.4 million hunters were expected to pursue deer in Pennsylvania this year, and one Pennsylvania Game Commission official has estimated that in recent years these hunters have spent about $100 million annually in the process.

Deer hunting is socially acceptable in most of upcountry New York State and Pennsylvania. My brother and I, for example, had stopped at the Antrim Lodge in Roscoe, New York, in the Catskills on our drive to Blossburg, and most of the evening crowd was hunters.

Although hunters were much in evidence in Roscoe, their numbers increased when we reached Blossburg (population about 1,700), where every motel and diner was jammed, and where many, as we did, had to locate private homes—dozens of the town's housewives pick up pin money in this fashion—in which to stay.

By the end of the first day of the Pennsylvania season, deer were hanging from outside beams provided by many of the motels in the Blossburg area.

As one might expect, many of the men of Blossburg are hunters. J. P. Ward Foundries, Inc., the town's largest employer, about 500 workers, gives its people two paid holidays during the buck season and one during the antlerless deer season.

The influx of hunters into this region—Tioga County is one of the state's top deer countries (Potter County is No. 1 in this respect)—also keeps the local telephone company hopping, and after dark every day during the deer season one might have to wait several hours to place a call to the outside. A spokesman for the firm, the Commonwealth Telephone Company, said, "It's our busiest time of the year."

Guided to the Waterfowl

When the first duck, a green-winged teal, streaked by shortly after dawn, I was not ready for it, being engaged in lighting my pipe.

"Shoot," our guide, Bob Hester, had said, and the others with us, Jerome Robinson, of Canaan, New Hampshire, and Joel Arrington, of Raleigh, North Carolina, could not respond because the bird was off my end of the blind.

"I'm sorry, Bob," I said. "It takes me a while to get used to a new situation and my pipe is an essential ingredient in that adjustment."

He regarded me with a vaguely troubled air. Waterfowl guides encounter an incredible variety of personalities in their clients, ranging from the fellow who shoots at every duck that goes by, even if it is out of range or more properly the target of one of his companions, to the man who seems unable to pull the trigger.

Mr. Hester was also worried, I think, about my armament, a 20-gauge over-and-under chambered for 3-inch shells and bored, improved and modified. For the uninitiated, a shotgun of this genre is quite properly considered a quail or grouse gun, being a little small and choked too loose for some waterfowling.

There was a time when I went after duck and geese with a full-choke 12-gauge or even the larger 10-gauge, but in recent years I have given all my modern shotguns, save the 20-gauge, to my sons. The 20 is perfectly adequate for decoying ducks and geese; a person only has to remember to pass up any shot over 40 yards. When flight shooting, it is a handicap because at least half the birds are passing at more than 40 yards.

My only exception to using the 20-gauge occurs when I go snipe or rabbit hunting with a little 28-gauge side-by-side muzzle-loading double, or waterfowl hunting with a 12-gauge muzzle-loading double.

This penchant for muzzle-loading shotguns (and rifles) is, I rather imagine, a way of easing into that time of life that moves many men to savor the pre-kill ritual of the hunt as well as the final act. Nearly all of us go through a period when shooting a limit of birds is a near obsession, but almost inevitably there comes a time when a brace of ducks for a well-planned dinner is utterly satisfying.

A short while after the teal escaped unscathed, I put Mr. Hester's doubts to rest, making a nice shot on another teal, and throughout the morning we performed in creditable fashion, taking seventeen birds, including teal, pintails, a mallard and one shoveler.

We were hunting out of Mr. Hester's Mattamuskeet Inn, which is located just east of Route 94 on the north shore of Lake Mattamuskeet, and our blind was in one of four flooded impoundments created by Mr. Hester, who is also a farmer.

Mr. Hester started building these impoundments, which range from 18 to 235 acres in size, about six years ago. The impoundments are planted with food many waterfowl crave, including sorghum and millet.

The low-lying area around Lake Mattamuskeet—most of the lake and its shoreline is within a national wildlife refuge—lends itself to the impoundment concept. Building impoundment areas and flooding and planting them is an expensive endeavor, but if they are properly hunted—not pounded every day—excellent waterfowling can result.

Mr. Hester runs a first-rate enterprise. He has fifty-eight blinds in all—eleven on the impoundments, five in areas of the lake open to shooting, two floating blinds in nearby Pamlico Sound and the remainder field blinds. He and his guides are expert at decoy layouts and calling and remain affable and eager after weeks of rising at 4 A.M.

Both the impoundment blinds and the stake blinds in Lake Mattamuskeet that my friends and I visited are also ideal for photographing waterfowl and in all instances it was possible for a man to set up with a telephoto lens in a "hide" of his own a hundred yards, or less, away.

The stake blinds—one wears waders to reach them—in the lake are also excellent locations from which to observe and photograph (the birds are protected) whistling swans. Approximately one-fifth, amounting to perhaps twenty thousand, of this continent's population of these magnificent birds winter on Mattamuskeet after journeying thousands of miles from the Northwest Canadian Arctic.

Canada geese are also present, as are a wild variety of puddle ducks and even diving ducks, including scaup. The lake is about 18 miles long and 6 miles wide and most of it is less than waist deep. There are various theories about how Mattamuskeet was formed, one being that it was caused by a fire burning down through peat. There were various plans to drain and farm the lake early in this century, but they were abandoned and it became a refuge in 1934.

Mr. Hester, as his impoundment-building indicates, is interested in improving the hunting opportunities in the area. He is also interested in the birds themselves.

One evening during our stay there we accompanied him to nearby Engelhard where a dinner, raffle and auction was held to raise money in an attempt to bolster the small population of blue geese, about 1,500, that have historically wintered on Lake Mattamuskeet. The endeavor, currently being led by Mr. Hester and Ben Simmons, Jr., of Fairfield, involves raising breeding pairs of the birds on land around the lake already leased for that purpose.

Hunting Canvasbacks Near New York

Pounding across the dark, choppy Hudson River a half-hour before dawn in a beamy skiff laden with three men, dozens of decoys and two dogs, I was intrigued by the lights that blazed along the western shore.

I had never before gone duck hunting in a place where the works of men were so much in evidence. But the Hudson is an ideal setting for such a seemingly apparent contradiction, a magnificent river that has remained vital—home, or part-time home, to striped bass, sturgeon, eels, blue claw crabs, shorebirds, ducks and geese—even when civilization's degradation of it was most relentless.

Twice—the first location being unproductive—we built makeshift blinds of netting and driftwood on the east shore, and the second location seemed illogical. There, the sharp southwest wind was in our faces and the black rocks upon which we sat trembled when passenger trains thundered by a few feet behind us, their occupants sometimes waving to the disreputable-looking trio below.

But my companions, John Vargo and Tom Carey, both of Verplanck, New York, who had arranged the hunt, knew what they were doing and within an hour many of the hundreds, maybe thousands, of canvasbacks that had hitherto avoided us visited our layout.

Five hours before, I had been sitting watery eyed and a bit disjointed in my truck in a shopping mall at 4 A.M., waiting for my companions to pick me up.

My condition wasn't caused by all-night revelry but by almost no sleep and much worry, smoke and excitement the previous evening and that morning.

I had been visiting friends in Croton, Mr. and Mrs. Daniel North, and a blaze that had apparently been smoldering for hours in the outside wall behind their fireplace broke loose at about 11 P.M. We called the fire department and did what we could to douse the flames with a garden hose before the trucks arrived. An hour later, all was under control—the damage being confined to the outside wall—and we set about cleaning up some of the debris and putting furniture back in its proper place.

As is always the case after a house fire, we felt a great need for talk and we talked until three. I went to bed fully clothed and an hour later was in the parking lot where my hunting partners soon arrived.

On the way to our launching site north of Croton, I explained the reason for my lack of verve.

"There's a good wind blowing and that should clear your sinuses," said Mr. Carey, whose activities include scuba diving and being a member of the Verplanck Fire Department.

He was right, and by the time he and Mr. Vargo, who have gone waterfowling together for years, were setting out the decoys and dawn was breaking over the wind-ruffled river, I had become sufficiently mobile to move around the rocky shore with some alacrity.

Large flocks of birds were soon visible high overhead, their wings glinting in the sun that had not touched us, and so far away I couldn't identify them. "What are they?" I asked.

"Canvasbacks," Mr. Vargo responded.

"My God, I haven't seen that many canvasbacks in thirty years," I replied.

"You haven't seen anything yet, just wait," said Mr. Carey.

We waited for perhaps half an hour for the canvasbacks to

come to our decoys, but they continued to fly south, in flocks of ten to one hundred birds, and paid us no heed.

"That's it," said Mr. Vargo. "I'm going to move the decoys."

"Wait a little, John," said Mr. Carey. "We haven't been here that long."

"Wait?" said Mr. Vargo. "I'm changing them. Sometimes just a little shift makes the difference."

He made the change and a short while later after three hundred more canvasbacks had gone by, Mr. Vargo said, "Enough is enough. We're moving."

"Be patient, John. Be patient," said Mr. Carey.

"Be damned with patience," his friend responded. "We're moving."

"Not yet," said Mr. Carey.

"Gentlemen," I interposed, "I'm in much too weakened a condition to successfully separate you."

Both laughed. "We do this all the time. It isn't serious," Mr. Carey said.

Our next and last location was the railway embankment previously mentioned, and the canvasbacks arrived, sometimes hurtling down from a thousand feet up, making two preliminary passes then coming in, wings set, about forty yards out.

Within minutes it was all over for us as far as hunting those birds was concerned. We each shot one, the legal limit, and the dogs, Rascal, a young male black Labrador and Kim, a middle-aged female springer spaniel, shared the retrieving honors, and for a few more hours we sat and watched canvasbacks come and go, hoping, uselessly it proved, that a few black ducks, mallards or scaup might come by.

Canvasbacks have a reputation for being particularly wary, but the need for caution on our part being removed by reaching our bag limits, we found that they would come to our decoys even when we sat on the rocks above the blind with only the lower portions of our bodies being covered. All we had to do was remain motionless and keep our heads down.

Among our largest and fastest-flying ducks—they have been clocked at over 70 miles an hour—canvasbacks subsist in the main on aquatic plants in fresh and brackish water, their favorite being wild celery. They are regarded by many as our best-tasting wild duck and my limited acquaintance with them tends to support this belief.

Canvasbacks have suffered greatly from drainage of the portions of their marshy breeding areas that are in the northern Great Plains, hence the one-bird limit. The birds are also particularly vulnerable to poisoning by spent lead shot because they pick up the shot when straining bottom muck for seeds of grasses and sedges.

Late that afternoon at Mr. Vargo's home, which is on a height of land over the Hudson, we drank a toast to our splendid day. My friends, knowing that I don't encounter canvasbacks often, generously gave me their birds and Mr. Vargo and his son Chris helped me pick them.

While we were so engaged, I noticed a mushroom-like structure about 8 feet tall in the yard.

"What does it look like to you?" asked Mr. Vargo who, among other things, is an inventor.

"Boletus edulis," I responded. "One of our most choice wild mushrooms."

"I just call it 'The Mushroom,'" said Mr. Vargo, who has no mycological leanings. "It's nearly ready to go. It's a climate-controlled phone booth and miniature office—unlocked by a credit card—with desk, good lighting and even a calculator."

I thought of the bitterly cold hours I have spent in outdoor phone booths trying to keep the wind from blowing my notes away, or of the blazing heat and the roar of passing vehicles I have had to endure when so engaged, and was impressed.

"I think I still have some dried boletus edulis I picked last summer. If I do, I'll add them to the gravy when I roast these canvasbacks," I said. "That would be a proper close to this adventure."

Singing the Praises of a Frugal Brugal in the Birth of the Booze

Crawling from my bunk at 4:30 A.M., tugging feebly at my longjohns with one hand and scratching my stomach with the other, I was confronted by a man of demonic energy, a man old enough to be my father, who thrust a glass at me and said, "Here's your Frugal Brugal!"

The man was Frederick (Pete) Blodgett of Dover, Massachusetts, a retired banker now turned to the good things of life: hunting and fishing. The Frugal Brugal is a morning potion designed to sweep doubt and indecision from one's mind and to turn the dreariest dawn into something bright and shining. The first sip set my teeth on edge and made my eyes water, the second was less onerous and the remainder of the drink seemed remarkably smooth, so smooth, indeed, that I volunteered to make biscuits for our deer-hunting party of seven.

Blodgett had brought many surprises to the camp, including black ducks and bluebills, quail doves, smoked Icelandic salmon, quahogs, and a magnificent slab of beef, and the Frugal Brugal was not the least of these.

The Frugal Brugal, a mixture of unsweetened grapefruit juice and a dry Brugal rum, was born some years ago in a fishing camp in a remote corner of Maine. Blodgett and a companion had been flying in for a day's fishing and had decided that one bottle would take care of their presupper toasts. They caught many trout and were ready to leave the following morning, but bad weather moved in and remained.

They caught more trout, and, despite belated rationalizing, soon had polished off their single bottle. The low clouds continued to hang over the lake and surrounding hills, and from time to time as the days went by, they could hear their plane crossing overhead, unseen, as the pilot tried vainly to find a hole in the murk.

The fishing remained excellent and the trout were good to eat, but there was nothing to drink. They remembered that some friends who also used the camp were wont to hide fifths of bourbon and scotch around the premises in anticipation of returning. They knew that these bottles were usually discovered by others soon after their owners departed. There was one man, however, Blodgett said, whose cache had never been found.

"That man was a very astute lawyer," Blodgett said, "And we knew he would have no ordinary hiding place. At first we thought he might bury it at the foot of a tree, but there were so damn many trees around the camp we decided that even a man of his intellect might become confused. Then it struck me. He would hide it under a fallen tree or log. There weren't many of those. I rushed out and under the very first log I tried, my hand closed around the neck of a bottle. It was Brugal rum. We found a can of grapefruit juice, and when my partner began to mix the rum and the juice I reminded him that the can was small and the bottle large. Be frugal with the juice, I said."

Blodgett says there is a Frugal Brugal Society in America with chapters in England and Canada.

When one has sufficient grapefruit juice, a good Frugal Brugal, at least for a beginner, is two parts juice and one part rum. It also helps if both the rum and the juice are chilled.

Waterfowling
Nuances

The surf—a half-mile to the south—was moaning and we were hunting waterfowl on Shinnecock Bay.

The surf has various voices, from its summer whisper on a gently sloping shore to its thundering mid-winter assault against storm-created escarpments of sand and jumbled glacial rocks.

When the surf moans, the ocean is only partially agitated by a moderate onshore wind or by a storm that passed by far at sea.

I dwell on the surf because so many of my waterfowling days have been spent within sight and sound of the sea, crouched in a blind in a sweet-smelling salt marsh. I dwell on it because as one grows older—an achievement of no value unless waning physical energy is replaced by a more muscular mind and a spirit that is less chary of soaring—the nuances of all endeavors, including the hunt, become as important as the climax.

This is not to say that to a thinking graybeard hunter the kill is pallid. It is merely that it has been placed in proper perspective.

Much, if not most, waterfowl hunting involves long periods of inactivity in the blind. The blind might be a clump of bayberry bushes, in which one fashions an impromptu hide with the aid, perhaps, of a bushel or two of dried eel grass, or an elaborate floating affair meticulously covered with bunches of marsh grass, such as my Long Island guide, Frank Downs, Jr., of Hampton Bays, and I were using. In many instances, one tarries in such spots from before daybreak until sundown. If one has a companion, there will be a spate of conversation after the first flurry of activity, the setting out of the decoys, is done, and that will be followed by sporadic talk and long periods of silence, the latter condition shattered, hopefully, from time to time by the arrival of ducks or geese.

Sometimes, but not often, the enforced idleness of a duck blind prods one to reveal more of his soul to a casual acquaintance than one would to kith of kin. But this is unusual, and commonly each man—women are rare occupants of duck blinds—retreats into retrospection.

The hours Mr. Downs and I spent in his blind produced an inordinate amount of retrospection. To be precise, we had only one chance to shoot, and I bagged one large mallard drake, a bird my guide said, because of its size, had newly arrived from Canada.

From time to time during the day, particularly in late afternoon, guns coughed to the west of us, but none of the birds that inspired that shooting came our way.

The fault wasn't Mr. Downs's, by the way. He is a highly accomplished waterfowler, as was his father before him, and his decoy layouts—we used several dozen blocks that day, including some magnificent and huge solid cedar Canada goose decoys—were carefully arranged.

One problem was that the southwest wind we had all that day was wrong for the part of the bay in which Mr. Downs has his blind and there was nothing we could do about that.

The wind was also rather gentle and in such a situation most waterfowl choose to stay on broad expanses of open water far from the hunters' guns.

The tide was rising all afternoon also, with the result that the waterfowl we most commonly saw, black ducks, began, an hour or so before sunset, to drop far behind us in the flooded marshes.

If we had had a low tide instead of a high tide, those flooded marsh areas wouldn't have been available, and our chances of success would have been much better.

Another handicap we encountered was brought on by me. I had arrived on Long Island shortly after four o'clock the afternoon before, via the ferry from New London, Connecticut, to Orient Point. Being a resident of Massachusetts, I needed a non-resident New York State hunting license. I had thought that somewhere between Orient Point and Hampton Bays, where Mr. Downs lives, I would find a sporting goods store that sold such licenses. Such was not the case, and by the time I began to think of various town offices, they had closed. The result was that we missed the early shooting the following day while I ran down what I needed at the town offices in Southhampton. On a truly wild day, whether high winds or high winds and rain or snow, an early start often isn't that important, but when the weather is mild, sunup and sundown are usually the best times.

One should also realize that when a duck hunting trip is arranged far in advance that one is at the mercy of the weather. The only hunters who consistently get out on good waterfowling days are those who live in the area and who can drop everything and go forth when conditions are right.

Ironically, our decoys were visited by many of the region's highly prized Atlantic Coast brant (Branta bernicla), but the season on them doesn't open until December 8 (it runs until January 6) in the Long Island area. Brant populations have been low because of severe winters and poor reproduction and the season on them in the Atlantic flyway was closed, with the exception of one year, from 1972 to 1980. This year, the daily brant bag limits two.

The brant is a black-and-white bird that appears larger than it really is. The mature brant is dark colored with an incomplete white collar on its neck and a somewhat pointed bill. An adult bird weighs only 3 pounds, slightly more than a large black duck, but its wing spread is 45 inches. The black duck's wingspread is about a foot less.

Branta bernicla (there is also a Pacific Coast species) frequent Atlantic coastal areas. The flight of these birds, members of the goose tribe, is irregular, dipping and weaving, and the flocks are usually small. The brant's voice is a guttural, honking sound which lacks the haunting quality of the cry of the Canada goose.

Brant are prized by epicures, although their value as table fare declined when they were forced, a few decades ago, to switch from their basic food, eelgrass, to sea lettuce. The near-demise of eelgrass along the Atlantic coast was not, to this writer's knowledge, ever fully explained, but in recent years eelgrass has come back and one must suppose that so has the cherished flavor of the brant. I cannot vouch for either the original or the present flavor, because I was never in a location—during nearly fifty years of waterfowling—to harvest enough brant to gain any appreciation of the gustatory pleasures they offer.

I've gotten the impression from my infrequent observations of them that they appear to lack the sagacity of many other waterfowl and that they will at least investigate a wide variety of decoys.

Cold Close to the Duck Season

If in your salad days you steeped your sons in the delights of waterfowling, be prepared to embrace manfully the results of that tutelage ten, twenty, thirty or more years later.

It is not enough to assemble the equipage and literature of the hunt; to, when your boys drop by, throw a fine double gun to your shoulder and swing on an imaginary duck, or to read them a few choice paragraphs from a long out-of-print waterfowling tome. They remember, as if it were yesterday, when you dragged them, runny noses and all, from the comfort of the hearth into a world of wildness and wet or ice and snow and wind moaning through marsh grass. They remember and they want deeds, not words. They want to see if the old man can still take it.

Their urge to do this is even more intense if you began their training at an unusually early age. I took my oldest son, Steve, duck-hunting for the first time when he was so young his eyes barely reached above the rim of the pack basket in which I carried him. Jeff, my youngest lad, did not enjoy the benefits of such an early start, mainly because we were living in a marginal waterfowling region at the time, but he does recall my leaving him—

during a deer-hunting expedition—sitting on a boulder on a snow-covered mountainside with instructions to keep a sharp lookout and under no circumstances to leave the post. The temperature was a few degrees above zero, and he was nine years old. He said, and I believe he exaggerates, that I told him I would be back in half an hour but didn't reappear until three hours later when night was falling and he was whimpering from the cold and fear that I had forgotten him.

A short while ago when a northwest gale with snow in its teeth was making the house shudder, Jeff showed up a little before three in the afternoon and opined that such weather was just what was needed to force waterfowl off the broad expanses of water and into various secluded coves.

"I've got the decoys in the truck," he said, "and we've got nearly two hours before dark."

I murmured that I had a writing deadline to meet, but that argument had little substance because I had been, when he came in, tinkering with a shotgun that had malfunctioned.

It is not, I should make clear, that I do not enjoy hunting with my sons, for they are splendid companions. It was—and only those over sixty can truly understand this—rather that my juices weren't flowing. I was slightly chilled—I pride myself on working in an office where the winter temperature doesn't get above the mid-60s—and the six or eight mugs of coffee I had quaffed in the previous four hours hadn't warmed me appreciably. I was, in truth, in a state best suited for contemplation of past delights.

"There are only a few more weeks of hunting left," my son said, "and we don't get many days like this."

Fifteen minutes later I was standing in a clump of bayberries and scrub oaks on the shore of a salt pond watching Jeff put out the decoys, a duty that at some point a father can, without fear of appearing inadequate, turn over to his sons.

He joined me in our hide, ruddy faced, emanating energy and obviously warm.

A particularly sharp gust of wind drove stinging snow against my face and I shivered.

Jeff shot a merganser that came in low over the water. The snow intensified until we couldn't see a portion of the shore 100 yards away. A lone bluebill emerged from the swirling white and was setting his wings over the decoys before I saw him. He fell when I fired, but it took another shot from me and one from Jeff to dispatch him.

Wind-buffeted in the gathering darkness, I knew I was too cold to properly mount and swing my gun if more ducks appeared, but I waited until my son suggested that we should leave, that it had gotten so nasty no birds would fly.

Once home it took ten minutes of soaking in warm water before my fingers worked well enough to type, and I remembered when as a trapper of muskrats in my youth I would set out on such days with no gloves, merely coating my hands with grease to deal with their repeated immersion in water.

The temperature fell to zero that night and was about ten degrees when he whom I had once taken duck hunting in a pack basket appeared late the next day.

"I got off work a little early," he said. "We can't let this go by. Most of the pond will be frozen, but there will be some open water in the channel off the point where you and Jeff were yesterday and some birds are bound to try to use it."

Once again I hunkered down in the bayberries and that time the cold was truly intense. The wind, still in the northwest, neared gale force at times and there were occasional snow flurries. Within half an hour I was hurting. Steve observed that he was a little chilly, adding that he had been in such a rush to go hunting he hadn't bothered to put on long underwear beneath his blue jeans.

Soon, each of us bagged a black duck, the limit for the species. Both shots were difficult, and we complimented each other. My performance involved a great deal of luck because, encumbered by bulky clothes and made awkward by the cold, I was unable to maintain a proper swing, and I knew that my bird had been hit with the tail end of the shot pattern.

During the breaks in the snow squalls, we were treated to a sight that gave us much pleasure: hundreds of black ducks—perhaps driven down from the north by the cold—were flying far out over the frozen surface of the pond, and we lingered to watch them although they were then off limits to us.

Sunset arrived and the day grew even darker when another

snow squall began. We were so intent on the black ducks that we would not have noticed—had it not emitted a single honk—until it was too late a lone Canada goose approaching us from the rear.

I turned and it was almost directly over my head before I fired. As with the black duck, I knew the cold had rendered me incompetent. The bird shuddered, set its wings and glided out over the ice. We watched it for perhaps 300 yards, then could see it no longer, and I cursed myself for having shot.

Steve's middle-aged black Labrador, Cass, had seen the bird, however. For nearly half a minute after we lost sight of the goose, she continued—intense and trembling—to mark its flight, then burst from the blind and ran across the ice, soon no longer visible.

Four or five minutes later she returned, moving at a trot, the still-alive bird in her mouth, and accepted our lavish praises with nonchalance.

A Hunter's Christmas Tale

Children of my children wild among your
   peers
and awash in crumpled paper, I have thought
of telling you to stalk delight with care,
but that would go unheeded. Rend wrap-
   pings, scream
at silly toys laid bare. Time enough for caution
when desire's tracks are blurred by falling
   snow
in the darkening, wind-filled woods.
And yet if you would listen, this aging man
at the room's edge, mug of coffee at his side,
calloused fingers idly plucking at a ribbons'
   bow,
could tell you of a gift that came after the days
when his April dreams skipped through the
   birdsong
dawn like flat stones flung across the water,
after the swollen, trumpeting time when he
   filled
the valleys—where a thousand dark-eyed
   Susans
waited—with the thunder of his blood.

Children of my children, after you hunt
your seasons away and the quarry's hooves
clatter on distant ledge in failing light,

know that the savoring years have come,
born of laughter at how deep imagined failure cuts.
It is then, cabined and fed, that you will smile
and hold that which you sought for all the while.

Orienteering, December 25

Carol-caught but with no Christ, I let choirs
Lead me where mind cannot go. Less lost than
  some,
More found than others, I have a map, more
  sketch than map,
For when the anthems end, but it shows no
  cliff's contours
Or streams from which to drink or where Po-
  laris gleams.
At times I walk with the prevailing wind, but
  winds
Are fickle and come from every quarter when
Mountains are about. Silent night or holy
  night?
I do not know if there is holiness in the hush
Beneath cathedral firs or above the empty
  pews,
Or silence only, beyond meaning and forever.

Some who pass seem as jubilant and sure as
  geese
Bound south, wings winnowing the stars,
But is it an intoxication whose morning-after
Is delayed until the final dawn?
Does faith leap with fierce grace from ledge
Above the traveler—a sudden sweet shudder
  as doubt

Is slain—or is it pursued to possession?
The questions are the answer. Hunted or hunter,
I am content enough when in cold so deep
It rives the oak, warm hands touch mine, when
As punctual as geese returning, alewives
Flail the shallows with a fury I once knew.

The bell calls. Festive lights adorn the church
And another lurks beside me looking in,
Heavy-browed and mouth agape with wonder. Stone drops
From hairy fist. For now, at least, no more, no less.

Gifts Are Mine and More Will Come

Gifts I would unwrap each Christmas are
    bound in twine
I cannot always cut in time to join the caroling;
twine tough as mindless dread—or wisteria
    that chokes
the tree it climbs—it must be slashed away
    each season.
The gifts it sometimes keeps from me were
    once seen
and savored: doubt's season slain by catbird
    song
in meadow fog at dayspring, making what
    might have been
impoverished by what was; black clouds rush-
    ing from
the west, the surf in wild disorder, five casts,
    one fish
and a race to beat the squall, that, even with
    the lee shore
gained before it hit, flung the canoe off course
    in bitter rain
almost too sharp to face; small rain on the
    Androscoggin,
spires of spruces for ranting preacher jays, an
    aldermanic beaver,
spawning brook trout shuddering on their
    gravel beds;

a lighted lamp within, and, in and out, both faces smiling
at the open door; an Irish poet's lament for his old bawd,
a grandson's grin. These gifts are mine and more will come,
but the keeper of the twine, working best on dark days
and pillow-punching nights, will seek to bind them up.

This Christmas I'll take a mind-forget blade honed
with thanks and touch its bright edge to all the silly strings.

Merry Remembrances

In the island town where I was a child, many Christmases were brown, and a new, shiny sled might hang unused in the toolshed most of the winter to be gazed upon and touched hopefully whenever black clouds hanging low over the gray sea and the sere meadows seemed too heavy to pass by without a gift of snow.

And when snow did come you had to make the most of it because in less than a week the wind would back from northwest to southwest. And even if it didn't rain the ocean's warm breath would set the trees dripping, and the tracks of rabbits weaving through thickets of scrub oaks would turn to pools of water on sodden leaves.

For those who wanted snow, the weather was perverse. Often after a three-day thaw had done its work, the skies would clear and there would be a time of bitter cold when ice would form in the salt pond until the only open water was at the mouth of its largest feeder brook—an ever-shrinking haven for ducks and geese, beside which Beany and I made a hunting camp from the crate in which my aunt's Christmas piano arrived.

We dragged the crate down to the pond

the very next day, nailed it against a wild cherry to keep it from blowing away, equipped it with a door, a sliding window, a bench and a plumber's candle. We spent much of the holiday vacation in it with our BB guns watching the birds come in, lighting the candle and playing cards when the last of the reflected light had left the water and the marsh beyond, and we could hear but not see the late-arriving ducks.

The BB guns were really no more than symbols of roles to which we aspired, but once, just once, we eased the window back and shot, the slow-moving pellets bouncing harmlessly off our prey. We knew we were breaking the law, but the law was far away and the temptation too much: three huge Canada geese gliding down from dark skies to land before us, so close we could see their shining eyes.

Twice in my childhood, 2 feet of ice covered the broad reaches of the salt pond at Christmas time and the young bucks of the town would drive their Model T and Model A Fords on it, and once one of them invited me to go along.

It was as much fun as sliding down Parsonage Pond hill in my seldom-used sled. We went on the ice at Muddy Cove at the pond's upper end and by the time we reached Big Sandy a half-mile away—where two old-timers spearing eels through the ice looked at us with disfavor—we were going faster than I had ever gone in my life. And when the driver put on the brakes we spun in great circles nearly all the remaining half of the pond, or so it seems to me now to the barrier beach.

There were only three girls and four boys in my part of the town and not many more altogether, and when Christmas vacation began there was no way to talk with Barbara, who lived 6 miles away. There was the telephone, to be sure. It sat, mouthpiece and dangling earphone, a forbidding black instrument, in the dark front entryway. I tried it once but became tongue-tied when dealing with a disembodied voice. I would have walked to Barbara's house, but I wasn't sure she wanted to see me.

One Christmas the snowless cold arrived and Barbara and other distant peers were driven by their parents to Parsonage Pond, which was less than a mile from my home, and that gave me a chance to help her put on her skates. Parsonage Pond is smaller and shallower than the nearby Mill Pond and always freezes first. I didn't go on the ice with her because I couldn't skate and was too shy to be seen learning.

When Barbara glided forth, I climbed the huge white pine on the hill overlooking the pond until I was swaying among the stars. There I clung as the church clock chimed the hours away, listening for her laughter and remaining aloft until all the skaters departed and the lights of the town blinked out.

That was the Christmas I earned my dollar by helping a neighbor cut wood for two days and learned that white oak killed by fire is so hard it makes a two-man crosscut saw swing. With that dollar, I bought Barbara a Baby Brownie camera—the most money I had ever spent for a present—for the eighth-grade Christmas party in our two-room schoolhouse. When she thanked me for it I was so overwhelmed I said, "What camera?"

That was also the Christmas when I received a shower of gifts, mittens and a sweater knitted by mother, a sheath knife, a lantern-like red flashlight to hang from my belt and an illustrated edition of *The Deerslayer*.

I took the presents to show Beany, and his mother, Mary, whom I dearly loved, pressed cake and cookies upon me with her Newfoundland-born accent that the years never blurred. I consumed more than a polite visitor's share, even though I had already eaten half a loaf of mother's bread fresh from the oven.

And then it was across the street to George's house where his mother, Lillian—even before I became her son's muskrat-trapping partner, she treated me as one of her own—fed me hot cocoa and massa sovada, a Portuguese sweetbread smeared with beach plum jelly, as I looked at the additions to George's ever-growing fleet of toy trucks.

It was then time to return home for the Christmas dinner prepared by mother in her little kitchen with its zinc-covered counter and black iron stove, and to marvel at my father's being able to take slices from the breast of the turkey that were as thin as the blade of the knife, and to listen to Miss Chignell who was older than anyone I knew and who always shared in our Christmas repast—tell of her travels in Europe. Fetched by father from her little cottage in a patch of white oaks in another part of the island where she lived alone—a British governess come to Canada and then this country—she could make do with greater skill than any Yankee.

When she grew too old to cut her own firewood, or no longer cared to bother, she fed her fireplace with long branches that protruded a broom's length into the room, pushing them toward the flames as they were consumed. Her aplomb was such that when having tea with her in winter, one was convinced that there was no better way to fuel a blaze.

Early that night I walked through the fields past the high bush blueberries and to the stepping stones across the brook below the pool where watercress grows. I could hear black ducks talking around the bend, and from the south there was a moan—more sigh than moan—the ocean sliding up and down the winter-narrowed beach.

I would have remained longer had it not been for *The Deerslayer* and the red flashlight, a compelling combination in the unheated west bedroom where, both for warmth and to escape detection—beds were for sleeping, my parents said—I would burrow under layers of wool blankets and a quilt, occasionally surfacing for air, and read the remainder of Christmas away.

Plans for a New Year

My New Year's roistering—two cups of black coffee; a chunk of cheddar cheese; three miniature hot dogs speared with a toothpick from a nondescript sauce bubbling in a miniature cauldron; half-heard, fixed-smile conversation with too many strangers, and to bed at ten—left me hungering for accomplishment the following warm and brilliant dawn.

I tried to celebrate the new year's gentle birth by writing, but even the simplest thoughts became unruly and the words with which I sought to corral them were equally recalcitrant. Is there a confusion here? Can thoughts and words be so separated?

Twelve Canada geese flew over the house bound from a salt pond to a corn-stubble field where they would glean what they could from the softening earth. I thought of sneaking through the woods to the meadow to see if I could bag one of them, but I was as ill-prepared for that endeavor as I was for writing, having forgotten to purchase a new hunting license, and license-issuing locations would be closed for the holiday.

This reminded me that research I might have begun that day—one can always gather material even if one cannot, at the moment, organize it lucidly—was also blocked because none of the state and Federal officials with whom I wished to talk would be at their desks. My first resolution of the new year emerged from this: I will henceforth mark holidays in black on my wall calendar.

A shotgun coughed three times from the direction of the meadow and five minutes later twelve geese flew back over the house to the pond. I rejoiced at that. No amount of preparation can compensate for ineptitude.

As the geese dropped down out of sight, I was reminded that the waterfowling season in the state in which I live is now closed except for geese and sea ducks: scoters, eiders and old squaws. A few days before on a late-afternoon bird walk I had seen several flocks of white-winged scoters riding the wind-ripped waves just beyond the breakers and had recalled that each fall for the past five years I had planned to build some floating silhouette scoter decoys so my sons and I could try for those hardy birds.

The crying of the geese could still be heard when I began work on the decoys, reasoning that something tangible would emerge from a project that would also give me a sense of having come to grips with my ever-increasing tendency to dawdle.

No longer indecisive, I entered my workshop and soon was running scraps of plywood through a table saw, cutting out 18″ by 11″ rectangles on which the outline of the decoy would be traced. There was a slight setback when I could not find the scoter pattern that I had tucked away half a decade before, but with pictures of them in various waterfowl texts to guide me I quickly sketched out another on a heavy piece of cardboard. I wound up with twenty-eight birds traced on wood, enough for two strings of five pairs each and one with four pairs. There are various ways to rig scoter silhouettes and the one I favor calls for the paired birds to be fastened together by two slats, such as furring, across the bottom fore and aft. The lead pair in a string is about 30 inches apart and the others are made progressively shorter so that they nestle into one compact unit. The paired decoys in each string are tethered together about four feet apart and each string rides on a single anchor.

I had cut out five of the silhouettes on a band saw before I remembered that I had promised one of my daughters that I would locate a piece of asbestos to go under her newly installed wood stove; because the light was failing and the asbestos was somewhere outside I went to look for it. I found it half-hidden in a snarl of honeysuckle vines at the rear of the garage, cut it to size and delivered it.

Had not mother called, I would have returned to the decoys. Her water pump, she said, was acting up, running almost continuously. Country folk with their own wells know that water pump summonses cannot be ignored. The pump was laboring mightily and hot to the touch when I arrived, the needle on the pressure gauge holding steady at 35 pounds. (As such shallow-well installations age, the sections of pipe driven into the earth to water accumulate rust as does the water-admitting screening on the lowest section, the so-called point. When this happens, the pump works longer to fill the tank to a certain level, or pressure, and begins to wear out. When replaced fifteen years ago, mother's pump produced 50 pounds of pressure, but last year slightly less than 40 was the limit.) I adjusted the pressure-regulating switch to cut off at about 32 pounds, which relieved the pump of its uselessness striving for an impossible goal, and called the plumber, reasoning that I would find him at home because it was a holiday.

"Mother needs a new pump and a new point and pipe," I said, adding that 32 pounds was now the best the system could muster.

"Did you try shooting it?" he asked.

"I tried that last May," I replied.

Shooting a well is part of the ritual attending its decline. One removes the cap on the pipe and fires two or three rounds down into its dark interior. The recommended cartridge for this is a .22 long rifle. The theory, and it sometimes works, is that the shock waves created by the bullet striking the water will jar the rust off the point's screening. The danger is that even the small .22 can blow a hole in the screening, rendering the point totally useless. I have shot a dozen wells in my lifetime and more than half of them expired. Occasionally, as with mother's well in May, a slight improvement results. There is always, however, a certain psychic release in administering such treatment to a failing well.

"I'm behind in my fall furnace-cleaning commitments," the plumber said. "My partner and I split up and I said to hell with everything and went deer hunting up north for a week."

"Did you get your deer?"

"Nope," he replied, "but I did get away from the furnaces." He paused, then continued: "How long you going to be around before your next trip?"

"About thirteen days. Why?"

"It takes two men to pull a well pipe and drive a new one and my partner is gone. You and I could probably do it in one day."

Because his logic was sound and because my being his helper would save mother money, I agreed.

With one day in the next thirteen consigned to the well, there was clearly no time to further indulge myself with decoy making and I returned—with immediate rewards—to the shaping of phrases. From this experience another resolution emerged: to strive to avoid whimpering about the writing deadlines without which I would soon become mute.

Going After the Varying Hare in Vermont's Snow Woods

It was cold, about six below zero. Deep in the woods, I was out of the wind, however, and comfortable even though standing still as I listened to the muffled baying of our beagle, Champ, who was plowing through the snow on the trail of a varying hare.

Champ was in the interior of a thick and extensive plantation of young spruces near Weston, on the northeastern edge of the Green Mountains. The plantation was too dense for a hunter on snowshoes to enter, so I was stationed on its outskirts waiting for the hare, or snowshoe rabbit, to emerge. Some distance away, also on the outskirts, were my companions—Bart Jacob of Winhall, Vermont, the dog's owner, and Niles Oesterle of Bennington, Vermont.

A vagrant gust of wind shot through the top of the tall spruce under which I waited, sending down a sparkling cascade of snow. The dog's voice rose and fell, and I tried in vain to pinpoint its location. I was unable to do so because on a similarly cold day more than thirty years ago, in the Battle of the Bulge, a German artillery shell exploding close by had ruined the hearing in my right ear. Receiving impulses from only one ear, the brain's computer cannot zero in on the direction of sound. So handicapped, I had no recourse but to remain where I was, hoping the rabbit would come my way.

I also knew that when there are several rabbits in a cover, some of the animals not being directly pursued by the beagle often move away from the sound of the chase, and sometimes in the course of a day's hunt these so-called "strays" provide most of the action. A half-hour after the dog had jumped the first rabbit, one of my companions fired twice, and in the hour following I heard two more shots. During all this the dog kept baying, so it seemed clear that either the hares had been missed entirely or strays had been taken. Ten minutes after the last of these shots, however, the dog fell silent, and I heard Jacob calling to me to come over to where he was. I shouted back that it would be simpler for him to come to me, and soon he and Oesterle appeared carrying three rabbits, Champ on a leash.

"I don't think Champ should hunt anymore," Jacob said. "He's got a sty on his eye, and he's cut it open."

The two hares shot by Oesterle had both been strays. Jacob's had not.

"I could have gotten a stray early in the hunt," Jacob said, "but I let it go. I often do this, because when the rabbit being chased finally is shot, I'll recall where I saw the stray and so will know where I can immediately put the dog on a fresh track. Of course, you can't always be sure you've got a stray coming at you.

"When I do shoot a rabbit I leave it there until the dog arrives— if he's going to arrive—because Champ enjoys finding something at the end of the line."

In the Northeast at the end of deer hunting (before the turn of the year) and waterfowl hunting (just after the turn of the year), cottontail and snowshoe rabbits are just about the only game that may still be sought. The larger and more athletic varying hare is a more challenging species to hunt than the cottontail rabbit, because the former runs faster and ranges wider, and because hunters usually follow it on snowshoes. Sometimes a few inches of new powder snow will cover a crust strong enough to support a man wearing only boots, but this does not happen often.

The snowshoe rabbit itself is not troubled by any snow

conditions, because in fall the soles of its feet develop a heavy growth of hair that, coupled with its huge hind feet, serve as "snow-shoes."

This hare adapts to winter in another way as well: In the fall its brown summer pelage begins to change to white, and the transformation continues until the only dark fur left is on the tips of its ears. The change is brought about by the shortening of daylight and will occur even if the days are warm and without snow. The reverse shift occurs in spring. Each alteration takes about eight weeks.

Deer hunters in the bare woods of November are well aware of the varying hare's pelage change. The snow-white animals show up for incredible distances in the brown woods. Indeed, late fall is just about the only time that the hunter without a dog will have any success going after snowshoe rabbits, for when they are sitting motionless in the snow they are nearly impossible to spot.

In New York State and northern New England the varying-hare breeding season begins near the end of February. The gestation period is thirty-seven days, and the latest litters—three litters a season seem to be the average—may be born as late as early October. The litter size varies from one to six, and the leverets, young hares, are born with full fur and eyes open, alert and able to walk and hop. Varying hares do not build nests; the female simply makes a depression on the forest floor.

Varying-hare populations dropped precipitously in all but the remotest regions of the Northeast when it was settled and land cleared for agriculture. Now, with farm land reverting back to woods in many places, good hare habitats are being created.

Varying hares require dense stands of conifers—spruces seem to be most favored—from 6 to 16 feet high as their base cover. They emerge from this base area at night to forage for food—a wide variety of plants, and buds of trees and shrubs—and during this foraging they use taller stands of conifers as avenues of travel. They dislike open spaces, and research has shown that even a two-lane highway is an effective barrier to them. The desire for overhead cover is undoubtedly born of a fear of attack from the air.

Once in a while, however, you will note where hares seem to

lose some of their caution. Not far from where we hunted, near an abandoned beaver pond, I found a set of hare tracks in the open, in a gully beside a logging road. The tracks went west until they encountered another set coming from the opposite direction. The two animals had met and cavorted in the snow for a while, and then one had plunged across the open road into the alder swamp beyond. The onset of the mating season almost certainly accounts for this exuberant behavior.

Only a few weeks are now left for snowshoe-rabbit hunting in Vermont. But Jacob said, as we shuffled up the last hill toward our car, that the final week of the season was often the best time, for, among other things, the warmer weather makes it easier for the dog to follow the scent.

Whether in January or March, however, varying-hare hunting has a singular appeal to those who like the woods to themselves. The deer-hunting hordes have departed, and one will usually go all day without seeing anyone save those in his own party. Sometimes the silence will be shattered by the snarl of a snowmobile, but the operator of this machine usually runs well-defined trails or logging roads, and a snowmobile cannot negotiate much of the thick cover the hare hunter must visit. Also, though one sometimes encounters cross-country skiers or snowshoers wandering through the trackless, snow-filled woods, most of them congregate at various skiing centers and dutifully pursue one another along marked courses.

Deep in a stand of young spruces, waiting for the sharp yelp of the beagle to signal that the chase has begun, one revels in a white silence broken only by the thumps of snow that have slid from heavily laden branches or the cheerful cries of chickadees that cannot resist a close inspection of the intruder in their domain.

Then, when such a hunt is done, some closing ritual is proper. In our case, as we lounged in the brilliant midafternoon sunlight, the ritual involved a few bottles of imported beer and a batch of fat oysters I had brought with me from Martha's Vineyard. Having spread a burlap bag on the hood of Jacob's car, I shucked the bivalves open, and Jacob, who is a partner in the Tabusintac camps, a hunting and fishing lodge in New Brunswick, pronounced them as good as those from Tabusintac Bay.

Eating raw oysters in the mountains is always a special experience; they seem particularly precious so far removed from the ebb and flow of the tide.

Our little feast done, we drank a toast to Champ, who had done remarkably well on a cold day, and as we parted my companions invited me to join them in Vermont's forthcoming spring season for wild turkeys.

Ice Fishing for Smelt

During a two-day introduction to ice fishing for smelt, I learned that those who are devoted to the sport have no truck with dawdling.

We rose—despite my protestations—long before dawn the second day in our rented cottage on the southeastern shore of Lake Champlain and even as I was enjoying my first cup of coffee, lighted lanterns could be seen bobbing across the snow-covered ice toward a cluster of shanties. I was spared a similar experience the first day because we didn't arrive until about noon.

I had questioned the early start because there seemed little point in venturing out when the temperature was eight below zero. Why not, I asked, wait for the sun?

"They often bite like hell during the first few hours of daylight," said Bob Kearney of Springfield, Vermont, the most accomplished smelt fisherman of our foursome, a pronouncement that left small room for dissent.

Many of the lantern-bearers were early for another reason: nearly all of us were using shanties towed out on the ice a few weeks before by Marvin Barrows, a dairy farmer who also owns several lakeside cottages, including the one we occupied. If one rents a cottage, as we did, one is guaranteed a shanty; otherwise it's a first-come, first-serve situation.

My other companions—Charles Spencer, also of Springfield, and Vic Pomiecko of Claremont, New Hampshire—had obviously been swayed by Mr. Kearney's hunger for action, so there was nothing for me to do but gulp down a second cup of coffee and follow them out on the lake.

I had become familiar with one of our two shanties the first day. It was a 6-by-8 four-holer, suitable for four men fishing one hole each, or a pair of anglers using two lines simultaneously. The holes, about 4 inches in diameter, were located in front of two benches set across the ends of the shanty. Mr. Barrows's shanties are equipped with kerosene heaters and ours also had four port-holes with sliding panes which proved helpful in getting rid of the fumes from the stove.

The smelt are caught with two-hook handlines, each of which carries a shiny, hookless jig weighing about 2 ounces. The bait is a small strip cut from a smelt. One either brings frozen bait or visits another shanty and borrows a fresh smelt.

The jig, or weight, is needed to get the line to the depths in a hurry. The water under the shanty was nearly seventy feet deep and we were fishing just above the bottom. The hooks we used were No. 6's, very fine and sharp with offset shanks. Many smelt anglers use monofilament line and the tendency is to choose a twenty-pound test or heavier, because there is less chance of the thicker line snarling. Mr. Kearney uses discarded fly lines. The leader bearing the two hooks, which is fastened below the jig, is usually much lighter, perhaps a 6- or 8-pound test.

Minutes after our first day's start, Mr. Kearney was catching smelt every time he lowered his line and Mr. Pomiecko was a close second. Mr. Spencer and I were doing very little. I because I was having trouble detecting when a smelt hit the bait, and he because he persisted in using a bobber, an unheard-of smelting technique. He had a simple explanation for his approach. He wished to re-capture, he said, the delight he experienced on his first fishing trip as a child with his father when the bobber was pulled under by a fish.

We suggested to him that while such nostalgia was understand-able, there wasn't a smelt alive that could submerge the float he was using—it nearly filled the hole—but he persisted, hunched over it with fierce concentration, occasionally yanking upward when it trembled on the water. He managed to catch a few fish in that manner the first day and the morning of the second day he eschewed the bobber and caught the first smelt and the first double—a smelt on each hook thereby winning the dollar pot which we had established for that achievement. He was kind enough to share that pot with me because exactly three seconds after his two smelt came up out of the hole I also caught a double.

By the end of the first day, my smelting technique had improved enough for Mr. Kearney to opine that I would be able, on the morrow, to fish two holes simultaneously, an approach to the sport that I found much more rewarding. Toward the end of the second day I was able to predict whether I had one or two smelt on a line, and whether a single fish was foul-hooked.

A brilliant sun shone both days, and I ventured outside several times to chat with other anglers, including those who were not using shanties. They ranged from couples in their seventies to family groups with children barely old enough to walk. From noon to about two o'clock, the cold was a comfortable haven when the sun hovered above the distant Adirondacks in the west. This was particularly true on the first day when, shortly before 3:30 P.M., a northerly gale sprang up instantly and moaned down the 107-mile-long lake, nearly obscuring three nearby fishermen in swirl-ing snow.

Vermont places no limit on the number of smelt one may catch with hook and line. It is possible for two men to fill a 12-quart bucket, about 30 pounds of fish, in a days' angling, but most would be satisfied with a third of that or less. The smelt in Champlain average about 7 to 8 inches long, although so-called foot-long "jack smelt" are fairly common.

Smelt—whether marine, anadromous or freshwater species—are long, slender fish with incredibly sharp teeth. They are excel-lent eating but because of the high oil content of their flesh they must be kept cold after capture, something that poses no problem in winter. Some anglers are so dedicated to the species that they fish for them in summer, and now, having learned how to catch them, I am thinking of various trout lakes where I might do the same during the portion of the day when angling for the primary quarry is slow.

I am thinking of this because the gutted and beheaded smelt Mr. Pomiecko and I had for supper at the close of our trip were superb. I dipped them in beaten eggs, rolled them in spiced (Italian) bread crumbs and deep fried them at 370 degrees for three to four minutes. They were served with parsley and lemon wedges. One surprising aspect of this feast was that the bones were so soft that the entire fish could be eaten, something that doesn't happen with whitebait (silverside minnows and sand eels) of similar size from marine waters.

Ice fishing for smelt in the location we visited is short-lived. The ice isn't usually safe for shanties until late January and they must be off the ice by the last Sunday in March at the very latest or sooner, which usually happens, if a thaw arrives. Mr. Barrows, whose telephone number is (802) 475-2487, usually has to call it quits before mid-March.

Ritual of Swapping

I am now engaged in ridding myself of various rods, reels and guns that once seemed essential to my activities afield.

This late-winter ritual would have unquestioned merit if out of the wisdom of advancing years I was paring away excess equipage, but that is not the case. I will simply swap each item for another of its genre.

The hunger that goads many fishermen and hunters to purchase just one more gun or one more rod is well known, and when I finally struggled free of penury, I accumulated a mountainous pile of gear, more than I could ever use. Rods remain in their cases season after season, and the only time I handle many of my guns is when they are periodically cleaned and oiled to protect them from the salt-air climate in which I live. Overcome by late-arriving guilt at spending money in this fashion, but periodically seized by a desire for something different, I turned to swapping a few years ago.

February and March are ideal swapping months for the hunter and fisherman in the northern latitudes. Barred by snow and ice and closed seasons from most of their pursuits, they have time to take inventory of themselves and the tools of their avocations. I, for example, am becoming increasingly interested in black powder hunting, something I first tried thirty years ago.

Black powder was the propellant in the muzzle-loading rifles, pistols or shotguns of yesteryear. With them, and their modern replicas, one pours a proper powder charge down the barrel, which is followed up, in the case of the shotgun, by a wad, a load of pellets and an over-pellet wad. This charge is ignited—creating a marvelous shroud of dense smoke that momentarily obscures the target—either by the hammer's striking a percussion cap or the sparks from the more primitive flintlock. Today, the term "muzzle-loading" is more accurate than "black powder" because of the development of a more stable explosive, called Pyrodex, which many gunners use instead of black powder.

When I first began black-powder shooting, there were almost no modern replicas of such firearms being manufactured and the literature on the subject was scanty. That is no longer true, and there is now a national muzzle-loading organization as well as special seasons in deer hunting states for those who wish to handicap themselves with such firearms.

I have one muzzle-loading rifle and three muzzle-loading shotguns, which obviously fulfill most of my hunting requirements, but I don't have a muzzle-loading revolver. My brother does, and a few days ago I offered him a modern deer rifle, equipped with telescopic sight, in exchange for it. An accomplished swapper, he diffidently responded that he would think about it. I know that he is giving my offer serious consideration because he has expressed interest in that rifle several times.

I am at a disadvantage because I made the initial offer and now must not press, must leave the next move to him. Sometimes this waiting period is so protracted that the would-be swapper loses interest. It's something like looking at a much-desired item in a catalogue for so long that it becomes commonplace.

My reason for wanting the revolver is essentially absurd. I might bag an occasional snowshoe rabbit with it, but its major role would be to hang on the wall among the artifacts associated with such weapons: the powder horns and flasks, bullet molds, shot pouches, cappers and ditty bags of fringed deerskin, all symbols of a long-gone era for which, like Miniver Cheevy, I long.

The longing began when as a lad I was given an illustrated edition of *Robinson Crusoe,* and it was intensified by my subsequent reading of *The Deerslayer.* Now when I am melting pieces of lead pipe scrounged from the town dump in an iron pot in the wood stove and molding my own bullets, I am one with those stalwarts. I am also with them when I am high on a mountain ridge with my muzzle-loading rifle in hand or huddled in a duck blind wondering if the stinging rain has rendered my antique shotgun impotent. I gather less game when I am so equipped and I sometimes wonder if that is my real intent.

The rifle that I wouldn't trade away, a lever-action Winchester .243, is a splendid long-range weapon suitable for game as large as deer. I bought it for antelope hunting in Wyoming ten years ago, have never killed anything with it and have taken it afield only half a dozen times since.

Although swapping eliminates cash outlays, one can, if one is too impetuous, trade downhill, which makes no difference at the moment of acquisition but which inevitably weakens one's bargaining power when additional exchanges are contemplated. Most of my trading has fallen into this category as will, if consummated, the deal with my brother.

I do have one glorious swapping victory to my credit, however. When I was fourteen, an aunt gave me an alcohol-fired toy steam engine for Christmas. It was a lovely thing with a brass flywheel and a piercing whistle.

On Christmas Day I took it down to Beany Alley's house because I knew that he had an unusual interest in things mechanical. He was activated by it, visibly saddened when we ran out of fuel, and when I left he casually suggested that we might make a trade. I pondered his proposal on the walk home. Beany had bested me in a marble swap the previous spring, taking advantage of my fascination with a type of marble we called a "realie." This time, I told myself, I will make up for that. I bore the steam engine to his house every evening for a week until, bedazzled by its gleaming, whirling wheel and its wailings he was without judgment. It was then that I told him I would take his muskrat traps, all twelve of them, in exchange. My proposal was preposterous. The traps were worth much more than the engine and he had worked a good portion of the previous summer, mowing lawns and hoeing corn for ten cents an hour, to pay for them, but, possessed by a demon, he acquiesced.

My brother will not be so malleable, but when he does get around to talking of my offer I will remind him of the big buck that stood 300 yards away on the eastern slope of Black Mountain, an easy shot for the .243, but far out of range of the .30–.30 he was carrying.